Great Forgers
and
Famous Fakes

★ ★ ★

Books by Charles Hamilton

Great Forgers and Famous Fakes (1980)
The Signature of America (1979)
The Book of Autographs (1978)
Big Name Hunting (with Diane Hamilton, 1973)
Scribblers and Scoundrels (1968)
The Robot That Helped to Make a President (1965)
Lincoln in Photographs (with Lloyd Ostendorf, 1963)
Collecting Autographs and Manuscripts (1961)
Braddock's Defeat (1959)
Men of the Underworld (1952)
Cry of the Thunderbird (1950)

Great Forgers and Famous Fakes

★ ★ ★

THE MANUSCRIPT FORGERS OF AMERICA
AND
HOW THEY DUPED THE EXPERTS

Charles Hamilton

A HERBERT MICHELMAN BOOK

CROWN PUBLISHERS, INC.
NEW YORK

Inquiries should be addressed to Crown Publishers, Inc., One Park
Avenue, New York, New York 10016
Printed in the United States of America
Published simultaneously in Canada by General Publishing Company Limited
Library of Congress Cataloging in Publication Data
Hamilton, Charles, 1913-
Great forgers and famous fakes
"A Herbert Michelman book."
Includes index.
1. Forgery of manuscripts—United States—History.
I. Title.
Z41.H35 1980   098′.3   80-13516
ISBN: 0-517-540762
Book design by Deborah B. Kerner
10 9 8 7 6 5 4 3 2 1
First Edition

Contents

Introduction

There is a darkling romance in the crime of literary or historical forgery. To fabricate the handwriting and thoughts of another person requires much more than adroit penmanship. The successful faker must disjoint himself from his own age and become a part of another time and place. He must think the thoughts of another era and use its language. He is truly a historian without portfolio, a resurrectionist of lost literature and history.

No European forgers ever put quill to foolscap who could equal the ingenious fabricators of America. Not Baron von Gerstenbergk in Germany, who immersed himself in Schiller and forged the letters of the great poet. Or Count Mariano Alberti in Italy, who set his talents to manufacturing false Tassos. Or Vrain-Denis Lucas in France, who faked letters of Cleopatra and Caesar in modern French. Or William Henry Ireland in England, who turned out Shakespeares that foxed the experts at the British Museum. Or Antique Smith, who composed letters and poems of Robert Burns. No; these notorious forgers were in no way the equal in skill and villainy of our American masters of manuscript fraud.

The art of forgery is as old as the alphabet. Anything that is handwritten and has value is worth forging, and I daresay that Caesar and Cicero, Virgil and Catullus had their manuscript counterfeiters who plagued the philographers of ancient Rome. Today the voracity of collectors for documents that give us an insight into the secret motives of men and women has brought about a bull market in forgeries. Every year new and enterprising fakers put forth their wares.

Many of the forgers whose malefactions are recorded in this book were never before trapped betwixt covers. Their evil creations were long anonymous and in many cases unsuspected by scholars.

Because there will always be clever men with misguided ingenuity who find it profitable to duplicate or invent historic letters and documents, the philographers of the future must be forever alert. I have not the slightest doubt that even as I write these words there is somewhere in America a nimble-fingered fellow touching a goose quill to parchment and concocting an exciting document that will fool at least one or two myopic historians and perhaps even a whole gaggle of scholars.

Great Forgers
and
Famous Fakes

★ ★ ★

1

Twelve Forgers of Honest Abe

The old mariner stood awkwardly in my gallery with his grizzled rough face glistening in the sticky heat of August. He certainly didn't look like an autograph-seeker or -seller. From his damp T-shirt bulged huge muscles adorned with tattoos that portrayed voluptuous women of far-off lands.

"I have something here which may interest you," he said, and his voice was soft and pleasant.

He handed me a worn sheet of paper.

A glance told me it was a fabrication of the handwriting of Abraham Lincoln by Joseph Cosey, the notorious American forger. Not even the stains and frayed edges and tears of this apparently venerable document could mask its spurious nature.

"I've carried this little note with me around the world many times," said the sailor. "It's my greatest treasure."

I asked him where he'd got it.

"I was sitting in a waterfront bar in New York about forty years ago," he said, "and I got to chatting with a little old man whose father had served in the Civil War. The man took this paper out of his wallet and showed it to me—Lincoln's own order to suspend the execution of his father, who was only sixteen and had fallen asleep at his post. When the old guy said he was hard up, and needed money bad, and twenty dollars would buy this note, I jumped at the chance. It's been my good-luck piece for years, but I'm between ships at the moment and I've got to raise a little cash."

I broke the bad news to the tattooed seaman.

"Who'd have thought it," he said. "Such a nice old man, too. Well, I'll just hang onto this for a while longer."

Lincoln is only one of the scores of celebrated Americans whose handwriting has been forged by the fraternity of manuscript fakers whose careers will be described in later chapters.

Two or three times a month, at least, I am approached by hopeful owners who proffer Lincoln forgeries. Many vendors are, I must add, not aware of the unsavory pedigree of their prized wares.

There is something about the humble, unpretentious handwriting of Honest Abe that tempts swindlers to try their luck in counterfeiting his script. His letters and documents have been more often forged than those of any great man in history.

Joseph Cosey specialized in Lincoln letters and legal briefs. He could dash off Lincoln's signature as fast as his own. He got so proficient at Old Abe's scrawl that he even wrote lengthy legal briefs and disdained to sign them, letting the handwriting speak for itself. A supply of Monnier's 1851 pale blue paper helped him, for scholars often refer to Lincoln's legal period as his "blue" period because of the blue folio sheets he used at that time. Cosey wrote enormous numbers of legal briefs on the paper manufactured by Monnier.

For all his skill, Cosey never quite mastered Lincoln's handwriting. If he had paused, even for a moment, to analyze Lincoln's signature, he would have noted that almost invariably the *A.* extends below the *Lincoln,* and that the *Lincoln* itself is formed in a series of two steps, with the *ln* on a higher level.

An awe-inspiring product of Cosey's pen is the forged itinerary of the Lincoln-Douglas debates, ostensibly written by Lincoln on a hand-drawn map, with the results of each debate briefly described. This great forgery belonged to my friend Samuel Moyerman of Phila-

Joseph Cosey. Forgery of a handwritten letter signed by Abraham Lincoln, about 1932. Notice the unLincolnesque tautology, "For which this shall be her warrant." Lincoln never used an extra word in his letters and his forgers often found it harder to imitate his terse style than his homey script.

Abraham Lincoln. Handwritten signed letter. Notice that Lincoln's own handwriting is much more difficult to read than Cosey's imitation.

delphia. I once owned an amazing, authentic Civil War account book, to which (on blank pages in the original) Cosey had added some fascinating observations on behalf of an imaginary Lieutenant C. R. Rogers of the 109th Ohio Infantry. Most of Cosey's notations in this slender, leather-bound 1860 volume are modest inventions, but under the printed date *Tuesday 20* there begins an intriguing tale:

Last night Lieut. Kemp and myself captured a rebel who was spying on our position not one hundred yards from our position. He was a young man barely 20 years old and had

apparently a good schooling and a good home, as he showed the earmarks of a good bringing up. He explained that he was a deserter from the Rebels and was coming north to join the Union army, and did not want to show himself in the day-time for fear of being shot down on sight.

As that was the usual story told by captured spies, in both armies, we told him he could join our regiment by obtaining a pardon from President Lincoln.

He was almost starving and we fed him of the little we had, and he greedily and gratefully drank the hot coffee.

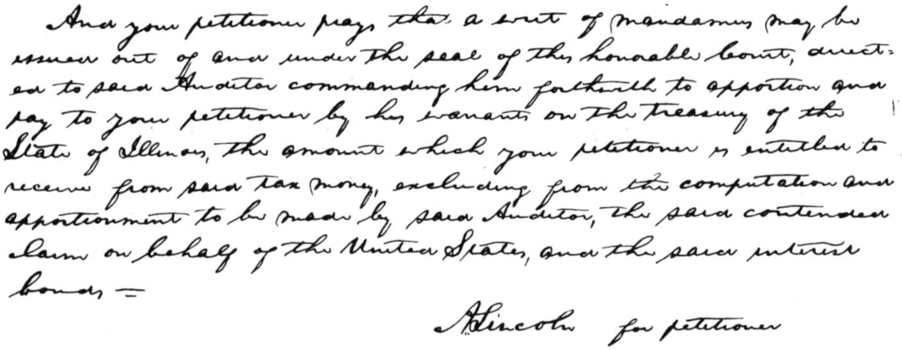
And your petitioner prays that a writ of mandamus may be issued out of and under the seal of this honorable Court, direct-ed to said Auditor commanding him forthwith to apportion and pay to your petitioner by his warrants on the treasury of the State of Illinois, the amount which your petitioner is entitled to receive from said tax money, excluding from the computation and apportionment to be made by said Auditor, the said contended claim on behalf of the United States, and the said interest bonds —

A. Lincoln for petitioner

Joseph Cosey. Forgery of a Lincoln legal brief. A skillful imitation, with accurate legal terminology, penned on Monnier's 1851-watermarked blue paper of the variety used by Lincoln.

This capture I knew would insure me the leave of absence I sought which in reality was to secretly hurry home and see if all was well—which I can do in two days—and return again—contented. I had not the faintest idea, however, what it would lead up to. But listen! I again made application for a leave of absence and my superior signed the application; and upon hearing of the rebel who was so bold, the commanding general approved my pass and I was granted 8 days leave of absence.

I went to Washington and saw Mr. Stanton who informed me that the President's pardon was necessary in the case of the rebel to prevent his execution. Execution by firing squad was the penalty on both sides for espionage.

Three days passed before I was able to see President Lincoln, and when he walked into the room where I was seated I was aware of a strange feeling of inferiority or something coming over me. I arose and saluted but the president waved his hand to the chair and said: "be seated, sir."

He listened carefully and very attentively to my story of the apparent education of the rebel, who was now under guard in our camp, and then told me it was a very serious thing for an enemy spy to venture within 100 yards of a Union position. He gave no credence at all to the "deserter" story, but pondered it over in his mind and then suddenly asked me if my leave of absence was to plead for the life of the deserter or was it to visit my people in violation of the 59th article of war! In all my previous and subsequent battles I have never been in such a fix. If I told him the truth I would be branded, however, secretly, by the

Abraham Lincoln. Authentic handwritten legal brief signed by Lincoln with his partnership name, *Lincoln & Herndon*.

Abraham Lincoln. Authentic signature as President.

Joseph Cosey. Forgery of a handwritten statement signed by Abraham Lincoln on autograph collecting from the spurious journal of Lt. Rogers.

Joseph Cosey and Abraham Lincoln. The signatures in the top row were forged by Cosey. Note that these signatures are penned on the same plane, but the signatures of the Civil War president in the bottom row are all written on a series of three levels, the capital *A.*, the *Linco* and the *ln.* Cosey's failure to observe this feature of Lincoln's signature makes his fakes easy to identify.

Joseph Cosey. Freehand forgery of a letter handwritten and signed by Lincoln, with the text copied by Cosey from a printed copy.

Abraham Lincoln. Second page of Lincoln's handwritten letter signed to Trumbull, 1856. Although Lincoln's script is more difficult to read than Cosey's imitation, the forger has done a remarkable job of creating a forgery without reference to the original manuscript or a facsimile of Lincoln's original letter.

Abraham Lincoln. First page of Lincoln's celebrated handwritten letter signed to Lyman Trumbull, 1856.

President as selfish—actually taking advantage of a man about to be shot to further a selfish aim—and if I lied and said I came to plead for the life of the rebel, I forfeited all chances of seeing my people till the end of the war, however long it might last.

So I thought quickly, and knowing from hearsay what kind of man the president was I told him the truth, but I softened the boldness of it by saying that if the choice was given to me to go home and see my mother and family or go back to camp with a pardon for the rebel I would unhesitatingly choose the latter.

The president without a moment's hesitation asked me for a piece of paper—my pass, or any piece of paper, and I stood at attention and handed him this book. And in this book he wrote the rebel's conditional pardon and granted my leave of absence, so that I was not charged with the time so far used.

I sold this remarkable Civil War forgery for several hundred dollars in 1969, and it now rests in a distinguished collection where its true character is recognized.

Not long ago a woman came into my shop with a fistful of Lincolns—all products of Cosey's facile pen—and although she finally conceded they weren't genuine, she refused to sell them as fakes. Sooner or later I'll see them again, I suspect, after they are palmed off on some unsuspecting librarian or antiques dealer. In the endless swirl of manuscripts, documents and letters keep coming to the surface until finally they are incorporated into the collection of some great library or institution.

When Cosey was arrested on February 4, 1937 for trying to pass off a Lincoln fake on a book dealer, he explained: "I found about one hundred of these Lincoln letters and documents in an abandoned house in Long Island." He told detectives that "my usual price is seven-fifty each." Today you would be lucky to buy a Cosey forgery of Lincoln's hand for ten times that amount.

A contemporary of Cosey, and a "rival" in the Lincoln manufacturing business, was Charles Weisberg, "the Baron," of Philadelphia. Weisberg specialized in gilding authentic documents of small value with annotations by Lincoln. "I remember Weisberg well," one of his bookseller victims told me. "He used to stroll into my store, a brash young man with a heavy build. From his pocket he would extract a few choice Lincoln documents, endorsements on letters, and within a few moments they would be mine at a modest price."

"Did you sell them?" I asked.

"No," said my friend. "I kept the transaction a secret. I didn't want anyone to know I had a pipeline to history. Here I was getting batch after batch of Lincolns for only a few dollars each.

"Then one day I got a letter from Weisberg. 'I'm in a hotel in Philadelphia,' he wrote, 'and I need $400 right away to pay my bill. I'm on the track of the biggest cache of Lincolns you ever saw—a whole trunkful, just like the two examples I'm enclosing. An old lady owns them and has them stored in her attic, and I can get the lot for a song.

Head Qrs. 4th Corps.
Camp near 7 Pines June 13th 1862.

General Orders
No 55.

In consequence of the great number of applications for leave of absence on account of Sickness, no further leaves will be granted unless accompanied by a Surgeons Certificate, Showing the absolute necessity, to save the life of the applicant.

By order Brig. Genl. Keyes
(signed) C. C. Suy dam.
Capt & A. A. G.

Head Qrs. Casey's Div.
June 18th, 1862.
Official

Wm. B. Lost
F. a. a. g.

Charles Weisberg. Forgery of a notation, "Approved—" signed by Abraham Lincoln, penned on an authentic Civil War document. The trivial nature of this general order, requiring a surgeon's certificate for certain leaves of absence, would certainly not have required the president's approval.

Approved —
A Lincoln

Abraham Lincoln. Handwritten note of approval signed as president. Lincoln's own writing is noticeably smaller than Weisberg's imitation.

Recommendation of Genl. Grant approved
A Lincoln
Jny 16. 1864

They're yours, every one of them, if you'll just send along the $400.'"

"Did you send the money?"

"Yes. You see, the examples he enclosed were the back of muster rolls, real Civil War muster rolls. Lincoln was pardoning soldiers for all sorts of crimes. I wanted the whole collection desperately. In those days four hundred dollars was like five thousand now, but I managed to raise the money."

"Why didn't you go to an autograph dealer and make sure the Lincolns were okay?"

Charles Weisberg. Forgery of a lengthy handwritten note, signed by Lincoln, written at the bottom of an authentic but very routine Civil War document regarding the promotion of an officer and three enlisted men. Lincoln's note suffers from the usual tautology characteristic of his forgers. Lincoln would never have repeated the word "sufficiently" in successive sentences. The phraseology is rather gauche and unlike Lincoln's. Further, Lincoln almost never wrote notes at the bottom of letters or documents, but preferred to fold them three or four times (for filing), then write a note at the top of the center section of the fold, so that when filed in a narrow, upright position in a file about four inches wide the note would readily be discernible for quick reference.

Because Weisberg failed to "size," or chemically gloss, this document for modern ink, his ink has feathered, or fuzzed, when it went on the old paper. Weisberg's imitation of Lincoln's script is in many ways more accurate than Cosey's. He was certainly aware of the ascending character of Lincoln's signature, a feature that Cosey never grasped.

The following names have been forwarded to Gov. Curtin of Pennsylvania for promotions

1st Captain E L Rogers for Major in place of Major John McGuire, who died of wounds received in action; to date from July 1 1862

2d Orderly Sergeant Charles G Cadwallader of Co K to be second lieutenant in the same Company, in place of Lieut Edward S McDowell killed in action; to date from July 1st 1862

3. Orderly Sergeant Edwin Fretz of C A, to be second Lieut in same Company, in place of Lieut Robert Holmes, Appointed Commissary of Subsistence Volunteer Service U S A to date from May 12 1862

4 Orderly Sergeant Francis M O'Neill of Company I to be second Lieut in same Company in place of Lieut J Matthias Evans, resigned; to date from August 1, 1862

Executive Mansion
March 10, 1862.

Hon. Gov. Curtin
My dear Sir
Capt E. L. Rogers career has been brought to my notice, and has sufficiently impressed me to induce me to recommend him to you. He is sufficiently resolute to him as a worthy soldier; and this known, it seems proper my asking for you to treat him as such.
Yours truly
A Lincoln

"I didn't want to let anyone else in on the deal. I figured I'd make a small fortune, provided I kept the source to myself."

"So Weisberg copped your money and split?"

"No, he didn't. He mailed me the Lincolns. It was exactly as he promised—an enormous collection. I knew then the time was ripe to sell, so I got ready to put out a mimeographed list of Lincolniana for collectors.

"But word leaked out about my 'find' and a big dealer, a specialist in autographs, showed up in my shop with a hungry look on his face. But the moment he set eyes on my horde of Lincolns the hungry look vanished and so did he. Not a word. Just turned on his heel and walked out.

"I was stuck good and proper. I gave the whole works to the New York Public Library.

"Weisberg was caught a few months later and my testimony helped send him to prison."

Although Weisberg died in prison in 1945, some of his forgeries are still

December 26. 1862

Gen. W. W. Davis:
  Sir:
        Two Maine officers and two from New York were captured at Hartsville, have been parolled; and are now at New York.
        This brings the N.Y. men substantially to their homes — I am strongly impressed with the belief that the Maine men better be sent to Maine, where they will be recruited and put in good condition, by the time they are exchanged, so as to re-enter the service.
        They did not misbehave, as I am satisfied; so that they should receive no treatment, nor have anything withheld, from them, by way of punishment
                Yours truly
                A. Lincoln

Charles Weisberg. Forgery of a handwritten letter signed "Abraham Lincoln," 1862, probably fabricated about 1941. A skilled imitation of Lincoln's script betrayed by the text, which is rambling and diffuse, lacking Lincoln's clarity and verbal precision.

Abraham Lincoln. Three lines from an authentic handwritten letter, signed.

Henry Cleveland. Forgery of a handwritten letter signed by Lincoln. An excellent fake, created in 1867, only two years after Lincoln's death. Cleveland also forged at least one U.S. Grant letter.

in a reasonable time, from a clerkship for him, I shall be greatly obliged to you.
                Yours truly
                A. Lincoln

Executive Mansion
Washington Feb. 10. 1865.

Hon. A. H. Stephens.
        According to our agreement, your nephew, Lieut. Stephens, goes to you, bearing this note. Please in return to select and send to me that officer of the same rank imprisoned at Richmond whose physical condition most urgently requires his release.
                Respectfully
                A. Lincoln.

Charles Weisberg. A remarkable forgery of a note signed by Lincoln (lower right) on April 14, 1865, the day of his murder, on the verso of a portion of a forged letter to Vice President Andrew Johnson, *left*. Beneath a dictated recommendation signed by Andrew Johnson (upper right), which bears a most skilled forgery of his signature, Weisberg has written a note of approval in the script of Lincoln's secretary, John Hay, and placed Lincoln's signature beneath it. One of the most expert forgeries I have ever seen, with a beautifully executed Lincoln signature.

Andrew Johnson. Authentic signature.

Abraham Lincoln. Authentic handwritten note signed as president.

treasured by colleges and historical societies who are unaware that they own Weisbergs and not Lincolns.

One of the most astute Lincoln forgers was Henry Cleveland, who in 1866 composed an exchange of letters between Lincoln and his old friend from Congress, then vice president of the Confederate States, Alexander H. Stephens. The text was plausible, the language terse and the phraseology not unlike Lincoln's. There are three Cleveland forgeries, properly identified, in the William L. Clements Library at the University of Michigan. They are dated November 30, 1860, December 22, 1860, and February 10, 1865. Similar forgeries of two of these letters, identified as fabrications, are in the Huntington Library at San Marino, California.

The forgeries of Cleveland were published as authentic by Nicolay and Hay in their great biography of Lincoln. They had not examined the original manuscript forgeries, but perhaps they would have tumbled for the skilled imitations. I once had a Robert Todd Lincoln letter in which he authenticated a forged signature of his father.

Eugene Field II, who specialized in fabricating manuscripts of his famous father, the poet of childhood, also adventured into the Lincoln forgery business. He forged Lincoln's signature in dozens of old books, usually with the ownership name of his grandfather, the

Gentlemen.

In response to your address, allow me to attest the accuracy of its historical statements; indorse the sentiments it expresses; and thank you, in the nation's name, for the sure promise it gives.

Nobly sustained as the government has been by all the churches, I would utter nothing which might, in the least, appear invidious against any. Yet, without this, it may fairly be said that the Methodist Episcopal Church, not less devoted than the best, is, by its greater numbers, the most important of all. It is no fault in others that the Methodist Church sends more soldiers to the field, more nurses to the hospitals, and more prayers to Heaven than any. God bless the Methodist Church—bless all the churches— and blessed be God, Who, in this our great trial, giveth us the churches.

A. Lincoln

May 18. 1864

Abraham Lincoln. Handwritten speech signed, 1864, especially penned in a large script so he could read it without his spectacles, not unlike the writing in Cleveland's forgery.

noted jurist Roswell M. Field, plus Lincoln's firm name, "Lincoln & Herndon." In every volume Field wrote: "This is my book/Abraham Lincoln." There was a note in the back of each book describing the "provenance." For example: "This set of two volumes of 'Bacon on Government,' having the original manuscript signature of Abraham Lincoln . . . in the original manuscript catalogue which my father made of his library . . . was described as 'very rare.'" Sometimes the books contain notarized statements testifying to their authenticity, and on rare occasions Field added as a lagniappe the signature of Mark Twain or Eugene Field.

Field's forgeries of Lincoln are excellent, but Lincoln would never have penned so childish and egotistical a statement as "This is my book," nor

would he have signed his name in full, a signature reserved only for official documents.

Sometime in 1930 or 1931, Eugene Field II apparently formed a partnership in the manufacture of Lincoln-signed books, pamphlets, sheet music and maps with Harry D. Sickles, a Chicago forger then living at the Congress Hotel. Sickles was not as skilled as Field, but his items had an equally good provenance. They purportedly came from Mrs. Lincoln's coachman, William P. Brown, a ninety-three-year-old black man living in Ravenna, Michigan. There was a notarized statement by Brown in each book or pamphlet swearing under oath that Mrs. Lincoln had presented it to him. Probably after the amnesiac nonagenarian had placed his shaky signature in the items, Sickles or Field had added Lincoln's

Eugene Field II. Forged Lincoln inscription in a legal book, also bearing a forged signature of Field's grandfather, the noted jurist in the Dred Scott case, Roswell Martin Field. Pinny (Eugene Field II) turned out scores of such inscribed volumes during his twenty-year career as a forger.

Eugene Field II. Certification of authenticity penned in the back of the volume allegedly inscribed by Lincoln. Sometimes such "authentications" were notarized. Any inscribed volume with an authentication by Pinny must be viewed with extreme caution.

Abraham Lincoln. Authentic handwritten note, signed. Compare Lincoln's rather diminutive and virile script with the bold and very legible simulation by Eugene Field II.

Private.

Springfield Ills
March 13ᵗʰ 1864.

Hon Michael Hahn —
     My dear Sir.
          I congratulate you on having fixed
your name in history as the first free-state Governor
of Louisiana. Now you are about to have a Convention which among other things will probably define
the elective franchise. I barely suggest for your private consideration whether some of the colored people may not be let in — as for instance the very intelligent and especially those who have fought gallantly in our ranks. They would probably help in some
trying time to come, to keep the jewel of liberty within
the family of freedom. But this is only a suggestion,
not to the public but to you alone.

                              Yours truly
                              A. Lincoln.

Eugene Field II. Forgery of a handwritten letter signed by Lincoln. In addition to this celebrated letter to Michael Hahn, Pinny also forged an important letter of Lincoln's to U.S. Grant, accompanied by a fabricated authentication.

signature. When queried later, Brown could not remember whether there was a Lincoln signature in each of the books and pamphlets when he sold them.

Sickles's imitations lacked the verve of Field's, but they were very legible and the "authentication" of Brown was very impressive.

Several affluent collectors were taken in by the Field and Sickles fakes, including Burt Massee of the Palmolive-Peet Company. On June 23, 1931, Paul M. Angle, the executive secretary of the Abraham Lincoln Association of Spring-field, Illinois, issued a warning about the forgeries to members of the association:

The officers of the Abraham Lincoln Association have just learned that several members of the Association have been solicited to purchase so-called Lincoln autographs which purport to come from one Brown, a colored man who is said to have been Mrs. Lincoln's coachman in the years immediately following Lincoln's death, and to have received the material now offered for sale from her.

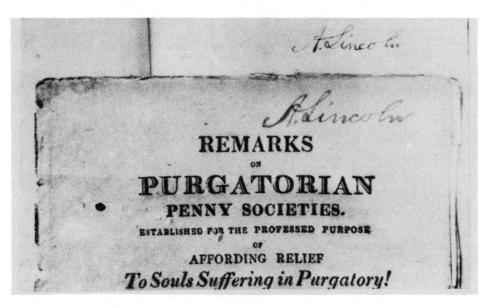

Eugene Field II. Two Lincoln signatures forged in old books. Many similar fakes are still on the market.

Abraham Lincoln. Authentic signature.

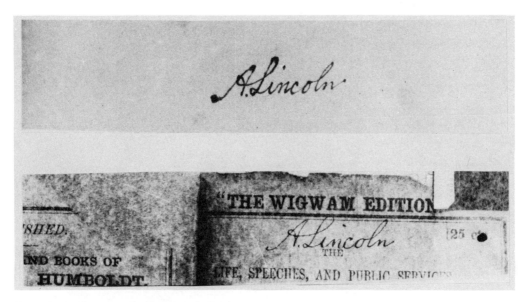

Harry D. Sickles. Forgeries of Lincoln's signature written in two books. Sickles's imitation is large and bold, lacking the rugged masculinity of Lincoln's own signature.

Abraham Lincoln. Authentic signature.

This material consists almost entirely of sheet music, old maps and rare books, usually autographed "A. Lincoln." Many of the items are of considerable value in themselves.

We feel, however, that we should fail in our duty to our members, many of whom will undoubtedly be asked to make purchases from this collection, if we did not point out several circumstances surrounding this material and the sale of it. In the first place, it is strange that a body of material so important as this should have remained unknown until this late date. In the second place, it is not known to the officers of the Association that

Lincoln was in the habit of collecting and autographing sheet music, maps and books. In the third place, several items from this collection have already been sold at prices much lower than the standard market value for genuine Lincoln autographs. . . .

Meanwhile, several victims who had become suspicious asked Judge Henry Horner of the Probate Court in Chicago to get an opinion from the renowned handwriting firm of Osborn, Osborn and Osborn in New York. Although an experienced philographer would have been able to identify the Field and Sickles items as fakes even clear across a room, Albert S. Osborn gave them "the full treatment" with blow-ups and caliper measurements and all the flashy paraphernalia so dear to amateur manuscript

Certification of authenticity for Sickles's forgery, signed by William P. Brown, who claimed to have been Mrs. Lincoln's coachman, with a notary's testimonial.

Abraham Lincoln 1863.

THE

HOSPITAL STEWARD'S

MANUAL:

FOR THE INSTRUCTION OF

HOSPITAL STEWARDS, WARD-MASTERS, AND ATTEND-
ANTS, IN THEIR SEVERAL DUTIES.

PREPARED IN STRICT ACCORDANCE WITH EXISTING REGULATIONS,
AND THE CUSTOMS OF SERVICE IN THE ARMIES OF THE
UNITED STATES OF AMERICA,

AND RENDERED AUTHORITATIVE BY ORDER OF THE SURGEON-GENERAL.

BY

JOSEPH JANVIER WOODWARD, M.D.
ASSISTANT SURGEON U.S.A., MEMBER OF THE ACADEMY OF NATURAL SCIENCES
OF PHILADELPHIA, ETC.

PHILADELPHIA:
J. B. LIPPINCOTT & CO.
1863.

Henry Woodhouse. Forgery of Lincoln's signature
in a book from Lanier Washington's library.

Abraham Lincoln. Authentic signature.

Abraham Lincoln

detectives. In a six-page pronuncia-
mento, fortified by an additional heap of
photographs, Osborn proclaimed the
Lincoln signatures by Field and Sickles
to be forgeries. It is to Osborn's credit
that he was able to spot the forest in
spite of the trees.

Osborn had questioned the notarizations and even the signatures of Brown,
which varied from item to item, but an
investigation by James W. Bollinger, an
attorney in Davenport, Iowa, where one
of Sickles's victims resided, indicated
"that Brown cannot write his name
twice alike, that Mr. Thatcher [the notary public] is clean and honest, and that
his certificate is true in all respects and
free from all fraud."

As my own hunch was the same as
Osborn's, I checked out Frank E.
Thatcher with the Muskegon County,
Michigan, clerk and found that Thatch-
er's record was as Bollinger described.

For nearly fourteen years the collection of forged inscriptions and signatures of Lincoln vanished from the
autograph market, with only one or two
now and then surfacing. But on April 14,
1945, the eightieth anniversary of Lincoln's murder, a Chicago attorney,
Raphael W. Marrow, mailed to nineteen
collectors a mimeographed list of signed
Lincoln items which he was offering for
sale on behalf of an unidentified client.
The list comprised one hundred eighteen books, pamphlets, maps and pieces
of sheet music, of which forty-one can
easily be identified as forgeries by Eugene Field II, all allegedly from the
library of his grandfather, the jurist, with
the signature of Lincoln, that of Roswell
M. Field, Lincoln's firm name and, in a
few cases, the additional forged signatures of Mark Twain or Eugene Field.
Presumably all of these forgeries were
bolstered by the authentications which
appear in all of Field's book fabrications.
The balance of the collection consisted

of seventy-one items signed *A. Lincoln,* all forged by Eugene Field II or Harry D. Sickles, with the authentications by the coachman, William P. Brown.

Unaware that the collection was composed entirely of forgeries, Ralph W. Marrow asked his nineteen prospects for "bids" within ten days, adding that the items "may be examined at my office, by appointment." Informed by the Abraham Lincoln Bookshop that every item was suspect, Marrow at once withdrew the collection from sale, observing: "Had I sold any of them I would have reaped a generous harvest of humiliation and embarrassment."

The books and other spurious items have again disappeared and I have not been able to locate them.

Most delightful and harmless of all Lincoln forgeries are the relics "dug up" on the site of New Salem, Illinois, about twenty miles from Springfield, where Lincoln spent four years of his young manhood. There from the earth were exhumed the grub hoe used by young Lincoln, his ox yoke, an ax helve carved with the rail-splitter's name and a flat rock, "discovered" by one William Green, on which is incised, "A. Lincoln and Ann Rutledge were betrothed here July 4, 1833."

What is appealing about these spurious relics is that they found their way into the collection of Oliver R. Barrett, noted Lincoln buff, and thence into the biography of Lincoln by Carl Sandburg. The poet who immortalized Chicago and fog and cool tombs was willing to suspend his critical acumen to admit these romantic fakes into his life of the emancipator. The frontispiece to the first volume of Sandburg's biography was the ax helve (which the big-city poet called an ax *handle*), a piece of wood bearing Abe's "jackknife signature" that had miraculously defied the corrosive effect of dampness and earth for over one hundred years. But the gem of the collection, also illustrated by Sandburg, was the flat stone recording what was almost certainly a mythical engagement between Lincoln and Ann Rutledge. The whole tale of this frontier love between Abe and Ann rests upon the tenuous word of Lincoln's law partner and biographer, William H. Herndon. In July, 1833, Ann Rutledge was probably still engaged to one John McNeil. But the movies, and the Chicago poets Sandburg and Masters, have wrought a beautiful American legend of the alleged love between Lincoln and the little New Salem girl who died in 1835—"Bloom forever, O Republic, from the dust of my bosom."

The apochryphal love of Lincoln for Ann Rutledge inspired still another forger whose creations would certainly test the credulity of even the most trusting historian. In January, 1929, *The Atlantic Monthly,* bulwark of staid philosophy and literary criticism, featured a number of "newly discovered letters, diaries and books" by Wilma Frances Minor entitled, "Lincoln the Lover. The Courtship." A mere glance at the texts of these forgeries reveals their blatantly false character. The letters are signed "Abe," a nickname Lincoln abhorred. In fact, Lincoln's wife, Mary, called him "Mr. Lincoln."

Ax helve with a forgery of Lincoln's carved signature.

The forged exchange of letters between Lincoln and Ann discloses almost every historical blunder it is possible for a forger to commit. Lincoln, the impeccable grammarian and master of English prose, writes in these letters like a retarded schoolboy. As the postmaster of New Salem he informs "My Beloved Ann" that "there is only five letters. if they keep the postage up to 25 cts for each letter poor people cannot avail themselves much. . . . however I am going over to Grahams as he is going to help me in my grammer. . . ." Ann is less polished than Abe. She sets forth her thoughts to "My Beloved Abe" in language that would have delighted Lincoln's favorite Civil War author, Orpheus C. Kerr, who made a literary style out of atrocious spelling. "I am trying to do as you ask me to praktise . . . if you git me the dictshinery . . . I no I can do both speaking and riting better. I am glad you sed that girls aint suposed to no

like boys . . . my hart runs over with hapynes when I think yore name. . . ."

There is little effort in these tedious forgeries to imitate the script of Lincoln; but since there are no authentic surviving examples of Ann Rutledge's handwriting I cannot fault the forger's chirography.

One of the most amazing Lincoln forgeries ever to land on my desk was fabricated to order for me. Early in 1960 I got a letter from Santa Monica, California, offering me a Eugene Field signature. "I have other autographs," wrote the vendor, "and if there is anything special you'd like just let me know."

I replied that Mark Twain was my favorite author and by return mail came a signature of Mark Twain. In enclosing payment, I asked: "Have you any *letters* by Twain?"

Back came a reply with an interesting letter by Mark Twain, as well as a brief note of Oscar Wilde's.

Forgery of a Lincoln letter signed "Abe," a nickname Lincoln abhorred and never permitted. A crude forgery, with little or no attempt to imitate Lincoln's script. Addressed to Ann Rutledge and written in stumbling English.

Forgery of a handwritten letter to Lincoln signed by Ann Rutledge, suggesting that Lincoln's legendary lover was virtually illiterate.

I was so amazed at my correspondent's ability to supply whatever I asked for that my suspicions were aroused. I took the Mark Twain letter to the window where the sunlight could fall directly upon it and examined it with a sharp and critical eye.

The letter was a forgery—and so were all the other autographs sent to me from Santa Monica.

After bestowing upon myself a few synonyms for donkey—but much less complimentary—I determined to set a trap for the Santa Monica forger.

"All my life," I wrote to him, "I have longed to own a truly great letter by Lincoln. If you have such a letter I should be eternally grateful for a chance to make an offer for it."

By registered post came one of Lincoln's greatest letters, often reproduced in facsimile, but this time in pen and ink on the very type of paper used by Lincoln and in the dark ink favored by him. It was a flawless freehand copy, not a tracing, so perfectly executed that it was almost impossible to tell it from Lincoln's original.

For weeks I tried to get the United States postal authorities to indict the perpetrator for mail fraud. Under pressure, they admitted to me that the Santa Monica forger had a previous arrest, but they refused to take any action.

When the forger's attorney wrote me a threatening letter, I redoubled my efforts to get an arrest and indictment. Finally, when I eventually gave up, I wrote a scathing letter to the postal authorities and accused them of fostering and encouraging the art of forgery.

Abraham Lincoln and the Santa Monica forger. *Top.* Authentic handwritten letter signed by Lincoln in 1861, a famous note that has been frequently reproduced in facsimile. *Bottom.* Forgery perpetrated in Santa Monica of the above note. A superb, very skilled freehand forgery, penned in an excellent imitation of Lincoln's very dark brown ink on paper of Lincoln's era.

All that was twenty years ago, and I now believe my efforts succeeded in stopping the forger, for I have not in two decades seen another faked autograph that came from Santa Monica.

Some of the quaintest Lincoln fabrications were vended by John Laflin, alias John Laffite, a forger who claimed descent from the famed New Orleans pirate. There is a remarkable family resem-

'LINCOLN' LETTERS FOUND IN TRUNK

Woman, Destitute, Seeks to Sell Notes to Grant, Mc-Clellan Dated 1864

The Judge was dead long since and his daughter was already elderly. The house upstate was in the hands of strangers—had been for years. The dressmaking business on which she had embarked after the death of her husband was likewise gone.

She sighed a little and tried not to cry. Yet the paper in her hand seemed to humiliate her merely because she had to touch it. It was a notice of dispossess. Things had come to that.

Her friend said nothing because silence was best, and together they went upstairs to pack.

Mechanically, the woman began sorting over the contents of a trunk.

"Look," she said, as she held out two picture frames. "I've carried them around with me for years."

The friend looked—and looked again.

Lincoln Letters Found

Out of the trunk had come two apparently authentic and possibly quite important Abraham Lincoln letters, one addressed to General McClellan and the other to Lieutenant General Grant.

Now, that is why Francis R. Laverty of 127 West Sixty-first Street today showed the letters to a representative of the EVENING POST.

"I don't know much about these things," he said. "I think they're genuine. You see, her father was a judge and a great admirer of Lincoln. It seems quite likely the letters are authentic. He was a judge, you know, and could have afforded to buy them for the comparatively small prices they brought forty years ago."

The Grant letter is date April 14, 1864. Grant had been commissioned a lieutenant general only the month preceding, and at that date was preparing his plans for the final campaign of the Civil War. At that date, too, he was about to leave to take personal command of the Army of the Potomac.

"Lincoln" Letter Is Found

Evening Post Photo

Note to General McClellan, signed by "A. Lincoln" and dated 1864, found by woman as she receives dispossess notice.

The letter reads:

Executive Mansion,
Washington, April 14, 1864.
Lieutenant General Grant,

Expecting to see you again before you leave. I am anxious that you have every assistance within my power. I know no points are likely to escape your attention as to the matter you mentioned. I must in candor say, do as you think best, for I have complete confidence in your judgment. Imploring the assistance of Divine Providence. May God assist you.

Yours very truly,
A. LINCOLN.

Important Topic Seen

"It would seem," said Mr. Laverty, "that they had been discussing something very important."

The McClellan letter is dated April 3, of the same year, the year whose autumn was to see the General contesting, as the Democratic nominee, the President's re-election.

The letter:

General McClellan,

I understand you wish to see me. If there is anything which is within my power, do not fail to let me know it. The sentiment which accompanied your letter meets my approval.

Yours very truly,
A. LINCOLN.

Mr. Laverty went on with his story, saying, "So I brought them down here. I thought you might like to write something about them. I thought, too, that there might be some one willing to buy them. Their owner would appreciate it."

An article from the *New York Evening Post*, January 28, 1933, about the "discovery" of several important Lincoln letters, all of which were forgeries. The letter to McClellan that is illustrated is a very inept imitation of Lincoln's virile hand. The letter to Grant, quoted in the article, was probably forged by Eugene Field II and is a copy of a famous letter frequently reproduced in facsimile.

Abraham Lincoln. Authentic handwritten note, signed.

Washington
April 18. 1863.

My Dear Mr Pickett.

I have seen your brother, and I am pleased to comply with your request, by inclosing you the paper you wish.

I would like to go to Rock Island, but the great pressure of official buisness prevents me from so doing at any very early date. As to the other matter you mention, I will give it my attention, and will be pleased to bear your wishes in mind.

Very truly yours,
A Lincoln.

Crude forgery of a Lincoln letter. The flatulent text is almost as unlike Lincoln as the script of the letter.

Executive Mansion
July 15, 1861
Hon. Sec. of Treasury
My dear Sir

The two Michigan Senators press me to appoint Arthur Edwards Supervising Inspector of Steam Boats, in the 8th District — The office is kept at Detroit, in their State; and unless you know some reason to the contrary, which is not known to me, let the appointment be made, at once —

Yours truly
A. Lincoln

Abraham Lincoln. Authentic handwritten letter, signed, couched in terse and forceful language.

blance in all of Laflin's forgeries, including those of his alleged forebear, Jean Laffite, and to judge only by the handwriting, Lincoln might have been the old pirate wearing false whiskers. There survive copies of several forged letters of Lincoln to "John," the originals of which were supposedly destroyed. Whether these forgeries were penned by Laflin or by a forebear is not known, but the attempt to capture the vitality of Lincoln's prose is even more inept than the imitation of Old Abe's script. In a forgery dated from Washington, November 11, 1847, Lincoln writes: "I don't mean to leave any one in doubt as to the course of my policy and paramount issue . . . You know we have in this nation an undivided [sic] house. Agitation for slavery on one side and freedom on the other . . ."

Possibly some Lincoln forgeries vended by Laflin alias Laffite still exist in private collections and libraries, but the forger's inimitably awkward script and clumsy style should not be difficult to detect.

Now and then the newspapers announce the "discovery" of an important and hitherto unknown Lincoln letter and frequently the letter turns out to be a fake. No exception was the discovery announced in the *Philadelphia Inquirer* on August 11, 1977:

With a wave of his hand, a Lancaster County physician, Dr. Arthur S. Griswold, recently signaled an auctioneer that he would pay $250 for a one-page handwritten letter purportedly written by Abraham Lincoln in 1860 before he became president, a document that could be worth four times more than the purchase price or simply a worthless forgery.

The purchase was, in short, pure speculation.

"Maybe it's a pig in a poke. Who knows? But I don't think so," the tall, grayish general practitioner said. "You can spend that much on liquor and women on a weekend and not have anything to show for it, so what the heck."

John Laffite, born Laflin, collection. Forgery of a handwritten letter signed by Lincoln, Washington, 1847. The writing is a poor imitation of Lincoln's hand, and the text is diffuse, rambling and incoherent. The forger even blunders in his anachronistic paraphrase of a speech of Lincoln during his debates with Douglas: "You know we have in this nation an undivided house. . . ."

Springfield, Dec. 1st 1841

Friend Weed:

Yours by the hand of Mr. Davidson was duly received — I will have your declaration filed and will taken to-morrow, according to Gunter —

Your case of Nicholas v. Herbert, stands on the Docket No. 57 — assigned to no particular day, for trial — If the opposite party will be ready to try it, as soon as the court will, my opinion is you may come right along — My recollection is, that I have never known a case in this court assigned the time beyond the first week, where both parties were ready for trial —

*Yours truly
A. Lincoln*

Abraham Lincoln. Authentic handwritten letter signed by Lincoln and penned during the same period as the date on the Laffite forgery.

The letter—written in longhand and in German—was sent to a Pennsylvania Dutchman by the name of Jacob Gingrich, who is something of a mystery man. . . .

The article quotes a part of the letter, a rambling and rather silly epistle making "a pitch for Gingrich's vote in the presidential election of 1860":

Esteemed Friend Jacob Gingrich: Although we are not personally acquainted with each other, nevertheless I have heard so much about you as also an old rail-splitter, that I desire to make your acquaintance.

Hence I send you herewith a very good picture of myself which, if you are so disposed, you may hang alongside of your splitting tools . . . I take it for granted that you have a wife. I have one that is much better looking than I. Mine sends kindly greetings to yours and has pleasant anticipations of the splendid pumpkin butter. It is possible she may treat us to some of her excellent spruce beer to drink with it.

This unLincolnesque letter concludes with "your friend, the old rail-splitter, Abraham Lincoln."

Aside from the fact that Lincoln could not read or write German and never signed his letters "Abraham Lincoln," the whole effect of this meandering letter suggests a very amateurish forgery.

My suggestion to Dr. Arthur S. Griswold, evidently a pleasant, good-natured man, is: "When next you have two hundred and fifty dollars to spare, spend it wisely, spend it on women and liquor."

Many years ago I owned the original manuscript of the most famous—and profitable—forgery ever perpetrated, and it was easily the worst. Retraced, labored, erased and thoroughly unconvincing. It was the celebrated letter of Lincoln to Mrs. Bixby in which Old Abe consoled her for the loss of "five sons who have died gloriously on the field of battle." In it, the forger had stumbled badly. The paper was not of the variety used by Lincoln, the ink was modern, the folds were not correct to accommodate envelopes of Lincoln's era and the letter itself had first been drawn in pencil and then retraced in ink. Yet this forged missive has been published in facsimile in scores of history books and hung in the parlors of half a million homes.

Nobody knows whether Lincoln really composed this great letter or whether, if he did write it, it was ever mailed.

New Salem, Ills.
Nov 21. 1835

My dear John,

I have a vivid recollection
of it yesterday when I first met you at St.
Louis. On my trip to New Orleans the relief and
assistance you rendered, I do not remember
so much about that gentleman in New
Orleans— you referred me to. I do know
his name was Alex Yours— it is about
his. 'Tis years since he is dead, it was my
understanding to assume the bill and the
money remitted by accepting you. I did
talk about the captains hospitality. He
paid the women about my fortune tell
them that day I have turned very bitter
against the slave block— of course I feel
fully entrusted over those two women
telling my future events. I am still in
debt, but I wish others to know that I
am to pay captain young in your behalf
the captain advised never to mention
his name anywhere but said he had
a brother living at Baltimore— My
conscience is strong and wish to have
his good name paid, as he was low

away with high honors and a hero for
the defence of the country. I struggled
with Wm. Berry, we met into failure,
and into debt. I can not conceive of
no other way to pay the money in
full; only to put in many twists to
front by packet. I spoke to you about
Mr. Green, who will spirit me with a
note for my future account. I do
not remember about that French
man you spoke of in Baltimore—
I would be glad you communicate
some facts to him— suppose you can
for a good turn to take a few things
over to a better way and a good
course from me. There is not much
up out May.

Come up when ever you can.

Your friend as ever
Abe Lincoln

Mr. John Mortimore
15 and 16 Biddle Street.
St. Louis, Missouri.

_pas devenir actif ni montrer N'emporte
Mr Lincoln. Je me sens Sure et Sain
et Conscient qu'il efseüra D'imprégner
principes Sur le Champ politique De cette
Nation. Son esprit pense toujours plu
qu'il ne pent agir. Il est sceptic, r
parleur rapide lorsque il est provoqu
convaincu Complètement par des faits
enant auf principes De Ceux Qui gagn
uruient Du Gagner.
Je suis sur mon chemin de
J'espère que les Deux petits Garcons font
Dans leurs études à L'école.
Votre Mari et pere famille_

John Laffite collection. Portion of a forged letter by the pirate Jean Laffite mentioning Lincoln. Note the similarity in handwriting between the forgery of Lincoln's script and the forgery of Laffite's script. Many letters, such as the *o, e, l,* capital *J* and others are almost identical, in spite of the fact that the forger was imitating two different handwritings in two different languages.

Lincoln's secretary, John Hay, once claimed the authorship of the letter. At least five or six times a year I am offered "the original" of the Bixby letter by eager owners who are convinced they possess a priceless relic, but I remain unmoved by such offers, for I am weary of viewing the ancient fake.

I once perpetrated a Lincoln forgery myself, but quite by accident. I was in Dayton, Ohio, working with the noted Lincoln expert Lloyd Ostendorf on a book about Lincoln photographs when he casually observed: "I'm offered forgeries of signed photographs for my collection almost every month. But they are usually poorly done—the ink isn't right or the forger hasn't got the hang of Lincoln's writing. I guess it's just about impossible to forge even a simple signature on a photograph."

"That's because the forgers never really study Lincoln's handwriting or the ink he used," I said. "Lincoln's signature breaks down into three component parts, and the forger must learn each of these parts so he can write them swiftly and accurately. Then he must join them as Lincoln did. And he must use a dark ink, almost black, like Lincoln's. Not the anemic brown of the amateur craftsman."

Genuine New Salem franking signature of Lincoln on a cover. Only five such covers are known to exist.

Free. A. Lincoln P.M.
New Salem Ill
Sept 22

Mr. Geo. M. Marsh
Portsmouth
N. H.

John Laffite collection. Forged addressed Lincoln letter cover, franked as postmaster of New Salem, Illinois. The postal markings are obvious fakes.

Express Mail
FREE
A. Lincoln P.M.
Dec. 21. 1835

ST. LOUIS DEC 24 MO.
NEW SALEM DEC 21. ILL.

Mr. John Mortimore
15 and 16 Biddle street
St. Louis, Missouri.

Lloyd listened carefully and practiced a Lincoln signature. His imitation was excellent. I complimented him and added: "If you have a cheap *carte-de-visite* photo of Lincoln around, and some good black ink, I'll take a crack at his signature."

Ostendorf produced an old photograph, vintage 1865. I waved the pen in the air a couple of times, limbering up: "I'm pretty rusty at this, but watch the component parts." I was writing as I spoke. "Part one, the up and down strokes of the capital *A,* placing the base of the *A* lower than the rest of the signature. Part two, the crossing of the capital *A* and the writing of the name up through the letter *n,* then picking up the pen from the paper. Part three, joining the letter *c* to the letter *n* and finishing the signature, making sure the terminal *ln* is on a higher plane than the rest of the signature. Finally, a single, quick rather sloppy dot under and after the capital *A.*"

"Pretty good," said Lloyd. He put the photograph away and we turned again to our work on the book.

Three months passed and I forgot about my signature of Lincoln on the old Civil War photograph. Late in 1963 I was opening the morning's mail in my office when the telephone rang. It was my close friend the Reverend Cornelius Greenway, whose collection of signed photographs was world famous. Connie's voice shook with excitement and joy. "I've got one at last! I've got one at last!" he cried. "I've got a beautiful signed photograph of Lincoln and I want to bring it over right now and show it to you."

An hour later, in from Brooklyn, Connie beamed as he handed me his prize. You guessed it! I found myself examin-ing the photograph I had signed several months earlier.

I demanded to know where Connie had got it. Connie named a prominent autograph dealer in a rather small city in Illinois. He added: "The price was only seven hundred and fifty dollars."

I at once telephoned Lloyd Ostendorf in Dayton. He explained: "Last week the dealer you mention was in to see me and asked if I had any Lincoln photo-graphs I cared to sell. I showed him a few, including the one you had signed. I

Genuine congressional franking signature of Lincoln.

Joseph Cosey. Forged address-leaf of a letter by Lincoln, bearing his franking signature as a member of congress. The postmarks, which reveal Cosey's creative ability, are patent forgeries. The noted stamp expert Herman Herst, Jr., said of Cosey's early attempts to create a philatelic cover: "The paper was almost like wrapping paper, quite unlike anything of the period. The postmark was made with the top of a bottle and the town name constructed of a child's rubber stamp outfit. . . . There was a gaglomeration of weird post-marks. . . ."

The notorious Bixby forgery. The original of Lincoln's alleged letter to Mrs. Bixby has never turned up and perhaps was never written by Lincoln. This crude forgery was the most profitable fake ever created. It was widely reproduced in facsimile and printed in history books, despite the fact that the imitation of Lincoln's script is halting and awkward and makes his forceful hand appear like a child's scrawl.

Executive Mansion
Washington, Nov 21, 1864

To Mrs Bixby, Boston. Mass,
Dear Madam.
I have been shown in the files of the War Department a statement of the Adjutant General of Massachusetts that you are the mother of five sons who have died gloriously on the field of battle. I feel how weak and fruitless must be any word of mine which should attempt to beguile you from the grief of a loss so overwhelming. But I cannot refrain from tendering you the consolation that may be found in the thanks of the republic they died to save. I pray that our Heavenly Father may assuage the anguish of your bereavement, and leave you only the cherished memory of the loved and lost, and the solemn pride, that must be yours to have laid so costly a sacrifice upon the altar of freedom.
Yours very sincerely and respectfully.
A. Lincoln

told him that since you had mutilated it with a phony signature I'd ask only ten dollars for it—and he bought it."

The dénouement? Connie decided to keep the photograph. "It will do until I get the real thing," he explained.

Some handwriting experts claim that the quirks and curlicues of handwriting can be inherited. And it's certainly true that there are hundreds, even thousands, of namesakes whose signatures look very much like those of their father's or grandfather's. So it is perhaps not remarkable that Abraham Lincoln II, grandson of the great Civil War president, wrote his name very much the same way as Old Abe. But there are tales that young Abraham Lincoln—known to his family and friends as "Jack"—got so proficient at scribbling the great man's name that he wrote *A. Lincoln* in old books and sold the inscribed volumes as authentic relics.

Abraham "Jack" Lincoln II was born on August 14, 1873, the son of President Lincoln's only son to reach adulthood, Robert Todd Lincoln. As a youth Jack played at the White House with the Garfield children. He was a cheerful boy and once got into trouble when he and a few friends accidentally swatted a baseball through a neighbor's window. The owner of the house burst out, furious, and all the boys fled except Jack.

"What's your name?" demanded the man.

"Abraham Lincoln."

The man looked startled, then his face ashened and he backed away.

Jack Lincoln was slated for Harvard and the law. He was bright and pleasant and his father adored him. But in the autumn of 1889 while on a holiday in France he got blood poisoning and a few months later, early in March, 1890, he died in England at the age of seventeen.

Many of the books bearing Jack's *A. Lincoln* signature were published after his grandfather's death in 1865, but those with an earlier imprint might easily be confused with the few, rare volumes from the president's library. At "Hildene" in Manchester, Vermont, the home of Robert Todd Lincoln, now a

Abraham Lincoln II. Flyleaf from a book inscribed by him "A. Lincoln," with his bookplate pasted beneath. The inscription and bookplate have lead to the mistaken conclusion that the book was inscribed by President Lincoln.

I now wish to make "the personal ac-
knowledgment that you were right, and I was wrong.
Yours very truly
A. Lincoln

Abraham Lincoln. Authentic handwriting and signature as president, from a letter to U. S. Grant.

LINCOLN AND HIS FORGERS

1	Authentic signature of Lincoln.
2	Eugene Field II forgery.
3	Charles Weisberg forgery.
4	Charles Weisberg forgery.
5	Joseph Cosey forgery.
6	Joseph Cosey forgery.
7	Abraham Lincoln II signature.
8	Santa Monica forgery.
9	Henry Cleveland forgery.
10	John Laffite (Laflin) forgery.
11	Bixby letter forgery.
12	Unidentified forgery.
13	Authentic signature of Lincoln.
14	Eugene Field II forgery.
15	Charles Weisberg forgery.
16	Harry D. Sickles forgery.
17	Henry Woodhouse forgery.
18	John Laffite (Laflin) forgery.
19	Unidentified forgery.

Abraham Lincoln II (1873–1890). Grandson of the Civil War president. His signature, "A. Lincoln," closely resembled that of his grandfather, and it is believed that young Lincoln may have sold his own autograph to gullible tourists, representing it as that of the great emancipator.

MAX PLATZ. CHICAGO.

fascinating museum, are preserved several dozen books signed by Jack, some of them also adorned with his *A. Lincoln* bookplate. As Jack got older his signature grew more and more to look like that of his celebrated grandfather. Jack's imitation was excellent. Had he lived to manhood he could certainly have supported himself handsomely by scrawling once or twice a week, in some old book, the most famous name in American history.

Abraham Lincoln
1

Abraham Lincoln
2

A. Lincoln
3

A. Lincoln
4

A. Lincoln
5

6 A. Lincoln

7 A. Lincoln.

Yours truly
8 A. Lincoln

Respectfully
9
A. Lincoln.

10 Your friend as ever
Abe Lincoln

Yours very sincerely and respectfully.
11
A. Lincoln

Yours very truly
12 A. Lincoln

Yours truly
13 A. Lincoln

Yours truly
14 A. Lincoln.

Yours truly
15 A. Lincoln

16 A. Lincoln

Abraham Lincoln
17

Yours as ever
A. Lincoln
18

Very truly yours,
19 A. Lincoln.

2

The Nine Bibles of Stonewall Jackson

THOMAS CHANCELLOR

Thomas Chancellor was the South's answer to the carpetbaggers. He came out of Old Virginny with nine pocket Bibles, an agile pen, a fantastic tale on his lips and a remarkable pair of lachrymal ducts. With this minimal equipment he made a killing in one week by outwitting the sharpest rare-book dealers in New York City.

Nobody would ever suspect that Thomas Chancellor was a forger. He had a Southern accent as broad as the Potomac, the rough hands of a farmer, threadbare old clothes that didn't quite fit and the hapless look of a small-town boy lost in The Big City. It was the perfect equipment to take in the Yankee booksellers, because Chancellor was not really a very good forger. But he had a trick that most Hollywood actors would envy. He could turn on the tears at will. Even the toughest bookmen would melt when they saw a grown man weep because he was forced by poverty to sell the family treasure—a pocket Bible that Stonewall Jackson was carrying when the fatal ball struck him at Chancellorsville.

At eleven o'clock on Saturday morning, October 3, 1891 (the precise date is important, because it's a memorable one in the chronicles of Southern retaliation!), Thomas Chancellor mounted the steps to the second floor of 34 Park Row where A. S. Clark had his rare-book store.

"Do you know of anybody who buys autographs?" he drawled to the proprietor.

"I do, if they're good ones."

"Well, I've got a little pocket Bible here," said Chancellor. He unwrapped a worn volume from a newspaper and laid it on Clark's counter.

Clark glanced at the inscription inside the cover, "From my dear friend, Dr. R. H. Morrison. T. J. Jackson," and said, "This doesn't seem to be worth much."

"Don't you know who that is?" asked Chancellor, pointing to the signature, *T. J. Jackson.* "That's ol' Stonewall."

Clark perked up and studied the book.

From my dear Friend Dr KBC Morris. T. J. Jackson. Lexington, Va., Dec. 20th 1860

I will do my duty, and leave the rest to God T.J.J. Apr. 28. 1861

Thomas Chancellor. Forgeries of two inscriptions by General Thomas J. "Stonewall" Jackson in a pocket Bible. Chancellor's imitations are labored and much more legible than Jackson's own hand. This Bible was sold in 1891 to the prominent book dealer Charles L. Woodward, one of Chancellor's nine victims, and was presented by Woodward to the Lenox Library in 1894.

Ordered. See Letter book 15 mar

March 14th, 1863

General,

Please have two of Anderson's brigades moved up to the U.S. ford as soon as the roads will permit. And have such disposition made of them as will be best calculated to prevent the enemy from crossing the Rappahannock.

I hope to move my Hd qrs near you one next Monday

I am Genl your obdt sert T. J. Jackson Lt Genl

Brig Genl R. H. Chilton A A & I Genl Hd qrs Lt Col S. Valley

Stonewall Jackson. Handwritten letter, signed, 1863. Note how sloppy and rapidly written is Jackson's script compared with Chancellor's awkward fabrication.

The signature was scrawled with a rusty pen in the pale, grainy ink that the South was forced to use during the war. Even the original light hue of the ink had faded.

Clark then took a closer look at his Southern visitor. Twenty-six years in the rare-book and autograph business had taught him to be wary and during his career he had run into all kinds of fakers and con men, two of whom he had jailed for trying to swindle him. "He looked like a farmhand," Clark later recalled, "a typical hired man. He wore a coarse check shirt and an old, faded coat. His hands were covered with callouses which must have been caused by the hardest kind of manual labor. He wore a dark mustache. His eyes at first glance appeared to be crossed, but a second look showed they were only not mated. One was a little larger than the other, which gave him the appearance of being cross-eyed."

Almost convinced of Chancellor's honesty, Clark popped the big question, the one all interested dealers put to the vendor of a valuable article: "Where did you get this?"

"Well, sir, my name is Thomas Chancellor and my grandpappy, Melchisedec Chancellor, founded the town of Chancellorsville, Virginny. He owned the largest house in the whole village and was the oldest man there.

40

Thomas Chancellor. Forged inscription of Stonewall Jackson in a pocket Bible, dated the very day that Jackson was fatally wounded at Chancellorsville.

"When ol' Stonewall got shot in the dark by his own men, some soldiers carried him into my grandpappy's house. There was a battle going on outside and I was only ten years old, so I was hiding in the cellar with the womenfolk. I can still remember the terrible sounds and how scared I was, but I climbed out of the cellar, we all did, to look at the general.

"The doctors were there and they took off Jackson's coat to probe for the ball that had hit him. They threw his coat on a chair and this little Bible fell out. My grandpappy picked it up and put it at the end of the mantelpiece.

"The surgeons discovered that Jackson was badly hurt and in all the excitement nobody thought about the book.

"Some men came and took Jackson away but it was two or three days before anybody in our family remembered the Bible. When we heard the bad news that ol' Stonewall had died, grandpappy said he would keep the Bible as a souvenir.

"When grandpappy died he left the Bible to pop and when pop died he left it to me. This was all he left me, this and his silver watch."

Chancellor paused for a moment as tears glistened in his eyes.

Clark was sympathetic and impressed by all the inconsequential details in Chancellor's story. The Southerner went on: "I came up North to find work. There wasn't anything for me in Albany and I couldn't pay my landlady so she put me out. Then I had to sell pop's watch. It wasn't worth much, only the value of the silver, and all I could get was two dollars and a half."

Chancellor started to sob. "Now I

haven't got anything but this Bible left."

"How much do you want for it?"

"Well, I asked several people here about its value," said Chancellor, trying to control his tears, "but nobody could tell me anything. An uncle of mine in Washington offered me twenty-five dollars for it, but when I made the trip there just to sell it to him, he started to haggle and tried to beat me down. So I just walked away. I know you're an honest man, Mr. Clark, and I'll accept whatever you want to give me."

"Will you sign an affidavit that it's genuine?"

Chancellor nodded.

"Have you had any breakfast?" asked Clark.

Chancellor shook his head.

"Here," said Clark, handing a dollar bill to Chancellor. "Get something to eat and come back and then we'll talk about the Bible."

After the Southerner walked out, leaving the Bible with him, Clark dispatched his assistant uptown to check the Jackson inscription with several big autograph dealers. In the 1890s there were few or no dealers who could spot a forgery instantly, and the experts unanimously allowed the handwriting to be Stonewall's after a quick comparison with other examples written by Jackson.

Early in the afternoon Chancellor came back. He handed Clark the one-dollar bill. "I didn't want to buy any

Stonewall Jackson. Handwritten letter to Robert E. Lee, penned and signed just before Jackson was accidentally shot by his own troops at Chancellorsville on May 2, 1863. This was the last letter ever written by Jackson.

breakfast," he explained, "because you mightn't have bought the book. In that case you'd have wanted your money back and I wouldn't be able to give it to you."

Clark was completely taken in by Chancellor's apparent honesty. He had drafted an affidavit for Chancellor to sign and Chancellor signed it as the tears ran down his cheeks.

Clark paid him thirty dollars.

Four days later, on Wednesday, a book merchant from uptown ambled into Clark's shop and asked: "Did you get a Jackson Bible?"

"How the devil did you know about my Jackson Bible?" asked Clark. "I haven't told anybody about it."

"Oh," said the dealer, "everybody's got one. Why, even Charlie Woodward got stuck. He took an affidavit, too. Mitchell and Walsh and Hembreen and Gilsey and three others bought a Jackson Bible."

It then turned out that Chancellor had sold a few pictures of Jackson inscribed on the verso to his wife:

Dear Mary

God crowned our arms, with success yesterday. Brig. Gen. White & 11,000 troops are ours. I also recd. my pictures & send them to you

Yours Lovingly

T. J. JACKSON

OFFICE OF **CHARLES L. WOODWARD,**

DEALER IN

RARE BOOKS AND PAMPHLETS RELATING TO AMERICA,

78 Nassau Street, .

New York, *Oct. 3,* 1891

To whom it may concern:
This is to certify that the bible printed at Oxford in 1844 and containing the signatures of T. J. (Stonewall) Jackson was in the pocket of Gen. Jackson when he was shot and was taken from his pocket in the house of my grandfather, Melzi: Chancellor at Chancellorsville, Va. on the night of 3d May, 1863.

Thomas Chancellor

Thomas Chancellor. Handwritten and signed affidavit of authenticity for a pocket Bible in which Chancellor had forged three Stonewall Jackson inscriptions. Dated October 3, 1891, the same day on which Chancellor also sold an identical Jackson forgery to A. S. Clark, another well-known New York bookseller.

Higers Valley Dist
Harfers Ferry
Sep 16th '62

Dear Mary
God crown
our arms with
success yesterday
Brig. Gen. White
& 11000 troops are
ours, I also recd
my picture & send
them to you
Yours loving ly
T. J. Jackson.

Thomas Chancellor. Forged Stonewall Jackson letter to his wife, Mary, with the portrait of Jackson on the verso of which the forgery was written.

T. J. Jackson

Stonewall Jackson. Authentic signature.

again more than they do
their peculiar notions of
slavery, and that they will
prove it to us when satisfied
that we are in earnest
about leaving the Confederacy
unless they do us justice.
Your aunt joins me in
love to you all.
Write often.
Your affectionate Uncle
Thomas

Stonewall Jackson. Last page of an authentic handwritten letter signed "Thomas," January, 1861.

Mitchell in Philadelphia had shelled out a handsome sum for the inscribed picture. With it came a lengthy tale from Chancellor about how he discovered it while employed to help demolish the Jackson homestead.

The _New York Herald_ printed a story about the Jackson Bibles and on Saturday, October 10, 1891, Thomas Chancellor strolled into the shop of a book dealer named Fullerton on Third Avenue near Nineteenth Street. He unfolded an old newspaper and produced a pocket Bible.

"Do you buy autographs?" he asked.

Fullerton had read the story in the _Herald._ He glanced at the Bible and said to Chancellor: "Inspector Byrnes of the New York police is looking for you."

Chancellor was indignant. He was also hurt by the implication that he had committed nine dishonest acts. For nearly half an hour he protested to Fullerton. Then he asked:

"Where does Inspector Byrnes keep?"

"Three hundred Mulberry," replied the dealer.

"Well, then, if you'll just point out the route, I'll go right down and see into this."

Fullerton took Chancellor to the door of his shop and pointed out the direction.

And Chancellor strode off briskly, whistling, jes' a country boy from the South with his pockets full of Yankee dollars.

3

George Washingtons to Order

ROBERT SPRING

Moses Pollock was uncommonly shrewd and could hide his emotions with great skill. Yet on this occasion the noted Philadelphia rare-book and autograph dealer of the 1860s felt his fingers tremble as he looked at the pass a stranger had just placed in his hands. Pollock had bought and sold scores of Washington documents, but this Revolutionary pass was actually made out to one of his own ancestors! Pollock longed to own it and he tried to appear casual as he chatted with the owner.

"Where did you get this?" he asked.

"I found it in an old hair-trunk," replied the vendor, a refined, middle-aged Englishman with an impeccable accent.

Pollock studied the faded document for a few moments, admiring the grace and beauty of Washington's script—a little shaky perhaps, but it had been hastily penned during the war when every moment was precious and there was no time for elegance.

"How much?" he asked.

"To you, Mr. Pollock, only fifteen dollars."

"Fifteen dollars!" Pollock was genuinely shocked. "Why, for fifteen dollars I can buy a full handwritten letter of Washington."

"I'm sorry, sir," said the visitor. "That's my price." There was a firmness in the British accent.

Pollock sighed and then counted out the money. But as soon as the Englishman left, he gloated over his treasure.

It was not until many years later, when Pollock showed his prized ancestral pass to Ferdinand J. Dreer, a distinguished collector from Philadelphia, that he learned he had bought the document from Robert Spring, the notorious forger.

Dreer chided him in a tone of amiable disgust. "Mr. Pollock, you, of all men, should know better! This thing is an arrant forgery—it's worth less than nothing."

It might have consoled Moses Pollock, one of the great book dealers of his time and the uncle of Dr. A. S. W. Rosenbach, if he could have known that this despised forgery of Spring's would someday, as it is now, be worth many times the price he paid for it, merely as a curiosity.

And it would doubtless have consoled him even more had he known, and perhaps he did, that dozens of Philadelphians from old mainline families had gratefully invested ten or fifteen dollars in forged Washington passes made out to their Revolutionary ancestors.

Pollock always kept the pass as a reminder of his youthful folly. Years later he said: "Buying the Robert Spring fake was one of the best investments I ever made. It put me on guard for the rest of my life and in time saved me thousands of dollars."

Robert Spring was the first forger to personalize his fabrications. Although he adventured now and then into manufacturing Jeffersons and Franklins, sometimes mere tracings from lithographs, most of these were less deceptive so he stuck mainly to Washingtons. Using a goose quill and his own special mixture of "antiquated" ink, he practiced constantly to capture the spirit and verve of Washington's handwriting. He was extremely successful. One of his Washington forgeries was ostentatiously displayed in Independence Hall. Even today the field of Revolutionary War collecting and study is still booby-trapped with Spring's forgeries of the man who "could not tell a lie."

Very little is known of Spring's life before the law caught up with him. He was born in England in 1813 and as a young man came to America where he opened a bookshop in Philadelphia. From here he carried out his transactions—legitimate and illegitimate. He bought and sold a few books from Washington's library, and the profit was so great that he decided to widen the profit margin on some of the slow-moving volumes in his stock. So he improved on them by simply adding Washington's signature to the title page. To his delight, the expensive fabrications sold just as quickly as the genuine articles, and soon Spring was launched on a career of manufacturing Washingtons. He did not, however, totally neglect the honest end of his business. To ministers in Pennsylvania and adjoining states he addressed the following communication, perhaps the first of its type ever sent out in America:

CIRCULAR

Washington

Respected Friend:

I am passing through the States, purchasing Old Books, Old Letters, Old Pamphlets, and Old Engravings. For any of such I especially want, I can afford to pay a HIGH PRICE. Many families have OLD LETTERS, BOOKS, PAPERS, &c. hid away in garrets and bye-places, of little account to them, but that would be deeply interesting to the Scholar and Historian, and contribute to throw a light on events of "other times" now shrouded in mist and uncertainty.

Should sufficient new matter be collected, a further history of this great country would be forthcoming, and it is judged correctly that much useful information may be obtained in this way. Do, therefore, allow me to look over any Old Books, Letters, &c. you would kindly, to further this pa-

The subscriber, Agent for several Public and Private Libraries, Historical and Antiquarian Societies in America and Europe, is desirous of purchasing Old Books, Rare Books, Old Engravings, Paintings, Coins, Autographs, &c., for which he is prepared to pay a high price and to a large amount.

Old Books and Pamphlets—especially those relating to American History—early imprints, &c., WANTED.

Autographs, Old Letters written by eminent men, such as Washington, Signers of the Declaration of Independence, Presidents, Military and Naval Heroes, celebrated Civilians, in fact the handwriting of every distinguished American—PARTICULARLY WANTED.

Parties receiving these circulars, who have in their possession collections of Old Books and Letters, will confer the greatest favor by permitting the subscriber to look over them. A line to his address will meet with the promptest and most respectful attention. He will, with pleasure, visit any part of Maryland or adjoining States.

ROBERT SPRING, 38 Spring Row,

☞ Please show this circular to any one likely to be interested.   Baltimore, Md.

YOUNG, PRINT

Robert Spring. Printed broadside issued by him, October, 1863, asking for rare books and autographs. Spring was the first American autograph dealer to use this method of advertising.

triotic undertaking, be willing to part with. I often pay a dollar for an old letter or pamphlet, looked upon by its possessor of no other worth than to kindle a fire.

Very Respectfully,
ROBERT SPRING

During the 1850s and 1860s Spring continued to turn out circulars and announcements, peppering the country with pleas for rare books and autographs. In an undated circular from Maryland (about 1865), Spring described several of his adventures in searching for rare books and manuscripts:

I beg to submit the following Remarks:—

There is nothing known that annoys a tidy housewife more, who has a quick Eye for dirt, and whose Equipose is so instantly disturbed, than by a descent from the garret of a lot of grandpa's old rubbish. How many Old Letters, Old Pamphlets and Old Books are daily gathered up and consigned to the fire, which if they had fallen into the hands of the scholar and historian, would have been of the greatest benefit. How often have these records and relics of the heroic past been snatched up and hurried to the flames, with a congratulatory "Thank goodness They're gone" as though they were Evil spirits and cumbered the Earth. . . .

About a year ago, I saw in the city two large wagons filled with huge bags, just leaving a wholesale junk warehouse, and from a few pamphlets a son of the Emerald Isle was stuffing into a bursted and refractory bag, I rescued one which for nearly eight years I had been trying through the land to find. . . . I asked my Irish friend what I should give him for the privilege of calling it mine. Taking it from me with a curious leer he glanced at it puzzled for a moment or so . . . no doubt thinking to himself, "its not worth nare a cint" returned it to me with a curious cunning leer and remarked, "its chape at fifty cints." Thinking so too, I presented him with that amount and withdrew a few steps eager to investigate a certain portion of its contents, but still watching Paddy out of one corner of my eye, saw him after sundry nods and winks to the driver of the other waggon, tap his forehead very significantly and casting a pitying look at me, remarked "Saft by jabers."

To oblige a friend and obtain information, I made a journey of over five hundred miles in the storms of winter to consult an old funeral sermon, which probably had not been looked at for a hundred years; but a point was wanted in a certain case, involving a large amount. It contained all the evidence required and incontrovertibly settled the case: who would suppose so much good could be extracted from a little pamphlet so ungainly to the sight. . . .

Among a large lot of old letters sent to me in sugar hogsheads written from 1750 to 1797, I discovered most valuable information. . . . I feel gratified that through my instrumentality one unrecorded historical incident has been rescued from the insatiable grasp of the Paper Mill . . . such instances are bright spots in a life of rebuffs and anxiety. Many look upon the collecting of such old matter as a symptom of insanity. Many of my

Robert Spring. Handwritten signed letter, Baltimore, October 17, 1863, offering forgeries of Washington checks. "Some time since I was so fortunate to obtain the papers belonging to the branch of the old U.S. Bank of this City. Among them I found many autographs of distinguished men and quite a number of the immortal Washington's.

"I have been advised to send you one. Enclosed please find two my price is $10 each $20 for both. . . . I sent several of the Washington checks to England and recd for all sold £5 sterling each. . . ."

most intimate friends treat me with but little more consideration than they would if I was crazy but harmless, yet, I do not regret I have made it my business, and although not profitable, yet to me it is an intensely interesting one.

By the 1850s Spring was well established as a bookseller—and as a forger. Curiously, his own letters are rare. Penned in a florid script, the few notes that survive discuss books or autographs, mostly his own fakes that he was trying to sell to unsuspecting customers. Once he presented a favorite client with a letter of Martin Luther, doubtless fabricated the previous evening.

Unlike other forgers, Spring used two methods: tracing and freehand. When he could get authentic letters of celebrities, he traced them on a sheet of paper removed from the front or back of an old book, then stained his product with coffee grounds to make it look ancient.

No doubt this is the way he created his Martin Luther. But with Washington and Jefferson he was more adept. Spring had spent so many hours practicing the handwriting of our first president that he was familiar with every curve and flourish and could write Washington's script almost as swiftly as his own.

Spring's favorite was a Revolutionary pass. He usually offered this by mail, and the sales were most gratifying:

> Permission is granted to Mr. Ryerson, with his negro man, Dick, to pass and repass the picket at Ramapo.

> Go: Washington

These adroit Ryerson-Dick fabrications were widely accepted among collectors and even dealers. In his sales publication, the *Autograph,* published in New York, January–February, 1912, the famed autograph expert Patrick F. Madigan unwittingly offered a Ryerson-

Robert Spring. Forgery of a pass by George Washington for Mr. Boudinot "with his negro man Tom to pass and repass the picket at Ramapo," one of the many variations of the Ryerson-Dick Ramapo pass. The handwriting is notably small for Washington, cramped and a little quavery. Spring never quite got the hang of the *Go:W* in Washington's signature. The peaks of the *W* should be sharp, but Spring blunted them. The crossing of the *t* by Spring lacks the bold, flourishing sweep of Washington's. The signature itself is less than two-thirds the size of Washington's and hasn't the grace and beauty of the original model.

I _George Washington. Commander in chief of the armies of the United States of America_

do acknowledge the UNITED STATES of AME-
RICA, to be Free, Independent and Sovereign States, and
declare that the people thereof owe no allegiance or obedience to George the Third, King of Great-Britain; and I re-
nounce, refuse and abjure any allegiance or obedience to him;
and I do _swear_ —— that I will to the utmost of
my power, support, maintain and defend the said United
States, against the said King George the Third, his heirs and
successors and his or their abettors, assistants and adherents,
and will serve the said United States in the office of _Com-
in chief as afores_: which I now hold, with fidelity,
according to the best of my skill and understanding.

Sworn before me
Camp at Valley Forge
May 12th 1778
Sterling Major Genl

Go Washington

George Washington. Authentic, original oath of allegiance, signed, with the first two lines at the top in Washington's hand.

Dick pass. He described it as "an interesting item" dated from Head Quarters,
Bergen County, September 5, 1780, and
priced it at twenty-five dollars.

Eighteen years later Patrick's son,
Thomas F. Madigan, one of America's
greatest autograph dealers, who had obviously profited from his father's
blunder, wrote:

Heaven knows how many times the
indefatigable Spring caused "Mr. Ryerson and his negro man, Dick," to pass
the picket at Ramapo—so often, I am
sure, that the two might have con-
stituted the first traffic jam in American history. Times without number
during the past twenty-five years this
identical Spring forgery has been offered to me, and invariably the owner
has insisted that the precious docu-

ment had been in the possession of
his or her family for fifty years or
more. I have never doubted the claim
for a moment—as Spring died more
than fifty years ago.

One wag who got stuck with a Ryerson-
Dick pass said: "I have thought it would
be a good idea to call a convention of all
owners of copies of this pass to meet on
the banks of the Ramapo and tell how
they got caught."

Almost as common as Spring's passes
are his holograph checks of Washington,
all drawn on the Office of Discount &
Deposit, Baltimore, and dated between
1795 and 1799. How many thousands of
these Spring turned out is hard to guess,
but they are very plentiful today and
turn up constantly at auctions where all
lots are sold "as is." If Washington, even

as a wealthy plantation owner, had actually written all the checks forged by Spring, they would not only have overdrawn his account but bankrupted him. Like most Spring fakes, these checks may be identified by a shaky, rather diminutive handwriting and the reddish-brown ink, quite unlike Washington's, used by the forger.

In his book *Talks about Autographs,* published in 1896, the genial English collector George Birkbeck Hill illustrated one of the gems of his collection, a Spring forgery of a Washington check, adding that "it is all in Washington's hand and is the more interesting as it was written in the last year of his life."

Finally, in 1859, the forgeries were traced to Spring and he was arrested. Spring employed both piety and wit by

Robert Spring. Forged check of George Washington from the collection of George Birkbeck Hill, Washington, May 16, 1799. Most of Spring's forged checks are dated from 1797 to 1799, in the last three years of Washington's life.

George Washington. Authentic handwritten signed check, Mount Vernon, 1798. Notice how large and powerful Washington's script is compared with the cramped, diminutive writing of Spring. Like most forgers, Spring shrank the handwriting of his subject in an unconscious effort to make detection of the fake more difficult.

admitting his guilt and vowing to reform. But the moving finger having writ moved on, this time to Canada, and under the alias of Emma Harding. Emma, it appears, had a large collection of rare autograph letters, inherited from her late husband and, being destitute, was willing to part with them. She was to be addressed in care of Dr. Samuel Hawley, another of Spring's aliases. Quite a few replies, many containing money, were received by the bereaved Emma, who obliged by furnishing forgeries to order.

While hiding out in Canada, Spring also posed as Harriet Copley, another destitute widow. Writing on mourning paper from Montreal, Spring sent two Washington documents to his prospective victims. The enclosures were the infamous pass for Mr. Ryerson and his Negro man, Dick, with the names occasionally varied to "Mr. McKean with his negro man, Ben" and a letter of Washington dated from Headquarters in New Windsor, February 23, 1781, ordering the discharge of a prisoner. Spring asked twenty-five dollars for the pair and sent out dozens of solicitations. His letter, identical in every case, read:

Canada East, May 28, 1866

Sir:

My beloved husband, who died lately in Europe, was a collector of literary curiosities, and when in affluent circumstances he expended large sums in the accumulation of what was rare: but lately, in consequence of the

Robert Ripley. "Believe It Or Not!" cartoon about Robert Spring. Every statement in this cartoon is an error. Spring lived and forged not in England but in Philadelphia and Baltimore, with a brief jaunt into Canada and England. He forged only American autographs, with several rare exceptions. His own letters are scarce, but their rarity has been greatly exaggerated. They are not nearly so valuable as those of Washington, Franklin, Jefferson and John Paul Jones, the men whose letters he most often fabricated.

civil war, in which he was dangerously wounded, he became greatly reduced—in fact, completely impoverished—and with the expectation of retrieving himself, sold our once happy home in Virginia and left for Europe; but disappointed in his expectations there, and destitution staring us in the face, it broke his heart, and his wound opening afresh, he sickened and died, and left me with four small children, without a protector in great distress and in a foreign land. No words could express my feelings when the dreadful reality became apparent. Gladly would I have died also; but when I looked upon my helpless orphan children, determination to live and struggle on for their sakes sustained me; and now, if my health is spared, I fondly hope to be enabled to support and educate them by teaching music, and my needle.

Among my lamented husband's papers I found many related to the interesting past. At first I looked upon them as of little value, but when in Paris I offered a few to several American gentlemen there, and they were delighted to have them, and it was through their kindness we were enabled to return so far on our way home. The sickness of a darling child and great distress detains me here.

I am told, Mr. ———, you are a kind-hearted, noble-minded gentleman, and an admirer of such things. I know my beloved husband paid twenty-five dollars for one; but if you will kindly send me twenty-five dollars for both, or loan me twenty dollars till I can redeem them, you will, indeed, so greatly assist me.

It is a long way to send, so pray reply by return, and please send a U.S. Treasury note. The letter will reach me safely, and I can use the currency here directly. Bless you, sir, I shall prayerfully await your reply.

I am, sir, your obedient servant,

HARRIET COPLEY

I reside three miles from Frelighsburgh, so that you had better enclose your letter, sealed, in cover directed: Dr. L. Bartlett, Frelighsburgh, and the Doctor will send it me immediately.

From Canada, Spring proceeded to Baltimore, where he operated under the name of Fannie Jackson, daughter of the late General "Stonewall" Jackson. Although Jackson had no daughter, the alias proved extremely successful. Spring got a list of British holders of Confederate bonds and, explaining that he was in dire need of money, offered Washington documents for sale. Pity the poor British, their portfolios already loaded with worthless Confederate bonds, now stocking up on Spring's Washington bank checks!

Possibly Spring thought he could profit even more by a personal visit to his native land, so he journeyed to England. The British were not taken in by his fakes and he was quickly exposed. Spring defended himself by explaining that he had "never done a dishonorable act" in his life and was only "innocently contributing to the gratifications of the amiable weakness of those who are fond

Special Announcement!

———◆◆◆———

☞ The OLD LETTERS, OLD PAMPHLETS, OLD BOOKS, &c., I allude to, are generally packed away, very often for more than forty or fifty years in garrets, out-houses, lumber rooms, in trunks, old barrels, sacks, &c. Do oblige me, and bring them out to the light of day, then after being ticketed to my address, convey them to the near-est point of transportation, drop me a line through the Post Office, and I will engage they come safe, on receipt and im-mediately I can know their worth: I will remit to you by next mail.

I will with pleasure, and to look over a large lot, visit within five hundred miles.

For Large and Small Packages, the better conveyance is the Express Company.

☞ *A few Old Letters, or Pamphlets can be sent by Mail.*

ADDRESS
ROBERT SPRING,
(Agent for Public & Private Libraries.)
38 SPRING ROW,
BALTIMORE, MD.

Robert Spring. Printed broadside issued by Spring, about 1864. Spring was an inveterate searcher for rare letters and manuscripts and no doubt helped to rescue many precious historical docu-ments from the paper mill. During his last years he was beset by poverty and many of his letters deal with his urgent need for money. On August 14, 1871, he wrote to the Philadelphia finan-cier and collector Gordon L. Ford, offering to travel in the Eastern states on Ford's behalf to search out "the immense number of old letters . . . stored away in garrets and cellars." Spring asked Ford to advance some money for the trip: "I will work faithfully for you and I know in less than a month you would be pleased. . . . no better chance will ever be offered you to make a noble collection, *and at a trifling outlay.* Fifty or one hun-dred dollars would be sufficient to start with. . . ."

Robert Spring. Conclusion of a signed, handwrit-ten letter, October, 1871.

Robert Spring. Variant signature, about 1863.

of autographs." He was not prosecuted and soon returned to America where he renewed his career as a forger with some fresh aliases—Robert Speering, Thomas French and William Emmerson.

Sometimes Spring, who used half a dozen post-office addresses and as many criminal pseudonyms, asked his victims to "just send me what you think the enclosed document is worth," and sometimes he requested his usual fee of ten or fifteen dollars.

Although Spring nearly always scored with his Washington forgeries, the fab-rication of Franklins and Jeffersons at first seemed to pose insoluble problems. But where there's a quill there's a way, and before long Spring was turning out acceptable Franklins, one of which even passed muster under the falcon eyes of William B. Sprague, America's greatest pioneer philographer. After examining a forged Franklin letter dated from Passy, April 22, 1779, fresh from the pen of Spring, Sprague wrote:

Albany, 23 Nov. 1865

My dear Sir,

My first impression, on looking at the letter you have sent me, was that it was not an original, as the handwriting seemed to me less free than that of Franklin: but upon comparing it with some of his writing of about the same period, I find so near a resemblance as to have no doubt of its genuineness. I should not hesitate to accept it as a veritable autograph of Franklin.

Very truly yours,

W. B. SPRAGUE

Spring had more difficulty with Jefferson and was never able to master his script. There is, in fact, a marked similarity between the writing of Spring himself and his imitation of Jefferson's. Spring has the same method of making the *p*'s; the terminal double *l,* as in *will,* has a shorter second *l;* the lines of his own writing and those of his Jefferson fakes are the same distance apart; the habit of curling up the terminal *e* in words like *the* is the same in both scripts; the formation of the word *if* is almost identical and the number 7 is written in the

Robert Spring. Forgery of a hand-written letter signed by John Paul Jones. An extremely well-executed fake, with the handwriting (as usual with Jones) much smaller than his large, egoistic signature.

Country, will be to me a duty, and need I say, the greatest satisfaction when accomplished;—

I am my dear Sir,

Yours Truly,

B Franklin

Robert Spring. Four lines and signature from a forged handwritten letter signed "B Franklin." Note the striking similarity between Spring's imitations of Jones and Franklin. The word *will* is identically penned in both letters, as are other common words, such as *and, the,* and *me.* The authenticity or falsity of a document can most quickly be established by a comparison of such key words, found in abundance in any example of handwriting.

John Paul Jones. Authentic handwritten letter, signed, 1790.

John Paul Jones. An exceptionally bold, authentic signature.

same way. These are only a few of the many similarities which mark Spring's fabrications of Jefferson.

On November 4, 1869, Spring was again arrested in Philadelphia by a Detective Franklin, the same officer who had apprehended him a decade earlier. The forger was brought before the mayor. Detective Franklin stated:

A complaint was made here a few days ago, in reference to a man named Spring, who is a dealer in autographs, charged with defrauding certain parties, by passing upon them fraudulent autograph letters. I went down to his house to see him, and found a number of manuscripts. He was earlier arrested in 1859, and came before

Passy, April 22, 1779

My Dear Sir,

will you call upon me this afternoon,
I have just received my letters from Boston, among
them one from Mr Quincy, mentioning you in the
kindest manner;– I am sorry a very severe attack of
the gravel prevented my accompanying you, and the
Marquis de la Fayette yesterday to Versailles, but do not
imagine the old mans company was greatly missed;– I
regreted my sickness for I have always met with the
reception
kindest, from their Majesties, and feel great pleasure
in paying my respects to them, but disease and
pain, are better away, tho' some would endure more;
for a less friendly reception than I should have
received;– come if you can.—

Yours affectionately,

B Franklin

Mr Bradford

Robert Spring. Forgery of a Benjamin Franklin letter, Passy, April 22, 1770. This forgery was examined and pronounced authentic by the pioneer philographer William B. Sprague.

Mayor Henry, charged with dealing in forged letters of General Washington. He then lived in Anita Street, near Tenth. I bought one of these letters myself. The paper he uses for these letters is prepared by himself, being generally stained with coffee. He frankly acknowledged his guilt yesterday when arrested. He also, earlier, wrote me a letter at my request.

"Will you please read the letter?" asked the mayor.

Detective Franklin read:

Philadelphia, Oct. 4, 1869

Sir:

Hearing there have been several complaints made I beg to state to you, from the remembrance of your fair and honorable treatment of my case with respect to the bogus Washington autographs, in the year 1859, that since I have resided in this city (June 6, 1868), I have never, by word or act, wronged any person in the United States, though I have obtained, in several instances, small sums from England, driven to such from dreadful home affliction, and to aid in supporting a large family of seven children, the youngest of whom died twelve months ago, at a moment when I had not a dollar.

I have tried by every effort to obtain a creditable livelihood, and it was only to spin out my short-comings that I solicited and obtained the small assistance I did from England about ten months since. I promised I would

Benjamin Franklin. Authentic handwritten, signed letter. Notice that Franklin's script is more fluent and less legible than Spring's fake. The capital *B* in Spring's signature of Franklin is labored and shaky, but Franklin's *B* sweeps easily in its curves, with not the slightest tremor.

never do another dishonorable act, and with the exception of receiving replies to letters written to Europe before that period, and which, from my urgent affliction and often absolute want, I could not resist the temptation to keep, I have kept my promise. You know, Mr. Franklin, the affliction to which I allude. I am writing this under the greatest distress. I write this to you at four o'clock in the morning.

I am willing you should know all, and have it in your power to stop in future any dishonest attempt should

Mr. Short

Dear Sir   Monticello Sep. 6. 08.

I avail myself of the last moment allowed by the departure of the post to acknolege the receipt of your letters of the 27th & 31st ult. and to say, in answer to the last, that any one of the three persons you there propose would be approved as to their politics, for in appointments to office the government refuses to know any difference between descriptions of republicans, all of whom are in principle, and cooperate, with the government. Biddle we know and have formed an excellent opinion of him. His travelling and exercise in business must have given him advantages. I am much pleased with the account you give of the sentiments of the federalists of Philadelphia as to the embargo, and that they are not in sentiment with the insurgents of the North. The papers have lately advanced in boldness & flagiciousness beyond even themselves. Such daring and atrocious lies as fill the 3d & 4th columns of the 3d page of the U.S. gazette of Aug. 31. were never before I believe published with impunity in any country. However, I have from the beginning determined to submit myself as the subject on whom may be proved the impotency of a free press in a country like ours, against those who conduct themselves honestly, and enter into no intrigue. I admit at the same time that restraining the press to truth as the present laws do, is the only way of making it useful. But I have thought a nicer hand first to prove it can never be dangerous. Not knowing whether I shall have another occasion to address you here, be assured that my sincere affections & wishes for your success & happiness accompany you every where.

Th: Jefferson

Robert Spring. Forgery of a handwritten letter signed by Thomas Jefferson. The script in the forgery has a remarkable resemblance to Spring's own handwriting and is, on the whole, a very poor imitation of Jefferson's. The text, however, is lively and interesting, a good simulation of Jefferson's literary style.

Robert Spring. First and last pages of a signed handwritten letter, Philadelphia, August 14, 1871, to antiquarian Gordon L. Ford, commenting on Spring's poor health, poverty and desire to search out rarities in New Jersey, Delaware and Maryland.

I make any. In November, 1868, I wrote about eighty letters [offering forged autographs.] The replies were to be sent to Richmond, Va., and Baltimore. The Postmasters of Richmond and Baltimore were requested to redirect to Camden, N.J. I received, as far as I can remember, seventeen letters, three containing money. They were in the name of Dr. S. R. Hampton, and, of course, are all run out.

My second attempt was the [daughter of Stonewall] Jackson letters, which were immediately exposed in England, though not before I had received several letters, two containing money, £5 and £5. At the same time I wrote ten letters almost similar to the Jackson, from which I received £10.

Anyhow, I promise you, without any reservation, never again to use any dishonorable means to procure money. I will rather starve first.

Yours, in great affliction,

W. E.[MMERSON]

When Detective Franklin finished reading the letter, one of Spring's victims, a druggist named Robert Coulson Davis, living at Sixteenth and Vine streets, testified:

Monticello Mar. 9. 23.

I thank you, Sir, for the copy of your geography which you have been so kind as to send me. I have examined the Statistical part to which you particularly refer my attention, and I find it truly a very valuable addition to the book, and constituting a convenient Repository of the matters of which tabular views are presented. there is yet one table which has never been given, and would be equally curious and interesting. it is that of the produce or exchangeable matter of each state respectively exported either to other states or to foreign countries. the tables pa. 624. 626. furnish some views towards it, but too general for special comparisons.

In your list of colleges pa. 645. you have omitted that of William and Mary in Virginia, founded by the sovereigns of those names about 1692, and probably the most liberally endowed of any one in the U.S. it is now much reduced by ill management of it's funds, and less resorted to on account of climate. it has generally had from 60. to 80. students and has furnished constantly from it's first institution it's full quota of distinguished characters.

You ask for such hints as I could furnish on the subject of these tables; but, good Sir, I am past that service. the torpitude of 80 years has relaxed the habits of research, and two crippled wrists render writing the most tedious and painful operation I can undertake. with my regrets therefore that I cannot be useful to you in this way be pleased to accept the assurance of my esteem and respect.

Th: Jefferson

Thomas Jefferson. Authentic handwritten, signed letter, 1823. The third president frequently begins his sentences without using a capital letter, and his script and signature are very different from Spring's awkward imitation.

I have known the prisoner personally for a good many years. I became acquainted with him through having a fancy for collecting autographs and things of that nature. He was residing in Lombard Street when I first knew him.

What led me to know about these forgeries was that they were repeatedly handed to me by the parties to whom they were addressed, I being an expert in distinguishing such matters. I have also had several conversations with the prisoner in relation to the forgeries some years ago, but have not seen him since 1862 or 1863 when he left here and went to Baltimore.

Davis showed the mayor an album that contained a number of Spring fakes, including two of his old favorites, the Ryerson-Dick pass and a check drawn on the Office of Discount and Deposit, Baltimore. Spring admitted the forgeries, and at the conclusion of the testimony, the mayor set bail at five hundred dollars, which Spring could not furnish. Ironically, the album of fake Washingtons that Davis had acquired from Spring would probably fetch today several times the sum that Spring needed, for rogues always have an eager following, and skillful forgeries are avidly sought by present-day philographers.

Spring served a final hitch in prison and when he got out vowed to reform. In 1875, not long before his death, he wrote from 1809 Lombard Street in Philadelphia to Charles Lindsley: "Since loss of fortune, now an old man painfully stricken with asthma, I have struggled on dealing in a very small way (too poor to avail myself of bargains when offered) in rare Books, pamphlets, Autographs &c but have never been able to realize therefrom more than the merest pittance." Spring urged Lindsley to buy "the accompanying trifles," adding that the purchase "will indeed be a kind and benevolent act."

Nobody knows whether Spring kept his vow to reform. If he did, however, the reformation provides an insidious moral for all forgers. The aging fabricator fell upon evil times. Honesty did not pay and he died in poverty in the charity ward of a Philadelphia hospital on December 14, 1876, seventy-seven years to the day after the passing of the great American whose autograph he had so often forged.

4

The Dapper Baron of Fakedom

CHARLES WEISBERG

They called him "the Baron" because he was a snappy dresser and sported a trim goatee or a neat mustache, but he really looked more like an opulent gangster. His name was Charles Weisberg. He also had a string of colorful aliases with which he blazed a trail from Philadelphia to New York.

Weisberg started out as an honor student at the University of Pennsylvania where he evinced a keen interest in history. No sooner was he graduated than he put his education to use by forging a few Lincoln documents.

The "Baron" first got his name on the police blotter in 1933 for forging a mail order. In 1935 he was convicted of using the mails to defraud by bookselling swindles under the firm name of Eli and Levi Kane. He spent eighteen months in prison and was then placed on parole for six years, but broke parole. Under the hideout name of Charles Levitt of Upper Darby, Pennsylvania, he continued his mail fraud by selling forgeries and offering nonexistent books, for which he collected cash in advance.

Weisberg was arrested in 1941 for peddling forgeries and twenty-nine witnesses were brought to Philadelphia for the trial. The government spent nearly five thousand dollars to get a conviction and Weisberg was sentenced to two and a half years.

The moment "the Baron" got out of jail he resumed his old trade of forger and rare-book swindler. Using the picturesque name of Brand Storm he turned out a fresh batch of forgeries, and when arrested in Philadelphia on October 2, 1944, he posted bond for one thousand dollars. Weisberg then skipped town, abandoning his wife and child. He was traced to his old hangout in New York and seized by postal authorities.

Weisberg's great successes in the forgery business were with Stephen Collins Foster manuscripts, Washington and Lincoln letters and original surveys of Mount Vernon. His last forgery was an inscription by Katharine Mansfield in a copy of her book *The Dove's Nest*. The imitation of Mansfield's script was flawless, but Weisberg tripped up on a foolish anachronism. The buyer discovered that the book was published posthumously and complained to the cops. In Philadelphia Weisberg was tried and sentenced to two and a half years in Lewisburg Prison, where he died on May 4, 1945.

Even in high school, Weisberg evinced the talent that was to make him infamous. A classmate recalled: "I used to see him stop on the street and dust a letter or document to give it the appearance of age. He composed a diary of an imaginary silversmith, one Elfreth, who worked in early Philadelphia. It was so perfectly contrived that any craftsman could make silverware after reading it."

A Philadelphia collector, Samuel Moyerman, was so infuriated at Weisberg for brazenly peddling his fabrications that he wrote him an accusatory letter. In a reply dated September 10, 1940, the forger lashed back: "Anytime you feel like 'taking a swat' at me, I am ready, ready with 225 lbs. of pretty desperate strength, seasoned for five years in as muscle-wracking an existence as a man ever led. I would not only never back away from a worn-out crow like yourself, but never for that matter from anybody. My career has taught me how to fight. I have never had one business deal with you and you have never been provided with one active, direct excuse to charge me with forgery."

Years ago Moyerman showed me Weisberg's letter and smiled quietly. "Lucky for Weisberg he didn't take on this worn-out crow," he said. "I was the middleweight boxing champ of Pennsylvania."

Charles Weisberg. Sketch by Constance S. Camner from a police mug shot (1943). "The Baron" had shaved off his goatee to disguise his appearance.

Mount Vernon, May 16, 1785;

Dear Sir,

In for a penny, in for a pound is an old adage. I am so hackneyed to the touches of the Painters pencil, that I am now altogether at their beck, and sit like patience on a monument whilst they are delineating the lines of my face. —

It is a proof among many others, of what habit & custom can effect. — at first I was as impatient at the request, and as restive under the operation, as a Colt is of the saddle — The next time, I submitted very reluctantly, but with less flouncing. — Now, no dray moves more readily to the Thill, than I do to the Painters chair. — It may easily be conceived therefore that I yielded a ready obedience to your request, and to the views of Mrs. Pine.

Letters from England, recommendatory of this Gentleman, came to my hand previous to his arrival in America — not only as an artist of acknowledged eminence, but as one who had discovered a friendly disposition towards this Country, for which, it seems, he had been marked.

It gave me pleasure to hear from you. — I shall always feel an interest in your happiness, and with Mrs. Washingtons compliments, & best wishes joined to my own, for Mrs. Hopkinson & yourself.

I am — Dr. Sir,
Yr. most obedt. & affect.
Servant

Fran. Hopkinson Esq.
G Washington

Mount Vernon Aug. 15th. 1786

Dear Sir,

Mrs. Washington is prevented from dining with you tomorrow by the arrival of a French Gentleman of Rank — Genl. Duplessis — who is introduced, and very warmly recommended to me by the Count de Estaing, the Marqs. de la Fayette &c. — in consequence I have persuaded Col. Humphreys to Postpone his visit to Abingdon. — Wishing to shew this Gentleman (Genl. Duplessis) all the civilities in my power, I should be glad if you & Mrs. Stuart would dine with us tomorrow. — Other Company are also invited from Alexandria at Dinner, at this time. — That Mr. Stuart may be accomodated, George Plater, & a pair of my horses (two others being sent to Fredericksburgh) is carried up by Charles. —

Yr. affect. &c.
Go. Washington

Charles Weisberg. Forgery of a handwritten letter signed by George Washington. Penned on old chain-lined paper in dark brown ink with just a tincture of red to betray it, this lengthy letter is an excellent imitation of Washington's script. The writing is slightly tremulous. For some odd reason Weisberg, after turning out this skillful imitation of Washington's chirography, omitted the *o* and the colon which immediately follow the *G* in Washington's signature. An obvious flaw by which Weisberg's Washington fakes can always be identified is that the capital *G* extends below the capital *W*. Possibly Weisberg developed this eccentricity because he forged a great many Lincolns, in whose signature the capital *A* does fall below the capital *L*.

George Washington. Authentic handwritten letter, signed, 1786.

Camden New Jersey
April 3, 1891

Miss Davis would be an author.
This is what you shale do:—
Love the earth and sun and the animals, despite riches, give alms to every one that asks, stand up for the stupid and crazy, devote your income and labor to others, hate tyrants, argue not concerning God, have patience and indulgence toward the people, take off your hat to nothing known or unknown, or to any man or number of men, go freely with powerful uneducated persons and with the young.

Walt Whitman

Charles Weisberg. Forgery of an imaginary Walt Whitman handwritten signed letter. As often occurs with forgeries, Weisberg's fabrication is much more legible than that of his subject. The pen pressure is much lighter in the forgery and one gets the feeling that if Weisberg had used Whitman's pen the fake would be a closer imitation.

Camden Feb: 6, '91
Dr B is better — is at office & seems all right again — the proof came & piece will be out in ten days or less — did I tell you that the Scribner man rejected my stuff & sent it back? — Abt same as usual with me (a horrible heavy inertia, lassitude) — write often as convenient — God bless you & Fran & my Boston friends — Walt Whitman

Walt Whitman. Authentic handwritten signed letter.

5

The Financier Who Turned Forger

HENRY WOODHOUSE

He was a dapper little man, less than five feet tall, a minuscule Beau Brummell who envisioned himself as a giant of industry and the prince of forgers. The second title he tucked away in his closet, but he never hesitated to proclaim his genius at commerce. He was born in Turin, Italy, on June 24, 1884. Years later he translated his Italian name, Enrico Casalegno, into English and came up with the oak-hewn name of Henry Woodhouse. For *Who's Who in America,* that dignified aggregation of prelates and pedagogues, he turned out an inflated account of his career. When we press the gas out of his entry we learn that Woodhouse came to America in 1904 and was naturalized in 1917. We also discover, if we care to take Henry's word for it, that he founded and published three aviation magazines, wrote or edited four technical books on publishing, was an advisor to the United States government on aeronautics and worked with Peary and Amundsen in organizing their Arctic expeditions. But his pretentious biography, one of the longest in *Who's Who,* does not even hint at the extraordinary skills with pen and ink that were to bring him posthumous fame.

Henry was a wheeler-dealer in a big

Henry Woodhouse (third from left), celebrating the inauguration of the first aerial mail, May 15, 1918, with some associates. Wearing his familiar gray suit and holding his gray fedora, Woodhouse is dwarfed by Postmaster Patten of New York City at his right.

way. "I'm working on a million-dollar deal" was his favorite observation. Actually, Woodhouse did make a fortune in real estate in Washington, D.C., but he lost all of it during the Depression. There were dark tales whispered about the little Italian who looked like a Valentine cupid. Some said he had murdered a man in Turin and fled to America to escape the vengeance of pursuers. Woodhouse lived and worked in an aura of amiable intrigue. Behind the engaging personality and disarming smile was a fierce, soul-consuming drive for wealth and power.

For a while Henry was sponsored by a faded *grande dame,* Alice Hunt Vartlett, an opulent dowager and poet who was fascinated by the cuddly little forger and put up the cash to sponsor his projects. She also headed many of the committees for promoting the arts that were organized by Woodhouse.

Few people knew Henry as intimately as Raphael Gould, the distinguished book dealer, who at eighteen met the forger early in the 1930s. "I admired him tremendously," said Gould. "He had a great knowledge of history. I guess he's still my favorite character of all time."

"Woodhouse turned over books and autographs to me that I was to sell for him on a commission basis and I quickly developed a knack for spotting his fakes. Most of the stuff he gave me was okay, but when he brought in forgeries, I merely put them away. We soon came to an understanding. He was aware that I knew about his forgeries, but I never mentioned them and he never mentioned them. He kept on giving them to

me and I just stored them in a big brown folder."

At my request, Gould exhumed the folder, a part of his private archives that he hadn't looked at in thirty years, and placed it at my disposal.

One of Henry's most ambitious schemes was the creation of a Henry Woodhouse Historic Exhibit in the Federal Hall Memorial Museum at Wall and Nassau Streets in downtown New York city. It was a showcase for his real and fake autographs. A tireless accumulator, Henry acquired many authentic rarities, letters of great Americans whom he genuinely admired. He was an avid collector of autographs of the signers of the Declaration of Independence, and when he had difficulty getting any rare specimen he just inked in a creation of his own.

Woodhouse used the Federal Hall Memorial Museum to display not only his genuine documents but the forgeries he wanted to promote. He worked out a big deal—all his deals were big!—with Gimbel's New York department store. The forger put a price tag on all his autographic rarities and sold them over the counter at Gimbel's. Henry was bringing history to the common man, putting a price on priceless documents. Gimbel's was the perfect front for his fakes.

Henry's favorite ploy was to tack a fraudulent signature on a genuine old document. If he had a request from one of Gimbel's customers for an autograph of Thomas Stone, one of the fifty-six signers of the Declaration of Independence, he simply forged the famous

John Adams' Boston Gazette for December 29, 1803, containing, page 1, (a) article from London paper voicing need of a "Nestor, a Fabius, a Washington, or a Cornwallis" to defend England from Napoleon's threatened invasion; (b) anecdote of Napoleon; (c) treaty between England and Sweden. Page 2 anniversary of Pilgrim's landing at Plymouth, Dec. 22, 1620.

from

The Henry Woodhouse Historic Exhibit

— in —

Federal Hall Memorial Museum

Sub-Treasury Building. Wall & Nassau Sts.

Open to the Public Daily 10 A. M. to 4 P. M.

Henry Woodhouse. Forgery of a John Adams signature on a *Boston Gazette* (1803), with Gimbel's price tag offering the fake for sale at forty-eight dollars and a description of the newspaper from the Henry Woodhouse Historic Exhibit.

John Adams. Authentic signature.

weus of usemange Dollars at four Shillings and Six Pence Sterling each, Pistoles, of one Weight at Septen Shillings and Six Pence Sterling each or English Coins or other Coins current in England, at the rates of their Currency in England with legal Interest thereon from the fourth Day of this Instant September at or before the fourth Day of September which shall be in the Year of our Lord Seventeen hundred and Twenty One then the above Obligation to be void else of full Force.

Sealed & delivered in the presence of

Tho: Stone

Dan. . . . Jenifer   *Dan. Dulany*

Henry Woodhouse. Forgery of a Thomas Stone signature on the bottom of an authentic eighteenth-century document. Woodhouse has added Stone's name as a witness.

Thomas Stone. Authentic signature from the Declaration of Independence, obviously the pattern for Woodhouse's forgery.

Tho: Stone

patriot's name as a witness on a worthless eighteenth-century deed or wrote his signature in an old volume. There were few signers of the Declaration who escaped the chirographic chicanery of Woodhouse, but he did draw the line at Button Gwinnett. The autograph of the rarest signer, the elusive nonwriter from Georgia, was selling in the 1930s for ten or twenty thousand dollars, but Henry resisted the temptation. No doubt he feared the intense scrutiny by experts that every freshly discovered Gwinnett was subjected to.

Many of the "signers" documents created by Woodhouse are still around. They limp from antique dealer to antique dealer, from country auction to country auction and occasionally crop up in libraries or at big sales in New York. They are the "I'm-not-quite-sure-about-this-one" items that impecunious collectors use to fill in their "sets" of the founding fathers. Some of the Woodhouse fakes come with grandiloquent pedigrees—official cards proclaiming they were once exhibited at the Federal Hall Memorial Museum and/or price tags from Gimbel's.

Raphael Gould recalls: "Woodhouse loved to acquire noted libraries. He would announce his purchase with much éclat in the newspapers. When he bought the library of Lanier Washington the event was proclaimed as one of the great book purchases of the century."

Colony of Rhode Island &c.

Newport March 19th 1763

I do hereby certify That Capt. George Jackson and Mr. John Jencks being the major Part of a Committee to audit the Accounts of Elisha Brown Esqr as a Member of the Committee of War did make Report to the last Session of the Generale Assembly that they had audited the said Accounts and presented the same to the Assembly with their Report thereon. And that thereupon the Lower House of Assembly having taken the same into Consideration found the Balance due from the said Elisha Brown to be One hundred & Forty-four Pounds and Four Pence Halfpenny Lawful Money.

Henry Ward Secy

William Ellery

William Ellery

ELLERY, WILLIAM, Signer of Declaration of Independence for Rhode Island. Document dated Newport, Rhode Island, March 19, 1763, signed by Ellery and Henry Ward, Secretary of the Colony, who also became one of the prime movers of the movement for American Independence. The document reveals that there was a Committee of War in Rhode Island in 1763 and that Ellery was connected with it.

The Henry Woodhouse Historic Exhibit
in
Federal Hall Memorial Museum
Sub-Treasury Building, Wall & Nassau Sts.
Open to the Public Daily 10 A. M. to 4 P. M.

Henry Woodhouse. Forgery of a signature of William Ellery, signed vertically in the margin of an authentic eighteenth-century document, Newport, March 19, 1763 with, *far left and vertically,* the authentic signature of Ellery from the Declaration of Independence. Woodhouse's fake is fairly accurate, but cramped and shaky, lacking the verve of Ellery's own signature. *Lower left.* Description of Woodhouse's forgery when it was on display at the Henry Woodhouse Historic Exhibit.

Nobody had the faintest idea who Lanier Washington was, but his surname was the most famed in American history and his first name was vaguely redolent of the bubbling music of the Chattahoochee river. The publicity on Henry's acquisition set scholarly tongues awagging, and the purchase supplied him with a "bottomless trunk" of "rare" material. For years afterward everything Henry sold was "from the estate of Lanier Washington."

Among the George Washington items in the bottomless trunk of Lanier were the wooden marker pegs used by the first president when a youthful surveyor for Lord Fairfax in Virginia. These ultimately went to Raphael Gould and he still treasures them as curiosities. They are tied together with red, white and blue ribbons. The clever Woodhouse got a lot of mileage out of the pegs, which he probably whittled himself. He even posed for the newspapers, demonstrating how Washington drove them into the earth.

THE

American Remembrancer;

OR,

AN IMPARTIAL COLLECTION

OF

ESSAYS, RESOLVES,

SPEECHES, &c.

RELATIVE, OR HAVING AFFINITY, TO THE

TREATY WITH GREAT BRITAIN.

VOLUME III.

PHILADELPHIA:

PRINTED BY HENRY TUCKNISS,
FOR MATHEW CAREY, NO. 118, MARKET-STREET.
—NOVEMBER 28, 1795.—

[No. IX.]

Henry Woodhouse. Top. Forged signature of James Wilson on a book published in 1795. *Bottom.* Authentic signature of James Wilson from the Declaration of Independence.

One of Henry's smartest tricks, recalls Gould, was to devise and copyright various titles in the hope that sooner or later someone of means would poach on his literary property. "I ran into Woodhouse one afternoon," Gould said, "and he joyously showed me a settlement check for twenty-five thousand dollars from Paramount Pictures in Hollywood. They'd 'infringed' on his title, 'Wings,'

Descriptive circular of the Historic Arts Association, founded by Henry Woodhouse in 1938, with a news clipping dated April 28, 1932, picturing Woodhouse demonstrating how Washington drove his wooden survey pegs into the ground.

Historic Arts Association

NEW YORK CITY OFFICE: 570 LEXINGTON AVENUE • TELEPHONE PLAZA 3-3800

HENRY WOODHOUSE, CHAIRMAN   AUGUSTUS POST, SECRETARY

THE activities of the Historic Arts Association were summarized in the following Resolution unanimously adopted by the Third National Arts Conference, held at the Hotel Astor, New York, September and October, 1938, to consider plans for holding authentic historic celebrations in the years 1939-1940:

"Resolved, that the Historic Arts Association and its President, Mr. Henry Woodhouse, be and hereby are highly commended for their valuable achievement in providing the only organization which has for over 20 years dedicated itself to making possible the celebration and presentation of authenticated historic events with accurate reproduction of historic personalities and places, scenes and episodes of home, artistic, literary, business, industrial, scientific, social, public, and spiritual life, with original exhibits. They make possible the realization of George Washington's pledge that posterity would remember the deeds of those who contributed to the nation's founding and progress; and make available genuine history, which has been as rare heretofore as it was in the year 1817 when Thomas Jefferson wrote to John Adams: 'A morsel of genuine history is a thing so rare as to always be valuable.' "

The Association has provided records and exhibits for upwards of 1000 celebrations, conferences, radio broadcasts, motion pictures, and pageants, including over 100 for the New York World's Fairs 1939-1940.

APR 28 1932

Washington's Surveying Pegs Are Used Again

FOUR collateral descendants of George Washington are here seen using the same surveying pegs he once used, to lay out the bit of ground on which a reproduction of the school Washington attended will be erected. At the left is Henry Woodhouse, collector of Washingtoniana. The women are (left to right) Mrs. H. H. Williams, great-great-great granddaughter of Betty Washington Lewis, only sister of George Washington; Mrs. Frank Taylor, great-great-granddaughter of Betty Lewis; Mrs. Margaret Turner, great-great-grandniece of George Washington; and Mrs. Catherine Knox-Gore, sister

of Mrs. Taylor and great-great-granddaughter of Betty Lewis. The school will be built on a site near little Hunting Creek on the plantation owned by Mr. Woodhouse.

which he had copyrighted only a year or two before Monk Saunders wrote his war-birds book with that same name. A typical Woodhouse caper!"

Henry had an imagination that would have excited the envy of Baron Munchausen. There was always some meat to be carved from every scrap of handwriting, and even the most pedestrian papers of the late eighteenth century, in Henry's hands, became important messages. Before me lies a letter in English dated September 27, 1776, postmarked from Rome, Italy and bearing the signature of one "James Smith." An expert could tell at a glance that it's the "wrong" James Smith, and not the patriot from Pennsylvania who signed the Declaration of Independence. However, under the magic of Woodhouse's imagination, this letter is transformed into one written by the great patriot, and it also appears that Smith (actually then in Philadelphia) was in Rome on a secret mission on behalf of the United States. The routine contents of the letter, in which the wrong Smith rhapsodizes over the paintings of the Italian masters, are artfully explained by Woodhouse as "a code to escape detection of British officials."

In the late 1930s Herman Herst, Jr., the noted stamp expert, visited Woodhouse at his office, a great cubicle crammed with steel shelves from floor to ceiling. He recalls Henry as "the most conceited man I ever met."

Woodhouse boasted to Herst about some of his financial triumphs: "I made a fortune when the Great War [World War I] ended in 1918. You see, when America entered the conflict in 1917 most big cities built parade grounds on which to train soldiers. To accommodate thousands of marching men they put down asphalt or concrete on a large area near the city. After the war was over I bought the paved land cheap because it wasn't any good for farming. Everybody thought I was crazy for investing in 'useless' property. But I knew then that the airplane had a great future and airports near each big city would be needed. Later I got a lot of money for

the paved areas. I owned the first airport in Richmond, a former parade ground.

"Another one of my big coups," said Woodhouse, "was when I utilized a little fact I picked up from the Bible. I had read a biblical tale about fire shooting out of the earth in Mesopotamia. That meant only one thing to me—oil! I talked Standard Oil into looking into the matter and of course they discovered oil. They gave me a royalty from every barrel taken out of the Near East oil fields."

In the early days of television, Henry developed a global concept in which great historical pageants would be presented, all documented by his collection of real and forged documents. He tried hard to sell this idea but never quite put it across with the moguls of the airways.

Although Henry had a true affection for early American history his heart and his pen were really in aviation, a subject about which he wrote extensively. Henry was personally acquainted with almost everyone in the field or out of it, and there were few famous men who had not at one time or another been beguiled into serving on one of his aviation committees. "Why," he used to boast, "I'm the man who introduced Tom Edison to Henry Ford, and I've got a signed photograph to prove it." Woodhouse really did know them all—pilots and polar explorers, industrialists and inventors, presidents and poets. Everybody was his friend. Orville Wright, Santos-Dumont, Amelia Earhart, Charles A. Lindbergh. He hobnobbed with Teddy Roosevelt, Woodrow Wilson and Calvin Coolidge. Arctic explorers joined him for dinner—Admiral Robert E. Peary, Roald Amundsen, Richard E. Byrd. The Staten Island poet Edwin Markham was a close associate. Woodhouse could have got their autographs. Easily. All he had to do was ask. But he preferred to forge their names. The tiny man who could scribble eighteenth-century flourishes with ease found the signatures of his own friends a cinch to imitate. Many of these chirographic malefactions he sold; others he squirreled away. He filled a big trunk with his contemporary fakes.

Woodhouse's aviation specialty was signing first-flight covers, those stamped envelopes carried on pioneer flights that commemorate great and sometimes not-so-great moments in the history of aviation. Whenever a pilot made a first airmail flight, say from Oshkosh to Hoboken, there was a commemorative cover put out and Henry would adorn it with a variety of choice signatures. If he didn't have a first-flight cover he put his forgeries on any airmail envelope that came to hand.

As a member of the Aero Club of America, Woodhouse was bombarded with air-post covers. He had them mailed to various addresses so he could gather a big collection without exciting a suspicion of cupidity among fellow members of the club. No sooner did Henry get the covers than he gilded them with signatures of his famous friends.

Any broadside, printed letter, first-day or routine cover mailed or issued by the Aero Club of America that bears signatures of famous persons is viewed with a jaundiced eye by knowing philographers. Years ago I owned a printed description of the "Roosevelt Memorial Arctic Expedition of 1919" with forged signatures by Woodhouse of Alexander Graham Bell, Augustus Post, Roald Amundsen, Admiral Robert E. Peary and R. A. Bartlett. Once Woodhouse slipped into a dramatic anachronism when he placed on a mimeographed letter of the Aero Club of America dated 1918 the signatures of Santos-Dumont, Augustus Post, Alexander Graham Bell, Admiral Robert E. Peary, Theodore Roosevelt *and* Amelia Earhart who, at the time, was still a college girl.

Woodhouse was a compulsive forger. His pen was never idle and he turned out so many fakes that he glutted the market. The surplus went into his private collection, much of it consisting of aviators and signers of the Declaration of Independence. The collection got so big that Henry put most of it, together with a lot of books, into a storage warehouse. Years later, when bad times overtook him and the tab was unpaid, the warehouse sold his vast collection. The purchaser discovered more than one hundred aviation postcards "signed" by Santos-Dumont and dozens of plain and fancy covers "inscribed" by illlustrious aviators and explorers. Henry's collection of Teddy Roosevelt inscriptions on covers had no equal. How many times the natty little forger wrote, "Congratulations on the great achievement," and added "T. Roosevelt," nobody will ever know.

Woodhouse was once presented with a fine studio photograph inscribed "To

Henry Woodhouse. *Top.* Forgeries on an Aero Club of America envelope, all executed by Woodhouse, of the writing of Admiral Robert E. Peary, Woodrow Wilson, Theodore Roosevelt, Postmaster General A. S. Burleson and others. *Center.* Authentic signatures of Peary, Roosevelt and Wilson. *Bottom.* Forgeries by Woodhouse on an Aero Club of America cover of Admiral Peary, Postmaster General Burleson and Theodore Roosevelt's writing.

Henry Woodhouse. Forgery of Calvin Coolidge's signature on "The American's Creed," also signed with an authentic signature of William Tyler Page, author of the "Creed."

Calvin Coolidge. Authentic signature.

Henry Woodhouse. Forgery of Admiral Peary's signature on a photograph. Although shaky, this fake captures the boldness of Peary's handwriting.

Robert E. Peary. Authentic signature.

Henry Woodhouse from his friend Edwin Markham," but when Henry realized he should have asked the old poet for a more intimate salutation, he simply added a lengthy encomium, adroitly imitating Markham's script, in which he lauded himself as a benefactor of mankind. On another occasion the agile-fingered financier composed a paeon to himself, also in Markham's script and with the poet's "signature," on a photograph of Millet's painting "The Man with the Hoe."

Because he was not a trusting man, Woodhouse made it a point to bone up on law. He loved to sue people. It was his joy and avocation. The records show that at the time of his death Woodhouse was suing more than thirty-five persons for real or imagined offenses.

Woodhouse was a conservative dresser. All his life he stuck to the same attire—a fedora set straight upon his head, Capone-style, and a sedate gray suit and overcoat that, as the years passed and his fortune waned, got more and more threadbare but lost none of their nattiness. To the very end Henry maintained a "headquarters" at 280 Madison Avenue in New York City, a tiny office crammed with files that overflowed with his personal fabrications.

Sometimes in his later years the impeccable and very shrewd Mr. Woodhouse visited the Argosy Book Stores where, as the friend of presidents and great aviators, he was royally welcomed. The proprietor, noted bookman Louis Cohen, recalls: "Once he examined some rare old maps and after he left the store an entire folder of treasures was missing. Misplaced, it was thought, for nobody suspected the distinguished Mr. Woodhouse. Not until he died in Bellevue at an advanced age. It was then the 'lost' folder turned up among his papers, every rare map still in it, just as it was the day he carried it out under his gray overcoat."

6

He Forged His Father's Poems

EUGENE FIELD II

"Now, Pinny," Eugene Field would say to his tiny son, "I want you to look sad and deprived. We're going to hit the cashier, Mr. Shackelford, for a 'fiver,' and the hungrier you look the better our chances."

And the famous poet would take his little boy, Eugene Field II, into the office of the cashier of the *Chicago News* to get an "unauthorized" advance on the salary that, by agreement, was paid every week to the family's financier, Field's wife, Julia.

Little Pinny, who got his nickname from the pinafore he wore as a child, was an expert at conning the cashier. Sometimes he would go alone, delivering the poetic appeals of his father to Collins Shackelford. Field's solicitations for relief from impecuniosity were delectably funny, and Shackelford could not resist them any more than he could

Eugene Field, the poet. Humorous appeal to the cashier of the *Chicago News* for a "five," delivered by his little son, Pinny. Field writes in his minuscule hand, here reproduced in actual size, "Oh, Shackelford, if you would see Your own true friend survive By this same small boy send to me A necessary 'five.' A-men!"

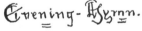

Pinny (Eugene Field). The future forger as a moody child.

Eugene Field II. Forgery of a handwritten poem signed by Eugene Field. An excellent fake, but lacking the precision and meticulous beauty of the poet's script.

turn away empty-handed the little messenger.

As Pinny got older, he improved his skills at fund raising and several times moved the "stony-hearted" editor and publisher, Melvin E. Stone, who was an avid admirer of Field, to increase his father's wages. Pinny was only fifteen when Field died in 1895 but within a few years he "acquired" part of his father's library and manuscripts. He made the most of this illicit acquisition and sold the books and manuscripts of his father for handsome sums. By 1920, a quarter of a century after Field's death, the poet's fame was at its zenith and John McCormack, the great Irish tenor, cheerfully laid out five thousand dollars for the original manuscript of Field's famous poem "Little Boy Blue."

Pinny was now, so the story goes, drinking rather heavily and had disposed of the last pen scratch of his celebrated

A Houtpoon went rowing out into the strait —
Out into the strait in the early morn;
His step was light and his brow elate
And his shirt was as new as the day just born.

His brow was cool and his breath was free
And his hands were soft as a lady's hands,
And a song of the bounding waves sang he
As he launched his bark from the golden sands.

The grayling chuckled a hoarse "ha-ha"
And the cisco tittered a rude "he-he"—
But the Houtpoon merrily sang "tra-la"
As his bark bounced over the northern sea.

Eugene Field.

Eugene Field, the poet. Authentic handwritten manuscript, signed. Although Field's writing was very tiny, compositors never complained about it.

Eugene Field.

Chicago, Sept. 14, 1895.

THE

TURNOVER CLUB.

Eugene Field II. Forgery of his father's signature, with place and date, in a copy of *The Turnover Club,* Chicago and New York, 1890. The volume bears an authentication by Eugene Field II penned, as was often the case, in green ink, testifying that the book was from the poet's library.

Eugene Field -

Eugenc Field, the poet. Authentic signature.

To -
Eugene Field —
With half Hoosier greetings
— James Whitcomb Riley

Eugene Field II. Forgery of an inscription to Field from James Whitcomb Riley, also in *The Turnover Club,* executed with great skill. The *James* is a bit shaky and the inscription is trite, considering the intimacy between Field and Riley, but it is a very deceptive fake.

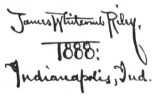

James Whitcomb Riley.
1888:
Indianapolis, Ind.

James Whitcomb Riley. Authentic signature.

namesake. But he had one last legacy, something his father never intended to leave him. That was the ability to imitate handwriting with extraordinary skill.

So Pinny began signing books with Field's name. In the back of each volume he added a notarized statement that the book came from the library of his father.

The books sold briskly. At first Eugene Field II specialized only in "signed" books and forged manuscripts of the poet, but soon he began improving the books with other and more salable signatures. Volumes "signed" by Eugene Field, Mark Twain and Bret Harte, all on the same title page or flyleaf, are not uncommon and they all bear the customary authentication of Eugene Field II.

Emboldened by his initial successes in peddling forgeries of his father, Pinny added Lincoln-signed books to his illicit productions, then sketches by Field and Mark Twain, usually copied from authentic examples. He even attempted to forge verses by Longfellow and Lowell, but these efforts were indifferent and not worthy of his talents.

By the mid-1920s Eugene Field II was disposing of large quantities of spurious autographs, including letters and manuscripts by Mark Twain, of whom he made a specialty. Many of these bogus documents found their way into public and private libraries, where the notarized—and sometimes not notarized—authentications of Eugene Field II still carried clout.

The facts of Pinny's life are lamentably vague and my most determined efforts have uncovered little about his personal

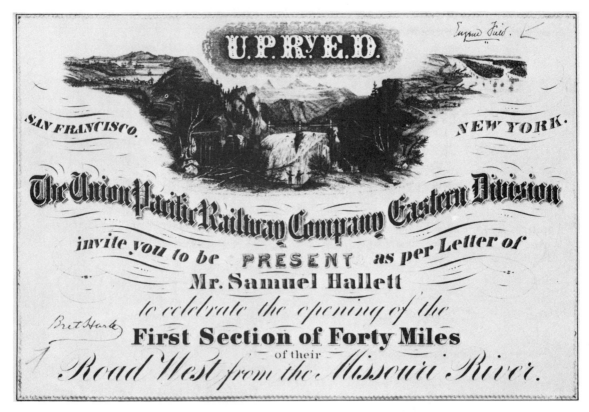

Eugene Field II. Invitation to attend a Union Pacific Railroad celebration, with forged signatures of Eugene Field, *top right,* and Bret Harte, *lower left.*

Bret Harte. Authentic signature.   Eugene Field, the poet. Authentic signature.

This original invitation came from the library of my father, Eugene Field.

Lit. Executor

Eugene Field²

April 29 – 1935

S. L. Clemens

(Mark Twain)

Eugene Field II. Authentication of the forgeries on the invitation to the Union Pacific Railroad Celebration, with a forgery of S. L. Clemens's (Mark Twain) signature.

Mark Twain. Authentic double signature.

Saml L. Clemens

("Mark Twain.")

activities. Where or when he died I do not know. There is, however, no uncertainty about the type and abundance of his forgeries.

For many years I occasionally ran across fabricated Frederic Remington signatures penned in books about the West. These signatures were ornamented with a bucking bronco. Over the years I saw enough of these broncos to supply a large rodeo. Only recently have I concluded that these ornamental Remington signatures are the invention of Eugene Field II. The handwriting in the phrase "My Book" is remarkably like that in other fakes by Field, and the gauche phrase "My Book" is one that Pinny favored. Add to this that Pinny

inherited a little of his father's artistic skill and liked to adorn his forgeries with sketches, and the evidence is just about conclusive.

In the early 1940s Field's career apparently ended, perhaps in the alcoholic or charity ward of a hospital or, one hopes, in the reformation and repentance that all the lovers of the poet of childhood would so ardently wish for.

A SCENE IN THE DAILY NEWS OFFICE.
From a drawing by Eugene Field.

Eugene Field, the poet. An authentic sketch depicting the *Daily News* office during the absence of "Nompy" (Field's nickname for Slason Thompson). This little sketch was illustrated in Thompson's biography of Field.

Eugene Field II. Forgery of the sketch above, gilded with a signature and with the locale transferred from the *Daily News* to the Office of the Chicago Press Club.

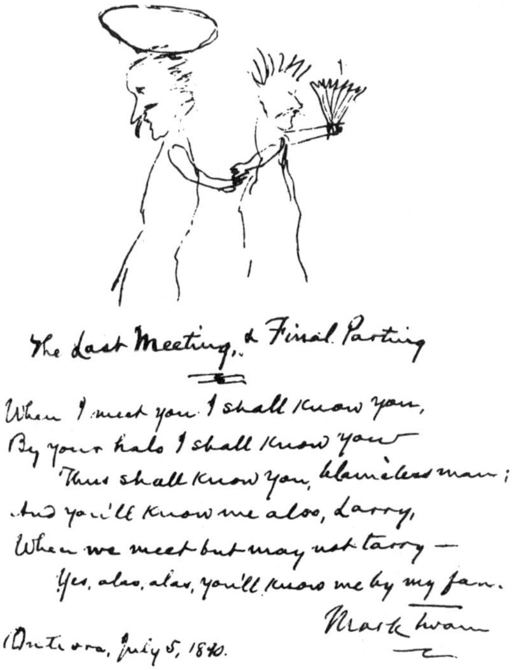
The Last Meeting, & Final Parting
When I meet you I shall know you,
By your halo I shall know you
Thus shall know you, blameless man;
And you'll know me also, Larry,
When we meet but may not tarry —
Yes, alas, alas, you'll know me by my fan.
Mark Twain
Onteora, July 5, 1890.

Mark Twain. An authentic sketch, with a humorous verse, in the visitors' book of the theatrical critic Lawrence Hutton.

Eugene Field II. Forgery of the Twain sketch. The handwriting of Clemens is well imitated by Pinny (Eugene Field II), but he has missed the whole point of the poem, which ends "Yes, alas, alas, you'll know me by my fan." Pinny has left the fan out of Twain's hand.

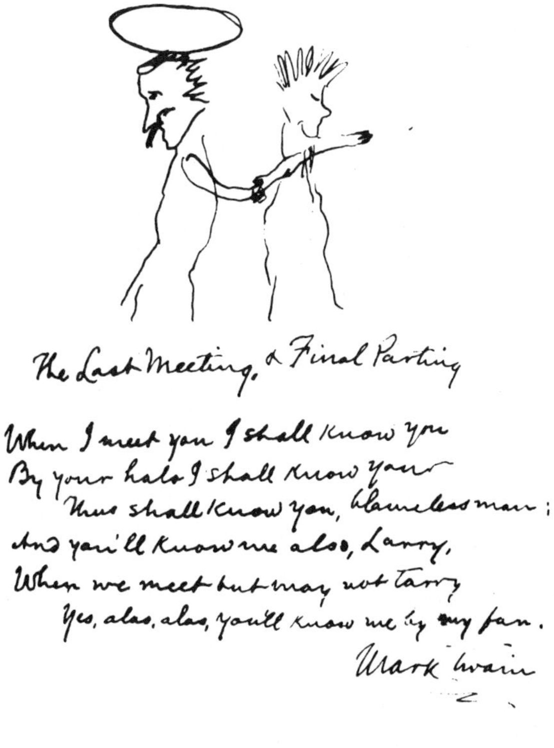
The Last Meeting, & Final Parting
When I meet you I shall know you
By your halo I shall know you
Thus shall know you, blameless man;
And you'll know me also, Larry,
When we meet but may not tarry
Yes, alas, alas, you'll know me by my fan.
Mark Twain

Each person is born to one possession which outvalues any he can earn or inherit — his last breath.

Mark Twain

Eugene Field II. Forgery of a handwritten quotation signed by Mark Twain. The writing is much more rounded and carefully written, and far more legible, than Twain's.

Eugene Field II. Forgery of a handwritten quotation signed by Mark Twain. The imitation of Twain's script in this fake is a little closer to the humorist's hand than the example above, partly because the writing is more cramped and less legible.

St. Louis, Mo.

May my namesake follow in my righteous footsteps, then neither of us will need any fire insurance.

Mark Twain

Let us save the to-morrows for work.

Truly Yours
Mark Twain

Mark Twain. Handwritten quotation signed in the shaky hand of old age. Most of Twain's quotations were, unlike those forged by Pinny, penned on small cards.

I hear in the chamber above me
The patter of little feet,
The sound of a door that is opened,
And voices soft and sweet.
              Henry W. Longfellow.

Eugene Field II. Forgery of a handwritten stanza signed by Longfellow. The writing is much too diminutive, too legible, and Field has not caught Longfellow's habit of breaking up the individual letters in a word.

I breathed a song into the air;
It fell to earth I knew not where;
For who hath sight so keen and strong,
That it can follow the flight of song!
              Henry W. Longfellow

Henry W. Longfellow. Handwritten stanza, signed. Notice Longfellow's custom of dividing his pen strokes into tiny dashes and dots, such as in the first line, the letter *t* in the word *the* has a downbar formed by two strokes; in the second line, the first word *It* has a capital *I* formed from two strokes; and in the fourth line, the second word, *it* has a two-dot crossing of the *t.* Because of his unusual script, Longfellow's manuscripts often look faded even when the ink is bright and fresh.

Eugene Field II. Forgery of a manuscript stanza signed with initials by James Russell Lowell. Except for the defect of being too legible, this is a very competent forgery. Lowell wrote these lines out rather often, and no doubt Field copied this poem right from an original.

This is my picture
Improved on by Rowse,
The sole one my victor
Allows in her house;
I don't give 'em ollers
But Fido is a friend
So, when he calls, it follers
My best I should send:
Straighten the hair now,
Gray the beard,— will
The likeness is fair now
Of yours
              J.R.L.
Elmwood: 30th Dec.r 1863.

James Russell Lowell. Authentic handwritten quatrain, signed. Notice that Lowell's own script is not so easy to read as Field's fake.

Ah, let us hope that to our praise
Good God not only reckons
The moment when we tread his ways,
But when the spirit beckons!
              J.R.Lowell.
29th Jan.y, 1871.

Eugene Field II (Pinny).

Eugene Field II. *Top.* Forgery of a drawing by Mark Twain. While the sketch resembles Clemens's work, it appears to be pointless, and Twain never put his pen to paper without some intelligent purpose. *Bottom.* Authentic signature of Mark Twain. Twain's signature differs in many ways from Field's forgery. Note that in the forged name, the terminal *n* of Twain was swung up to cross the capital *T.* This is a flourish the humorist never affected and apparently was inspired by exuberant overconfidence on the part of the forger.

The Truth
About
The Black Hills

By
H. Helen M. Bennett

My Book

Frederic Remington

Deadwood
Pioneer-Times
1907
**FRED G. BORSCH
BOX 527
DEADWOOD, S. D.**

Theodore Roosevelt. Authentic signature.

Frederic Remington. Authentic sketch of a bucking horse, signed.

Eugene Field II. Page of a book bearing a forged signature of Theodore Roosevelt, excellently executed, at the top of the page and a forged ownership, "My Book/Frederic Remington," with a sketch of a bucking mustang. Eugene Field II loved to combine on one page the signatures of several important persons and was aware that Theodore Roosevelt and Frederic Remington were close friends. Both were interested in the American West and might have owned this book. Roosevelt's signature was forged in blue ink and the Remington sketch and signature in brown ink. All the bucking-bronco sketches forged by Field that I have looked at were in brown ink, rather than the usual black ink used by Remington.

7

Wizard of the Pen

JOSEPH COSEY

First Joseph Cosey would show you his *B. Franklin*. "One of my best creations," he would say proudly. "I fooled the biggest library in America with one just like this."

If you praised his Franklin forgery and offered him a drink, Cosey would get expansive.

"Take a look at this *Mary Baker Eddy*. Just watch how fast I write it. A couple of dealers fell for this one." And Cosey would make a few eloquent flourishes in the air with his pen before putting nib and Waterman's brown ink to paper.

Like a poet who swaps ballads for beer, Cosey, a little Irishman with brown hair and a wen on his right cheek, would sit in a bar and whip out *Go: Washington*s and *Edgar A. Poe*s with inspired facility as long as the drinks kept coming.

But this was in his palmy days, in the 1930s. Earlier Cosey had been a commonplace thief, an ordinary crook almost ignored by the cops. Later he was to go on hard drugs and mainline his way into obscurity.

Cosey's real name was Martin Coneely. He was born in Syracuse, New York, on February 18, 1887, the son of an Irish cabinetmaker. An unruly youth, Cosey was, however, a clever student, especially partial to American history. But he left school and home at seventeen to become a printer's devil at a salary of three dollars and a half a week. He moved restlessly from one job to another, and the hatred for authority that he had manifested as a boy was intensified by a four-year hitch in the army (1909-1913), which ended when he was dishonorably discharged for assaulting the company cook. Years later, after he had discovered his true vocation, Cosey reversed this by forging an honorable discharge for himself.

Before he turned to forgery, Cosey had a long career as a petty sneak thief. He was barely out of his army uniform before he replaced it with an even more confining one. In 1913, in Sacramento, California, he stole a motorcycle. Under the alias of Joe Hallaway, he was caught and punished with a six-month's prison

Joseph Cosey. First page of a forged honorable discharge from the United States Army, dated July 26, 1920. Cosey actually got a dishonorable discharge in 1913.

Joseph Cosey. Second page of Cosey's forged army discharge, with his character noted as "Very Good," and with his own extremely rare signature in the lower left.

term. Then he turned up in 1914 as Frank Thompson, trying to cash a forged check, for which he drew a suspended sentence. But the following year he spent five days in a Seattle jail for carrying a concealed weapon. In 1916, this time as John Martin, he was tucked away in San Quentin for cashing a forged check in San Jose, California. Three more sentences, all under his alias of Frank Thompson, all for forgery, brought his prison years to a total of nearly a decade before he finally developed, around 1930, the forgery racket that rendered him almost immune to punishment. Almost, but not quite. He was convicted only once for the forgeries that made him notorious. On February 24, 1937, he pleaded guilty to petty larceny and was sentenced to Rikers Island, where he served less than a year.

"I owe my real start in life to the Library of Congress," said Cosey. "I wandered in one day in 1929 and asked to examine a file of historical manuscripts.

Benjamin Franklin. An authentic signed pay warrant, with the body of the document in the hand of a clerk. The writing is quite different from Cosey's script, the signature of Nicholson is bold and fluid and the chirography indicates the use of a quill, for the nib of the quill spreads in the downstrokes, such as in the heading of the document, *In Council.* In the authentic document the vertical notations, so characteristic of Cosey's fakes, are not present. Genuine Franklin pay warrants seldom come with authentications, but Cosey often accompanied his fakes with certifications signed by one "J. Edwards."

Joseph Cosey. A very early (about 1929) forgery of a Franklin pay warrant, one of the first fakes ever executed by Cosey. It has many technical defects. The paper is unusually thick and does not match the thin chain-lined paper so often used in the eighteenth century. The penmanship is gauche and large, and the Palmer-method script does not suggest the eloquent flourishes of the Revolutionary era. Cosey has written in Waterman's brown ink with no aging improvements. The name of David Rittenhouse as the addressee, in the lower left, was penned in a strange bluish ink very unlike that used by the founding fathers. Certainly no expert examining this crude forgery would suspect that Cosey was soon to become the most skilled and versatile forger of all time.

Joseph Cosey. Forgery of a pay warrant (about 1935) signed by Benjamin Franklin. In this advanced example of Cosey's art, the handwriting now resembles that of the Revolutionary period, the ink is a rich, dark brown, the paper is identical with that used in Franklin's time, the signature of Franklin is exactly the right size and the docket of John Nicholson is no longer disconcertingly inaccurate. In his search for perfection, Cosey has tastefully rounded the corners of his forgery, an added touch he often could not resist.

I was intrigued by them. When I left I took along with me as a souvenir a pay warrant dated 1786, signed by Benjamin Franklin when he was president of Pennsylvania.

"It wasn't stealing, really, because the Library of Congress belongs to the people and I'm one of the people.

"I offered the Franklin document to a dealer on Fourth Avenue Book Row in New York. He looked it over carefully, then curled his lip and announced: 'It's a fake.'

"His self-assurance infuriated me, so I decided to teach him a lesson. I bought a bottle of Waterman's brown ink from the dime store and started practicing the handwriting of famous Americans. I got quite expert at Franklin and could soon scribble his signature as fast as my own. Lincoln was another of my earliest specialties, and only a few months after this ignorant dealer had rebuffed me I had the satisfaction of selling him a Lincoln forgery for ten dollars.

"Despite my ability to forge Lincoln, Franklin pay warrants were my favorites. They sold readily and even a few smart dealers bought them. They still turn up at the auction houses, and I get a big kick out of watching them knocked down at high prices."

Like most creative men, Cosey was prolific. He whipped out his forgeries with great ease, never resorting to the amateurish device of tracery. The speed with which he penned his fakes is one of the reasons they are so hard to detect. They lack the usual marks of a forgery, retouching and labored or shaky writing. And once Cosey learned to mix rusted iron filings with Waterman's brown ink he was able to simulate almost perfectly the rich brown iron-gall ink of the Revolutionary period.

That the genius of Cosey could thrive under all the adverse conditions he daily faced is remarkable. He sold his forgeries for very little, usually from two to fifty dollars each. Today most of them are worth five times what their creator got for them. When in New York Cosey stopped at 268 Broadway, a flophouse with rooms no larger than closets, no furniture save a cot and a locker and no lighting except from the flickering yellow bulb in the corridor. The air smelled of creosote, an acrid disinfectant that brings tears into the eyes. And like the Bowery flophouses I knew when I first got to New York in 1939 it was infested with bedbugs so savage that only a body-spraying with Flit before retiring could discourage them. It was hard to be creative in this setting of misery and poverty, but Cosey managed to turn out convincing and often inspired forgeries.

In his pockets Cosey carried all the tools of his trade. Penholders, nibs of various sizes, doctored ink and sheets of antiquated paper ready for the outpourings of his creative art.

A mere chronicle of the names forged by Cosey is a testimony to his adventurous genius. His favorites were the Revolutionary big heroes—Washington, Franklin, Richard Henry Lee, Thomas Jefferson, John Paul Jones, Patrick Henry, John Adams, Samuel Adams, Alexander Hamilton, Aaron Burr, John Marshall, James Monroe—the list goes on and on.

Joseph Cosey. Forgery of Franklin's signature on a faked pay warrant dated 1787. The signature and paraph (flourish under the name) are bold and vigorous like the writing of Franklin's earlier years.

Benjamin Franklin. Authentic signature from a handwritten letter, 1787, at the age of eighty-one. The elderly statesman, who was to die in three years, had difficulty writing the capital F, and the n's lack the curvaceous clarity of his youthful script.

Benjamin Franklin. Authentic signature on a land grant, 1787. Notice the tremors in the capital F and the paraph. Franklin was eighty-one when he scrawled this bold signature.

Benjamin Franklin. Authentic signature from a handwritten check, 1787. Compare this feeble, tremulous writing with the bold imitation of Cosey at the top, also dated the same year.

Joseph Cosey.

But he did not neglect the later statesmen. Lincoln, U. S. Grant, Theodore Roosevelt, Cleveland and Calvin Coolidge were also objects of his creativity. Cosey did better with the earlier figures; his Roosevelts and Coolidges are not worthy of his great talent.

So expert was Cosey that most proud owners of his spurious wares would cheerfully wager a double eagle that they possessed the genuine article. Not long ago a courtly old gentleman bowed his way into my gallery and with great ceremony opened a swathe of silk to unveil a yellowing document. Reverently he placed it in my hands.

Joseph Cosey. Forgery of a handwritten letter signed by John Marshall. The original manuscript of this forgery was age-treated by Cosey and is foxed and stained, looking even older than its spurious date of 1804.

John Marshall. Authentic handwritten, signed letter. Marshall's own script was smaller than Cosey's imitation.

"It certainly does look like a genuine Franklin pay warrant," I said. "And it would fool anybody who wasn't an expert. But it's a forgery by Joseph Cosey, penned about 1935.

"There are dozen of libraries in the United States," I went on, "that prize in their vaults similar products of Cosey's pen. Not just fake Franklins, but Washingtons and Jeffersons. Scholars and historians study these pen-and-ink imposters and even quote them in their theses."

After my visitor's first flush of embarrassment subsided, he pressed me for more details, saying: "But the signature of Franklin perfectly matches a facsimile with which I compared it."

"It is a superb counterfeit," I said.

"Then how can you tell it's not genuine?"

"Notice the date of your document—1787—only three years before Franklin's death. Yet the signature is firm and bold, unlike the writing of an old man. Cosey never grasped the fact that like most handwriting, Franklin's disintegrated toward the end of his long life. It became shakier, almost tremulous. The

"A family heirloom," he explained.

The "heirloom" was a familiar sight. No more than a split-second glance was needed for me to identify a Cosey forgery of Franklin. I pretended to study the spurious paper while I gave the owner the bad news as gently as I could.

beloved "first".

"——— the human will which maketh and worketh a lie, hiding the divine Principle of Harmony, is destructive to health, and is the cause of disease, rather than its cure."

My own salutation has ever been — "Be of good cheer; & if you will trust in God for comfort you cannot go astray."

Lovingly —

Mary Baker Eddy

March 22. 1905.

Pleasant view.

Massachusetts Metaphysical College,

571 Columbus Ave.

Mary Baker G. Eddy, Pres't.

P. O. Address, 385 Commonwealth Ave.

"Science and Health, with Key to the Scriptures," by Mary Baker G. Eddy, the standard work on Christian Science Mind-Healing. Sold, wholesale and retail, at the above address. Price, $3.00; postage, 18 cents.

Boston, May 23 1889

My dear Student

Will you take my College for one year or more? I want to have it open, and I have given up teaching, for time to do other things that God demands. The translation of the Scriptures is needed. Answer me at once. Love to dear Mrs Bates

Lovingly Yours

M B G Eddy

Mary Baker Eddy

Joseph Cosey. Forgery of a last page of a letter of Mary Baker Eddy to Sarah Dean, quoting from *Science and Health. Right.* Authentic handwritten letter signed by Mary Baker Eddy (1889), and a full signature (1894). Cosey's forged writing is more legible than the erratic, jerky script of Mrs. Eddy, and Cosey unwittingly imitated her earlier handwriting even in the letters he forged and dated near the end of her life.

Valley Forge.
Jan! 6, 1778.
Maj. Howell,
    The Quarter master informs
me of the shortage of blankets.
What is the number available?
                    G? Washington
                    Com?

Joseph Cosey. Forgery of a handwritten letter signed by George Washington from Valley Forge, January 6, 1778.

George Washington. Conclusion of an authentic handwritten letter, signed. Notice that Cosey failed to capture the grace and beauty of Washington's script. His forgeries of Washington's signature are easily identified because the crossing of the *t* is a tiny, cramped replica of the sweeping flourish of Washington.

You will receive this
letter from the hands of Mr. Izard,
to whom I request you to pay attention, and make his visit to Mount
Vernon as convenient and agreeable
to him as may be in your power
    I am Your Friend &c"
                    G? Washington

Joseph Cosey. Forgery of a Revolutionary War pay warrant signed by Washington and Aaron Burr.

Aaron Burr. Authentic signature, 1776.

George Washington. Authentic signature. Notice that the top of the capital *W* is on the same level as the middle curve of the capital *G,* whereas in Cosey's forgery the *W* extends far above the middle of the *G.* This error is characteristic of most of Cosey's forgeries of Washington.

Aaron Burr. Authentic signature, 1795. Cosey has unintentionally imitated the later signature in the forged document above of Revolutionary date.

Joseph Cosey. Forgery of a letter of Patrick Henry to John Marshall, Washington City (at that time not in existence), 1779, sending an old map. The signature of Henry is poorly executed, and the handwriting in the body of the letter resembles most of the clerical scripts used by Cosey in his fakes.

Patrick Henry. Authentic signature.

"Mount Vernon"
June 12th 1779

Hon. P. Henry,
House of Burgesses.
Dear Sir,
Thank you for submitting this map
of ancient symbols.
I am sure that John Marshall will find
in it just what he seeks for his new book.
Cordially yours
Richard Henry Lee

June 12, 1779

My dear Mr. Henry,
There remains nothing for me to do but
add my approval, since Mr. Lee and yourself have
endorsed the drawings herein.
as ever —

G. Washington

Joseph Cosey. Forgery of a handwritten letter signed by Richard Henry Lee transmitting Henry's letter to John Marshall, with an approving handwritten letter signed by George Washington beneath that of Lee. The complimentary closes "Yours very sincerely," "Cordially yours," and "as ever" were rarely used during the Revolutionary era and must be consiered as careless anachronisms on the part of the forger.

Richard Henry Lee

Richard Henry Lee. Authentic signature.

George Washington. Authentic signature.

G. Washington

tremor is especially obvious in his handwritten documents, but even the huge signature which the aging statesman affixed to land grants and pay warrants reveals a slight quaver, easily visible without a magnifying glass.

"Yet, whether Cosey writes an early or late Franklin document, he never varies the handwriting. His scribbling Franklin is timeless, an eternal youth whose hand never trembled and whose handsome script remained firm and bold to the very end."

"But isn't this the paper of Franklin's period?"

"Yes, indeed. Cosey cannot be faulted on his paper. It is the typical, chain-lined, hand-laid pure rag paper of the Revolutionary era. No doubt Cosey stumbled upon a supply of it, or else removed blank portions of paper from insignificant or valueless documents.

"I am convinced, too," I went on, "that Cosey 'sized' or treated his paper chemically to prevent his fresh ink from blurring, since modern ink tends to fuzz or 'feather' when it goes on old paper."

"Did Cosey use a quill pen, like Franklin?"

"A good question," I said. "I doubt if Cosey ever plucked a goose. Aside from the fact that the ink trail left by Cosey's pen indicates a steel nib—and the steel pen was not widely used until the 1840s—his forgeries lack the unintentional little spurts or showers of ink which occurred when a quill's sharp nib caught in the paper. Missing from Cosey's writing, too, are the variations in width of the upsweeps and downstrokes of the pen."

When my visitor bowed his way out of my gallery, he took with him his family "heirloom," and I dare say it will come my way again, perhaps still wrapped in its sumptuous silken cocoon.

Cosey was far more than just an artist. He had the audacity and the *sang-froid* which characterize both the madman and the genius. His commonplace fakes—the pay warrants of Franklin, the letters of Mary Baker Eddy and John Marshall—all might conceivably have been fabricated by a talented artist. But many times in his life the alcohol-inspired Cosey reached great heights. Once he daringly forged a complete draft of the Declaration of Independence in Jefferson's hand. Every pen stroke, every word, every letter, every comma was perfectly executed by the master of fabrication. The ink was strikingly similar to Jefferson's and the huge sheets of foolscap were the same as those often used by Jefferson. It was with a feeling akin to reverence that I first examined this masterpiece of the forger's art. I bought it from the owner and years later, in an unguarded moment, put it up for sale.

Described in my auction catalogue of March 29, 1969, as one of Cosey's finest fakes, the Declaration was sold for four hundred and twenty-five dollars to Professor C. Ernest Cooke of Virginia Intermont College in Bristol, Virginia. Cooke was also the successful bidder on several other remarkable examples of Cosey's handicraft.

About six months after the sale I received a letter from one of the leading colleges in Virginia. "We have been offered Jefferson's original draft of the Declaration of Independence for $35,000," read the letter, "and we understand that it has been authenticated by you as a manuscript entirely in the hand of Thomas Jefferson. Would you please confirm this?"

I replied to the college that the document was a Cosey forgery and the proper repository for it was a wastebasket and that Professor Cooke was a mountebank and the proper repository for him was the nearest penitentiary.

Cosey often complained that his clients were as guilty of fraud as he, because they believed they were taking

Joseph Cosey. Forgery of a real-estate plat subdividing Tory lands, with a handwritten note by John Adams. Adams's forged script bears the usual similarity to Cosey's other rapidly penned hands, but the signature is a pretty fair imitation.

John Adams. Authentic handwritten note, signed.

Joseph Cosey. Forged handwritten letter signed "Richard Henry Lee" to Patrick Henry, Philadelphia, 1777, attacking the British for "an acrimonious and foolish display of Tyranny." Notice that Cosey employs in this letter the proper complimentary close for the eighteenth century, "I am with great respect dear Sir your most obedient and very humble Servt."

Joseph Cosey. Forgery of a handwritten, signed letter of James Madison, New York, March 4, 1787. Presumably the addressee was Timothy Dwight or Theodore Dwight, both of whom at the time resided in Hartford (not in Salem) and neither of whom was entitled to be addressed as "Honorable." Cosey frequently blundered in his historical data. A further and very obvious defect in this forgery is the misplaced, double wax seal, visible at the bottom of the letter with faint traces at the top. Had this letter actually been sent through the mails or dispatched by courier, the seal would be a single one, the letter would show the folds necessary to create an address-leaf and there would be a paper tear or a seal break where the letter was opened.

Dear Sir   *Montpellier Sept. 23 1821*

I have duly receiv'd the copy of your Memoirs which you were so good as to send me. Be pleased to accept my thanks for it. I have looked sufficiently into the work to be sensible of its value not only to those who take a more immediate interest in local details, but as a contribution also to the fund of materials for a general history of the American Revolution. Every incident connected with this great & pregnant event is already an object of patriotic curiosity; and will be rendered by the lapse of time more & more so. It is much to be desired that the example you have given may be followed in all the States by individuals who unite with industry & opportunities the requisite judgment & impartiality. Besides the more general obligation to engage in the task a special one will be found in the occasions for doing justice to individual merits which might otherwise escape the historical tribute due to them.

Be pleased to accept Sir assurances of my esteem and best respects.

James Madison

James Madison. Handwritten letter signed, Montpellier, September 23, 1821. Compare the regular alignment of Madison's script with the weaving of Cosey's fake, especially in line five of the forgery. Cosey was obviously concentrating on the formation of the individual words and lost touch with the alignment of the writing.

Aaron Burr. Authentic signature, 1807. This is the signature that the forger has mimicked, unaware that it was not characteristic of Burr's handwriting during the Revolution.

Joseph Cosey. Forgery of a document signed by Aaron Burr as a Revolutionary War colonel. The body of the document is in Cosey's familiar script and the two dockets on either side of the text are executed with his usual skill. However, the signature of Burr is unlike that of his youth.

Aaron Burr. Authentic signature, 1776, at the approximate period of the Cosey forgery.

Aaron Burr. Authentic signature, 1795.

Joseph Cosey. *Left and above.* Forged handwritten, signed letter of James Monroe to John Quincy Adams, Washington City, 1818. An interesting letter, but a very poor imitation of Monroe's handwriting and signature. *Under the forgery.* James Monroe. Conclusion of an authentic handwritten letter, signed. Note that Monroe's own script is very hard to read compared with the writing in Cosey's fake.

Albany N.Y.
June 6, 1909

Mr. W. H. Taft.
White House, Washington, D.C.
Sir,
Here is the only old map of the "Market Place" that I think is in existence. Your request to Col. Cassidy was referred to me, as he thought I had a collection of such items. It is a very old print, done by Mundell of Albany, and only a few were made as no one attached any importance to them. But the (Governor of New York) (Chas. Evans Hughes) also requested one, however, Col. Cassidy of the "Albany Argus" asked me to try and find one for you and here it is. I understand you want it for the N.Y. hist. room at Yale, and hope it will be acceptable.
I am Sir
Yours very sincerely
Mark Twain

Ten Broeck House
West Albany N.Y.

Joseph Cosey. Forgery of a handwritten letter signed by Mark Twain, June 6, 1909, less than a year before his death. The script is a very poor imitation, and the flourish under the name unlike that used by Twain. However, Cosey's imagination did not fail him. Notice the name of the addressee of the letter.

Mark Twain. First page of an authentic letter handwritten by Twain, age seventy-three. The writing and the signature are somewhat tremulous. Cosey was apparently unaware of the degeneration in Twain's script during his last years. Twain died at seventy-five in the spring of 1910.

21 FIFTH AVENUE (1904-1908)
Monday.
Dear Mr. Hapgood
I am so sorry I was not here to assure you in all sincerity that you haven't a thing to reproach yourself with. I did not make myself understood the other day: That was my fault not yours. Now I beg you to believe that which is absolutely true: that you have nothing in the world to blame yourself—
Truly Yours
Mark Twain

advantage of him. He also alleged that he was kind and generous. To illustrate his compassion, he told a story about one of his Poe fabrications. "I went to this bookstore with a Poe forgery. The owner was out, but his secretary told me she was a student of Poe and would be thrilled to see something in his handwriting. I finally sold the forgery to her for just three dollars, but only because I was broke. Well, my conscience bothered me about it for weeks, and the first time I had three dollars I went back to the shop to tell her it was a counterfeit and buy it back from her. But she

Joseph Cosey. Forgery of a petition to the Continental Congress by a group of merchants, requesting authorization to trade in cotton and tobacco. Signed by the merchants, and with the forged signatures of Richard Henry Lee, Edmund Pendleton, Joseph Hewes, Samuel Adams, John Adams, Edward Biddle and Benjamin Franklin.

This amazing forgery first came to my attention more than a quarter of a century ago when it was published as an authentic original in 1952 in a privately printed little book about autographs by Robert Williams. About a year after the book appeared, Williams died and his collection, containing this forgery which, from the illustration, appeared to be genuine, was bought on speculation by a farmer in Pennsylvania. I was crushed that I had had no opportunity to purchase any of the documents in Williams's collection, but my delight was great when I got a note from the farmer asking me to visit him in the country and look over his acquisitions. I scraped together what money I could and drove with my former wife, Doris, and my father-in-law to a little farmhouse in the country. I was particularly eager to look at this unusual document. A quick glance told me the bad news. It was a Cosey forgery.

It was twenty years before I saw this fake again. The new owner generously allowed me to photograph it, so that its migrations as an authentic document would at last come to an end.

Richard Henry Lee

Edm'd Pendleton

Joseph Hewes,

Sam'l Adams

John Adams

B Franklin

Authentic signatures of the forged names on the document opposite.

Joseph Cosey. Forgery of a handwritten note signed by John Wilkes Booth, popular stage actor and assassin of Lincoln, written on the verso of an authentic carte-de-visite photograph of a Civil War soldier. Cosey has cleverly penned an admission pass on the photograph of the very soldier who had presumably requested a free seat at one of Booth's performances.

John Wilkes Booth. Authentic signature.

14 Chestnut St.
Buffalo N.Y.
Aug. 10, 1905

Senator T.C. Platt
Albany N.Y.

My dear Senator

I have been informed from a very confidential source that Mr. T. R. has agreed with Wm Howard Taft to run again for the presidency upon his return from Africa, which will be a new departure — being a third term for Mr. R. One cannot of course foresee what may take place in the hands of the Republican party in the time between now and then. You know Mr. Taft has three years yet to go, and I understand there were some differences between them when he left for his big game hunting trip.

Present my best wishes to Mrs. Platt and my wife sends hers.

Yours Sincerely,
Grover Cleveland

Joseph Cosey. Forgery of a handwritten, signed letter of Grover Cleveland. The handwriting is the usual rapidly penned script of Cosey, very unlike Cleveland's. Cosey must have whipped this fake out for a special customer, one who was extremely trusting.

To the Assembly:

Assembly bill No 253 entitled "An act to amend Chapter five hundred and seventeen of the Laws of eighteen hundred and seventy, entitled 'An act to amend the Charter of the City of Buffalo,'" is herewith returned without approval.

Grover Cleveland
1894

Grover Cleveland. Authentic handwriting and signature.

Sangamon Hill,
Oyster Bay,
Mar. 10, 1918

My dear Archie;—

I am sorry to disappoint you, but I cannot possibly be at your exhibit this evening. I have just now received a large quantity of mail, some from Washington which I must attend to.

I understand negotiations are under way for an armistice. but I hardly think the Central Powers are ready as yet for any cessation of hostilities. Yesterday I had a cable from Quentin, and he makes no mention of it. Of course the cable was censored like all mail for the U.S. but as it was addressed to me I thought perhaps it might pass the censor. We shall soon know however. Now, to my mail. If there is anything of importance I shall let you know.

Please make my apologies to Dr. and Mrs. Kent, and the rest.

Yours very truly

Theodore Roosevelt

Major Archie Butt,
314 E. 94 St.
N.Y.C.

Joseph Cosey. Forgery of a handwritten letter of Theodore Roosevelt to his son, Archie, Oyster Bay, 1918. A poor example of Cosey's work which does not capture the force and masculinity of Roosevelt's rapid scrawl.

Theodore Roosevelt. Authentic handwriting and signature.

courtesy, and consideration for others.

Theodore Roosevelt

april 8ᵗʰ 1911

G. William Berquist, special investigator for the New York Public Library, makes his first report on Joseph Cosey.

File Number 36/001 J
From: Special Investigator
To: Curator of Manuscripts

Subject: Cosey Forgeries

1. This office is forwarding herewith samples of the work of Joseph Morrison better known as Joseph Cosey. He also uses the alias of Martin Connelly and various other names.

2. The enclosed manuscripts came from a good many different sources, some of which are indicated and all have been traced more or less definitely to Cosey.

3. Cosey came to my attention in 1933, and I saw him for the first time on January 11th, 1934. At that time, he was brought to my office by Mr. Heinle and a city detective. He had been picked up after trying to sell a Lincoln document to Mr. Edward L. Dean, a book dealer.

4. At this time, Cosey tacitly admitted that he was responsible for the forgeries and we took from him a bottle of ink, forged manuscripts of Lincoln and Poe and some signatures of Franklin and Button Gwinnett. He was allowed to go at the time because it was felt that there was insufficient evidence to convict him.

5. Subsequently, he came to my office on several occasions and told me that he had decided to give up this activity. However, there is no indication that he did because in January 1937 he was arrested for selling a Lincoln letter to a dealer in stamps. Later, he pleaded guilty and was sentenced to the city penitentiary for an indeterminate period of three years.

6. A complete and detailed record of this case is kept in this office.

GWB:L   G. William Bergquist.

May 12th, 1937.

June 16, 1924

Mr. J. E. Meredith
Harvard University.
Cambridge Mass U.S.A

Dear Sir,
            Your letter came and I am
grateful to you.
            The Lahore edition of Barrack
Room Ballads is I am sure long
since exhausted, and I believe, scarce.
You might write to Bernard Quaritch
in London or Dr. Rosenbach in New York.
If these cannot furnish you with a
copy you might write W.E. Moore & Sons.
14 King St. Calcutta (publishers). Failing
these I know not what you can do to
secure a copy. Have you advertised in the
various American periodicals?
            Thanking you for the expression of interest
in the volume. I am sincerely
                        Yours
Antigua   Rudyard Kipling
Leeward Is.
℅ British Consulate

Joseph Cosey. Forgery of a signed, handwritten letter by Rudyard Kipling.

William Winter.

John Gilbert

Whitelaw Reid.

S.L. Clemens

Thomas Bailey Aldrich

Very Truly Yours —
James Whitcomb Riley.
— 1887 —

Autographs given to me
on request at a dinner
party — Murray Hill Hotel, N.Y.
Nov. 17, 1887
Miss Adeline Cox

Joseph Cosey. Forgery of a group of signatures allegedly obtained at a dinner party.

‡ BURWASH
ETCHINGHAM

BATEMAN'S
BURWASH
·SUSSEX·

Oct. 10. 1904.

Dear Leonard,

That was a most timely — not to say oddreded — buck. It galloped up to the door just as visitors were arriving and we tried hard to behave as though venison were our daily fare. Likewise it arrived in perfect condition — and I have known venison that came, so to speak, roaring like a bull. I write, housewifely, to thank you on the wife's behalf as well as mine own. It's a comfort to think we shall meet on the road to the table.

Yours sincerely,
Rudyard Kipling.

S.L. Clemens

Mark Twain (Samuel L. Clemens). Authentic signature.

Thomas Bailey Aldrich.

Thomas Bailey Aldrich. Authentic signature.

Very truly your friend,
James Whitcomb Riley.

James Whitcomb Riley. Authentic signature.

Rudyard Kipling. Authentic handwritten letter signed.

112

Joseph Cosey. Forgery of a hand-written quotation signed by Mark Twain. Cosey commented to G. William Bergquist: "I did not do this very well."

New York Aug 5 '87

Taking the pledge will not make bad liquor good, but it will improve it,

Truly Yours
Mark Twain

To W. D. H.

Do your duty to-day & repent to-morrow.

Truly Yours
Mark Twain

Mark Twain. Authentic handwritten quotation signed.

for Deposit with Jay Cook & Co.
U. S. Grant.

Joseph Cosey. Forged U. S. Grant check endorsement.

Edgar A Poe

Edgar A. Poe. Authentic signature.

U. S. Grant. Authentic signature.

Joseph Cosey. Forged handwriting and signature of Edgar Allan Poe. Cosey's Poes are among his finest creations.

Edgar A. Poe.
Philada. Dec. 9. 1847.

The Poetic Principle (A lecture)

9 — land now situated on the Comanche Reservation —

10 — fifteen thousand acres under cultivation, and capable
of producing more than is provided for. An act of
Congress of 1847 prohibits the marketing of any
produce raised in this section unless agreed to at
seed time with the agent's approval.

11 — The sum of four thousand dollars ($4000.00) to be
expended as follows :-
Salary of Agent one year twenty-five hundred dollars
$2500.00; salary of assistant agent fifteen hundred
$1500.00; with fuel, light, and transportation.

12 — An additional $1000.00 is requested for emergency
purposes.

13 — An additional $2000.00 is requested for hospital supplies.

14 — An additional $750 is urgently needed for medical
attention, the actual rate of $500.00 being inadequate
and exhausted.

December 4th 1878
Fort Wingate,
Ter. N. M.

By William H. Howard, Deputy Agent

Attest: Walt Whitman Agent
Lieut. Leslie McElwain M Hosp. Dept } Dec. 4th 1878

Joseph Cosey. Forgery of page three only of a "Comanche" document signed by Walt Whitman. A bizarre fake that was bought from Cosey by a rare-book dealer, Alfred Goldsmith. Cosey's usual handwriting is readily recognizable. The signature of "Indian agent" Walt Whitman lacks its usual power and vitality.

Walt Whitman. Authentic signature.

> *U Declaration by the Representatives of the UNITED STATES*
> *OF AMERICA, in General Congress assembled.*
>
> *When in the course of human events it becomes necessary for one people*
> *to dissolve the political bands which have connected them with another, and*
> *to assume among the powers of the earth the separate and equal station to*
> *which the laws of nature & of nature's god entitle them, a decent respect*
> *to the opinions of mankind requires that they should declare the causes*
> *which impel them to the separation.*

Joseph Cosey. Forgery of Jefferson's draft of the Declaration of Independence (eight lines only), a remarkable freehand imitation of Jefferson's script. Cosey forged the entire Declaration.

Thomas Jefferson. Authentic handwritten manuscript in Jefferson's hand, a rough draft of the Declaration of Independence (first eight lines only.)

> *A Declaration by the Representatives of the UNITED STATES*
> *OF AMERICA, in General Congress assembled.*
>
> *When in the course of human events it becomes necessary for one people to*
> *dissolve the political bands which have connected them with another, and to*
> *assume among the powers of the earth the separate and equal station to*
> *which the laws of nature & of nature's god entitle them, a decent respect*
> *to the opinions of mankind requires that they should declare the causes*
> *which impel them to the separation.*

welcomed me joyously, and before I could confess, she said: 'You'll never know what owning that Poe letter means to me. It's the most exciting thing I've ever owned.' I didn't have the heart to disillusion her. So I walked out and let her keep it and believe in it."

Many times I have identified a document as a Cosey forgery only to have it offered to me again as an original within a few weeks by someone else. An amusing incident of this type occurred when I was called to distant Brooklyn to make an offer for a Poe letter about "The Cask of Amontillado." As I entered a dingy, half-lit room in an old house where Poe himself might have lived, I could see in a far corner a framed letter which, even from twenty feet, appeared to be the handicraft of Cosey.

"Is that by any chance your Poe letter?" I asked the hopeful owner.

It was, she proudly affirmed. I picked up the letter, worth about fifteen dollars as a curiosity, and pointed out the features that labeled it as a fabrication.

I'd have been spared a lot of trouble if I had bought the letter, but I said

notes cont'd

To — Calvin F. S. Thomas — Printer.

note 1. S. 1 "I have sent for thee holy friar". Of the history of Tamerlane little is known; with that little I have taken the full liberty of a poet. That he was descended from the family of Zinghis than is more than probable, but he is vulgarly supposed to have been the son of a shepherd, and to have raised himself to the throne by his own address. He died in the year 405, in the time of Pope Innocent VII. How I shall account for giving him a ~~friar~~ as a death-bed confessor I cannot exactly determine. He wanted someone to listen to his tale — and why not a friar? It does not pass the bounds of possibility — quite sufficient for my purpose — and I have at least good authority on my side for such innovations. — Poe.

note *

"no purer thought ~~dwelt~~ in a Seraph's breast". I must beg the readers pardon for making Tamerlane, a Tartar of the fourteenth century, speak in the same language as a Boston gentleman of the nineteenth; but of the Tartar mythology we have little information. — Poe.

note 39 "The mists of the Taglay have shed" &c. The mountains of Belur Taglay are a branch of the Immaus in the southern part of Independent Tartary. They are celebrated for the singular beauty of their vallies. — Poe.

Mr. Thomas.
                make any typographical corrections, but no changes in tent
"which blazes upon Edis shrine". A deity presiding over virtuous love; upon whose imaginary altar a sacred fire was continually blazing.   — Edgar A. Poe.

Joseph Cosey. Forgery of handwritten notes of Poe regarding "Tamerlane" (an early Poe poem), found on Cosey at the time of his arrest in 1934.

Edgar A. Poe. Authentic later handwriting and signature of Poe (1845), usually the script imitated by Cosey regardless of the date he put on his fakes.

Edgar A. Poe. Authentic early handwriting and signature. Cosey was unwittingly imitating Poe's later hand in his "Tamerlane" (1829) forgery.

At the request of Mr Thomas W. White, Proprietor of the Southern Literary Messenger" I take the liberty of addressing you, and of soliciting some little contribution for our Magazine.

It is our design to issue, as soon as may be, a number of the Messenger consisting altogether of articles from our most distinguished literati, and to this end have been promised,

Simpson, Esquire. The bequest was conditioned upon my taking the name of the testator; — the family, not the Christian name. His Christian or baptismal names are Napoleon Buonaparte. I am now Napoleon Buonaparte Simpson. I as-

Edgar A. Poe

Edgar A. Poe

Joseph Cosey. Forgery of a letter of Edgar A. Poe to the poet and critic N. P. Willis, with several forged notations by Willis. An excellent forgery, imitating Poe's formal and very carefully indited writing. Cosey often dyed his Poe forgeries with Tintex. The slight weaving up and down of the lines in this forgery reveal that Cosey was concentrating very hard on the formation of individual letters in the words. Many of Cosey's forged Poe letters were addressed to Willis, and as a result scholars have learned to be wary of all Poe-Willis correspondence.

"Pencillings by the way"
1st. Graham's
New York,
N.P. Willis
Dec 7. '47.

My dear Willis,

Having just returned from Philadelphia I thought to first drop in at the Home Journal Office and see you, but Morris informs me you have gone to Idlewild for the week end. As far as literary circles are concerned my visit was unsuccessful. Mr. R— was very attentive and interested, but when it came to subscribing he ...tated, suggesting that $3°° was not a sufficient sum for a Mag. of the kind proposed — that people who could pay $3°° would pay $5°°, and that is as far as I got with him. I met our old friend, N.C.B. of Baltimore, who has visions of a return of the "Museum" on a level with "Sartain's" or "God..'s at the same price as formerly.

Perhaps you may come out to Fordham on Sunday after... I shall be alone, except maybe Mrs Russ... and possibly Dr.F— might drop in. Morris assures me he will deliver this in time for you to let me know if I may expect you, so I shall not absent myself.

R.G. sends his compliments for "Pencillings By the ..."

Yours cordially
Edgar A Poe

N.P. Willis Esq?
Home Journal Office,
New York.

nothing further to the owner about it and confined myself to the purchase of a large collection of miscellaneous autographs that had been assembled by her late father.

Less than two weeks later, an antiques dealer burst excitedly into my gallery with a package under his arm. "It's a Poe letter," he said, tenderly untying the cords that secured his treasure.

I shared his excitement, but within a few moments I found myself again examining the Cosey forgery of Poe's letter about "The Cask of Amontillado." I let the owner down as pleasantly as possible, for his shabby clothes indicated that he was ill prepared to accept a loss.

"It's worth ten dollars to me as a curiosity," I told him.

He shook his head.

"Okay, I'll make it twenty-five."

"I wish I could sell it to you," he explained, with tears glistening in his eyes, "but I simply can't. I put two hundred dollars into it—and that's a fortune for me. I've got to pass along my loss to somebody else. I suppose that's dishonest but, after all, you *could* be wrong, couldn't you?"

Looking at this wretched man inspired me to the ready admission that I was very fallible. He packed up the letter, still in the same walnut frame, and walked out.

New-York. April 16. 46.

My Dear Sir,

You seem to take matters very easily and I really wonder at your patience under the circumstances. But the truth is, I am in no degree to blame. Your letters, one and all, reached me in due course of mail — and I attended to them, as far as I could. The business, in fact, was none of mine but of the person to whom I transferred the Journal* and in whose hands it perished.

Of course, I feel no less in honor bound to refund you your money, and now do so, with many thanks for your promptness & courtesy.

[*Broadway Journal - G.W.E.]

very cordially yours

Edgar A Poe,

G. W. Evelett Esq

Edgar A. Poe. Authentic handwritten letter, signed. This letter is in Poe's informal script, written with great rapidity.

Nathaniel P. Willis. Authentic signature.

About a month later I got a phone call from a prominent antiques dealer.

"What's a good Poe letter worth to you?" he asked. "And I mean a *really good* letter."

"About five thousand dollars."

"Well, hang on to your hat. I've got one, and it's a beauty. Unpublished, too. It's about 'The . . .'"

"Don't tell me," I interrupted. "It's about 'The Cask of Amontillado.' It's penned in pale brown ink. And it's in an old walnut frame."

"Why, yes. But how did you know?"

"Because I've already seen it—twice. It's a forgery by Joseph Cosey. My last cash offer for it was twenty-five dollars and that offer still holds if you want to sell it."

There was a long silence, then a click as the receiver was hung up.

For many years I pondered the fate of this unusual Poe forgery. Then on June 21, 1976, I got a letter from D. M. St. John, of Carry Back Books in Haverhill, New Hampshire, describing the sale at auction of a Poe letter about "The Cask of Amontillado" which, if genuine, would be valued at ten thousand dollars. The auctioneer had been able to coax only two or three bids from a skeptical audience, and the letter had been

The Raven

By

Edgar A. Poe.

Once upon a midnight dreary, while I pondered, weak and
weary,
Over many a quaint and curious volume of forgotten lore—
While I nodded, nearly napping, suddenly there came
a tapping,
As of someone gently rapping, rapping at my
chamber door.
"'Tis some visitor," I muttered, "tapping at my chamber
door—
Only this and nothing more."

V

And the Raven never flitting still is sitting, still is
sitting
On the pallid bust of Pallas just above my chamber door;
And his eyes have all the seeming of a demon's that is
dreaming,
And the lamp-light o'er him streaming throws his
shadow on the floor;
And my soul from out that shadow that lies floating
on the floor
Shall be lifted — nevermore!

Respectfully Yr. Obt. Ser.
Edgar A. Poe.

Joseph Cosey. First and last stanzas of a complete forged manuscript of Poe's "The Raven." A magnificent forgery, executed with great skill. Unfortunately for Cosey, in his eagerness to capture the flavor of Poe's era, he penned his fake on chain-lined Revolutionary War paper intead of the slick pearl-gray paper ordinarily used by Poe.

knocked down for just four hundred dollars. "Attached to the back of this framed letter," wrote St. John, "was an envelope bearing . . . a letter of validation . . . which certainly did not convince me. It was signed by Henry C. Roberts." The buyer was a venturesome bookman from New Ipswich, New Hampshire. Philosophized St. John: "Did he know something, one wonders, or did he buy a curio only?"

I once examined a complete Cosey manuscript of Poe's "The Raven," a superb forgery of this famous poem for which I offered the owner one hundred dollars. But Cosey turned out an even more masterful Poe forgery. Quite by accident, he discovered an account book with the stamp "Henry Anstice, stationer, cor. Cedar and Nassau Streets, opposite the Post Office, New York," a firm that Poe might well have patronized during his residence in New York. In this volume, Cosey created the genesis of Poe's "The Raven," copying out several stanzas, with manuscript corrections. On other pages he wrote an accounting of sums due to Poe for literary work, including an indebtedness for N. P. Willis, noted editor and close associate of Poe.

This elaborate and convincing fabrication, a work of art in its own right, he sold to Henry C. "Radio" Roberts, an old-time New York book dealer who had once specialized in radio parts and who served as an outlet for Cosey's fakes. Roberts consigned the account book to the Crown Art Galleries on West Twenty-second Street, where it was offered at auction with the estate of Max

D. Steuer, a swashbuckling art collector. In the maudlin assemblage of decadent art assembled by Steuer, most of which went for a fraction of what it cost him, the Poe seemed a great bargain. It was knocked down to J. J. Podell, a Wall Street lawyer, for one hundred and fifty dollars. A moment later a tardy book dealer rushed into the auction room and offered Podell a one-thousand-dollar profit on his purchase, but Podell felt it wiser to hang on to his "bargain."

During the next few weeks, Podell's conviction weakened to the extent that he consulted an expert and learned that he had been taken. The Crown Art Galleries refunded his money, and Roberts got his book back.

Roberts sold the book later for eighty-five dollars to a collector, who brought it to me for authentication. It was so perfect and exciting a forgery that I shelled out his investment for it and placed it in my personal collection of fakes. The late Colonel Richard Gimbel, a good friend of mine who owned the world's finest Poe collection, including the only known complete transcript of "The Raven" in Poe's handwriting, heard about my Cosey treasure and asked to see it. I made the error of showing it to him.

"What do you want for it?"

"Nothing in my personal collection is for sale," I told him.

"But I *must* have it! I'm putting my Poe collection on display at Yale, and I'd like to set this forgery side by side with the genuine manuscript of 'The Raven.'"

"I'll be glad to lend it to you."

But Gimbel was not to be put off. "No;

I've got to own it, because everything in the display belongs to me."

I had the feeling that Colonel Gimbel would have stayed and argued all day if he had to, to change my mind. And I also knew that he would be genuinely anguished if I refused to sell the account book to him. So I yielded to his plea and let him buy this masterpiece of Cosey's art. Maybe Colonel Gimbel had more of a right to it than I. And I'm sure Cosey would be pleased to know that one of his efforts found a place among the great Poe's authentic creations, now forever ensconced in the famed Free Library of Philadelphia.

About two years ago I was visiting with a fellow dealer, and while relaxing in his sumptuous office I said: "I'm working on a book about forgeries. Do you have any old fakes I could look at and perhaps use in my book?"

"A couple of Poes by Cosey," he answered. He walked to a nearby shelf and took down a small brown envelope, which he handed to me.

Inside were two Poe letters that I instantly recognized as originals worth thousands of dollars.

"Who said these were Cosey forgeries?"

"The great Dr. R. himself," said he, placing the error on the world-famous rare book and manuscript dealer, Dr. A. S. W. Rosenbach, who died nearly three decades ago.

"May I take them along with me?"

"Certainly. Do what you wish with them."

I slipped the old envelope into my coat pocket. When I called the next morning to tell my friend the good news that the letters were authentic Poes he readily agreed to let me offer them on his behalf at my next auction. They fetched slightly more than seven thousand dollars.

What greater tribute could be paid to the forger's genius than that a pair of the keenest and most expert eyes of this century mistook two original letters of Poe's for Cosey fabrications?

8

The Scion of a Pirate

JOHN LAFFITE

"Shake hands with the great-grandson of a pirate," John Laflin used to say. And his big frame would swell with pride as he extended his beefy paw. Then by way of validating his roots Laflin would tug from his pocket a yellowing paper and allow you a glimpse, a very quick glimpse, at a document signed by old Jean Laffite.

But there was a big difference between Laflin and his notorious ancestor, the terror of New Orleans. Laflin's weapons were not the cutlass and the horse pistol. They were a pen and a bottle of Waterman's brown ink, plus a stack of inherited forgeries of Jean Laffite's and other historical figures' handwriting that created more havoc in the world than the pirate and his crew of cutthroats.

There was still another difference between Laflin and his ancestral freebooter. Laflin never stole any pieces of eight or gold doubloons. He stole hearts, mostly ladies' hearts. Even when his women friends were confronted with the damning evidence that Laflin was a purveyor of forgeries, they rose in fury to his defense. "How dare you write anything to tarnish that wonderful man's name!" said one. "Try it, and I'll take you to court for libel."

When Laflin changed his name to Lafitte, and later to Laffite (by way of getting the spelling right), he only added a little piquancy to his glamor and won more friends than ever among the fair sex.

John Laffite had been around a long time, peddling promises to salivating historians, before I ever heard about him. Early in July, 1969, the seventy-five-year-old Laffite wrote to me about his collection of the old pirate's papers. He could hardly have found a mark more amenable. I was a pirate buff, immersed in the chronicles of Esquemeling, a closet admirer of Captain Kidd and Edward Teach. I answered his letter at once.

"When I was in New Orleans a few years ago," I wrote, "I became fascinated with the lore and legends which surround Laffite. On Bourbon Street, I think it was, I visited and explored the forge which was supposedly owned by Laffite and his brother and used as a 'cover' for their piratical operations.

"The order to purchase slaves is an original and interesting paper and I have a hunch it will greatly appeal to collectors and historians and there is really no telling what price it will fetch. I will illustrate it in my catalogue."

Laffite had sent me a Xerox of the slave document that from the somewhat fuzzy reproduction appeared to be genuine. Besides, I knew of no reason to doubt John Laffite's veracity. Was he not the descendant of the famed pirate and owner of the original journal of Jean Laffite?

In my letter to the pirate's descendant, I mentioned that the slave deed would fetch at least five hundred dollars and very possibly more. Armed with this evaluation and validation from me, and without my knowledge, John Laffite offered the collection to John H. Jenkins of Austin, Texas. On July 28 I got a telephone call from Jenkins, triumphantly announcing his purchase of a cargo of Laffite papers from the pirate's scion.

"I understand my purchase includes everything," said Jenkins. "Be sure to let me know if Laffite gets in touch with you."

I congratulated Jenkins on his "marvelous acquisition" in a letter dated July 28, 1969, and promised to let him know if John Laffite offered me anything of his ancestor's.

Within three or four days I got a package from Laffite that I opened with great excitement. It is always a surpassingly great thrill to me to look upon a truly rare document. My first split-second glance at a corner of the slave document as I started to take it out of the envelope told me what I did not want to know. The document was a bare-faced forgery. The paper was "wrong," the ink was "wrong," the handwriting was tremulous and labored. I was crushed and I was angry and I blistered the summer air with oaths. Then I packed up the forged slave document and returned it to Laffite, and I notified Jenkins that it was quite possible he was the owner of the largest collection of Laffite forgeries in the world.

Shedding letters and documents along the way, the Laffite collection of forgeries moved from Jenkins to William Simpson and finally into the archives of Governor Price Daniel in the Sam Houston Regional History Center at Liberty, Texas. Governor Daniel reportedly paid twenty thousand dollars for the collection. Unfortunately many documents were apparently removed from the original "haul" of Jenkins's. These fugitives from the collection turn up on the philographic market from time to time.

Not until five years later, when I received a letter from Robert C. Vogel, probably the world's greatest expert on Jean Laffite, did I again turn my attention to the blustering swindler John Laflin alias John Laffite. Vogel's painstaking and scholarly research into the activities of the modern Laffite had led him to the conclusion that Laffite was a confidence man, not actually descended from the pirate, but in possession of a huge collection of forgeries purportedly written

ye doit toute mon ingenuité à la grande
intuition de ma Grandmère Juive —
Espagnole, qui à été un témoin aue
temps de l'inquisition

John Laffite, born John Laflin. Forged inscription of Jean Laffite, the pirate, in a family Bible: "I owe all my ingenuity to the great intuition of my Grandmother, a Spanish Jewess, who was a witness at the time of the Inquisition." The writing and signature in this forgery are forced and labored, telltale signs of a fake. The fabricated signature differs in every letter from the authentic signature.

Jean Laffite, the pirate. Authentic signature from his instructions to the captain of *El Bravo,* a pirate vessel serving under his command.

by the notorious privateer. Much of the information I have about the life and misdeeds of John Laffite was furnished to me by Robert Vogel.

John Andrechyne Lafitte (or Laflin) was born on June 4, 1893, near Omaha, Nebraska, and died of emphysema on February 20, 1970, in Columbia, South Carolina. Between these two essential facts lies a great curtain of fog with only a few shafts of light. Laffite never finished high school, and although most of the forged documents he sold were penned in French and Spanish he could not read or write either language. He was an engineer on the Missouri Pacific Railroad until his retirement early in the 1940s, at which time he got a free pass and began his travels in search of easy marks for his collection of bogus autographs. His wife, Lacie Surratt Laflin, survived him, but apparently Laffite made friends with many women during his travels. He was courtly and portly and spinsters swooned over him. For a while he lived in Kansas City, Missouri, where he was well known to rare-book dealers for his intense interest in old paper. It is possible that Laffite had a secret associate who was quietly at work producing the French and Spanish documents.

Not long after his prosaic career with the railway ended, the rotund ex-engineer turned up in New Orleans with the story that he was the direct descendant of the notorious pirate and the custodian of the Laffite family papers. At this time he used the name John Andrechyne Laflin and lived on a very modest pension. No doubt he was delighted when, in 1942, he met Ray Thompson and his wife, a brace of authors in quest of fresh data about the New Orleans pirate. It was a great chance to freeload, and for well over two decades Laflin, or Laffite, as he soon renamed himself, kept the Thompsons intrigued with the constant hope that he would turn over to them for research the "family papers," including the original journal of the pirate and a Bible inscribed by Laffite. In a lengthy and very interesting letter Ray Thompson has described their association with Laffite:

Our first meeting with him was exciting, for if his story was true it would prove once and for all who Laffite was and where he died. We invited him to our home for several weeks. During that time we introduced him to a number of historian friends and professors. They interrogated him at length but concluded he was a fraud, and was just junketing around the country. . . . He claimed to have a "family journal" with him written by Jean Laffite but would not show it to anyone, saying "it would do you no good, it is written in French." . . . During this first stay with us he appeared to know very little about Jean Laffite, in fact, seemed more interested in examining records that we had, and was curious about Laffite's "buried treasure."

The one item he presented as evidence at this time was a small Bible with an inscription on the flyleaf purporting to be presented . . . to Mademoiselle Emma Hortense Mortimore and signed "Jean Laffite." We photographed the Bible and inscription—then compared the signature with two known signatures of Jean Laffite and they were quite dissimilar—worse yet, the inscription appeared to be written with a ballpoint pen!

The following year he spent several months with us, during which time we again tried to get him to show us his original journal, but again without success. This time he was much more glib about Jean Laffite, but his information was data that could be found in any book already written about Laffite. We introduced him to Lyle Saxon [a noted New Orleans historian] who had done much research on Laffite, and Lyle's opinion was that the man was a fraud. We took him to Grand Isle to meet the descendants of Laffite's smugglers. . . . They questioned him about things he should have known [and] their consensus was the same—he was not the great grandson of Lafitte. . . .

In 1958 he published "The Journal of Jean Laffite." In our opinion, this book is a complete hoax, much of it a condensed version of "The Corsair" [a work of fiction about Laffite by Madeline Kent]. Laflin undoubtedly had family journals written by someone posing as Jean Laffite.

In 1960 John Laflin asked us to write a book based on the "diary" which he had published in 1958. We invited him to visit us. . . . By now he was claiming to have visited the archives in Spain, Mexico and Cuba and had "much new material to show us." A neat trick since he neither spoke, wrote nor understood Spanish or French. Even neater considering that he had previously written us he could not afford to travel about anymore because he no longer had access to "free railroad passes."

Ray Thompson offered an interesting theory about the original forger of the manuscript of the Laffite journal: "It is quite possible that in 1832 Emma Hortense Mortimore [wife of a man named John Laflin], enamored with the romantic stories then being printed [about the pirate Laffite], inscribed a Bible to herself. Note that the Bible signature is 'Jean Lafite,' the way it appeared in magazine stories of that day. It is quite possible that Emma, after her husband's death, wrote the alleged journals or that John

Left. Jean Laffite, the pirate. Letter bearing his authentic signature. Notice that the pirate has penned his name with great rapidity, the final *ite* on a higher plateau than the rest of the signature, with even the terminal *e* above the *t.* This obvious characteristic of Jean Laffite's signature was not picked up by the forger in the bogus *Journal, above top* or in the final line from a receipt, *above.*

John Laffite. Forgery of a handwritten letter signed by Jean Laffite, the pirate, with a curious text indicating that the forgery was executed after 1865 and very likely after 1909. ". . . I have the manuscripts and I hope they will be presented to Mr. Abraham Lincoln. He has left the Senate [House of Representatives]. We can try Mr. Joshua Speed or that other intimate friend of his, Mr. Nathaniel Grisby. Personally, I do not wish to become active, nor appear, nor carry anything to Mr. Lincoln. I feel sure, sound in spirit and conscious that he will try to impregnate some principles in the political field of this Great Nation. Always his thought is quicker than his actions. He is skeptical, but a rapid talker when he is provoked and completely convinced by the facts appertaining to the principles of those who deserve it or might deserve it. . . ." The forger was apparently not well acquainted with Lincoln and his history. Lincoln's term in Congress was undistinguished and he was always known as a slow and deliberate thinker and talker.

126

Laflin [forebear of the forger], continued the hoax by writing his memoirs which turned up in another generation and was accepted as 'gospel.'"

However, in view of the presence in the collection of Lincoln letters that were obviously forged by the same person who forged the Laffite journal and documents of Manuel Lisa, it is my belief that the forgeries are of fairly modern date, perhaps executed in the 1920s or '30s. The postmarks on the Lincoln and other covers suggest that the forger was unfamiliar with postal usage before the year 1900. Add to this fact the keen interest shown by John Laffite in gathering old sheets of paper and it is hard to avoid the conclusion that he forged the journal himself, together with the Lincoln letters, or was working with some person who executed the forgeries, or provided the text from which Laffite wrote the journal.

The distinguished historian Charles van Ravenswaay, formerly the director of the Missouri Historical Society and now the director of the Winterthur Museum, has described his first meeting with the blustering Don Juan and peddler of the Laffite forgeries:

In 1948 a man came into my office who said he was John A. Laffite and claimed descent from the famous pirate. He said that he owned a great many letters, the diary, the family Bible and other material by the pirate. He would not permit me to examine the originals, but he did allow me to see some photostats of this material. These purported to show that the

John Laffite, born John Laflin.

John Laffite. A forged address leaf from a letter of the pirate Jean Laffite, with a plethora of spurious postmarks.

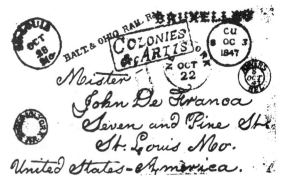

original Laffite did not die in Louisiana [during a hurricane in 1825] but that he moved to St. Louis, took an assumed name . . . and died in 1854 with burial at Alton, Illinois. . . .

Laffite was obviously trying to get his material in print and succeeded very well. In 1952 Stanley G. Arthur used these materials in his "Jean Laffite, Gentleman Rover," published by the Harmanson Press of New Orleans. In 1958 appeared the "Journal of Jean Laffite," which John A. Laffite apparently had published on his own account by the Vantage Press. There have been numerous local articles, new releases, etc., using this material, all toward the end of enshrining in print his obvious fabrication.

Van Ravenswaay added that none of the facts in the John A. Laffite papers checked with data known to be authentic, and the postal markings on the pirate's letters were denounced as forgeries by philatelists.

Letters and documents of Jean Laffite were not the only forgeries with which the retired engineer peppered the philographic market. There were fakes of Joseph Robidoux and Manuel Lisa, the St. Louis pioneers, and Abraham Lincoln. Curiously, as I have pointed out, the rounded, very legible script of the pirate looks strikingly like that of Lincoln, and the script of Lincoln looks like that of Manuel Lisa. Almost certainly the same man created all this group of forgeries.

But there are also several fraudulent documents sold by the burly engineer that were almost beyond question forged by him, a brief jingle by Andrew Jackson dated 1839 and a David Crockett note about his plans to go to

John Laffite. Forged signature of Joseph Robidoux.

Joseph Robidoux. Authentic signature.

John Laffite. Forged signature of Manuel Lisa.

Manuel Lisa. Authentic signature.

128

Of just such fun she had a
                              cape.
Tied up and down in front with
                              tape
So neat and tidy she did look.
        Andrew Jackson
              1839
        As neat and tidy as a book

John Laffite. Forged handwritten poem signed
"Andrew Jackson."

Andrew Jackson. Authentic signature from a letter.

John Laffite, born Laflin. Forgery of a handwritten
statement signed by David Crockett, 1835.

David Crockett. Authentic signature from a letter.

> *Laffite signatures to notarial sales civil courts and Laffite signatures supreme court of New Orleans and no catholic church records.*
>
> *That is as far as research will take anyone to above mentioned.*
>
> *If you cannot obtain the journal from New Orleans library — I will loan you one — I had '83 journal books — all went into smoke and ashes.*
>
> *That is about the only way anyone who is qualified into a book — is to dramatize the journal of about 43,000 words into a book of about 80,000 to 100,000 words The editors of large publishers will decide. An iron clad contract — and only with large publishers to advance royalties — No subsidiary publishers .*

John Laffite, born John Laflin. Handwritten passage from a personal letter. Notice the striking similarity between the forged scripts of Jackson and Crockett and the similarity between both of these scripts and the writing of John Laffite. Some of the words are identical. While there is doubt that John Laffite personally forged the *Journal* and other fakes of the pirate, as well as the documents of Robidoux and Lisa and the letters of Lincoln, there can be little question that the forgeries of Jackson and Crockett originated from his pen.

San Antonio in 1835. The handwriting of both Jackson and Crockett is very similar to John A. Laffite's own fastidious chirography. I have not examined the ink used in these fabrications, but I have no doubt it would turn out to be modern, a variant of the forger's friend, Waterman's brown ink.

How many of the spurious letters and documents vended by John A. Laffite were inherited from a miscreant forebear or forged by an associate of John Laffite or by him from a French or Spanish text furnished by an associate will always be debated. Which of the pirate's signatures are genuine and which are copies or forgeries will no doubt be argued for the next century. The supposed journal of the pirate will always have adherents—firm believers, no doubt, in Napoleon's jesting query, "What is history but a fiction agreed upon?"

9

The Nazi Who Forged "Home, Sweet Home"

GEORGE A. VAN NOSDALL

Two black, greasy handprints defiled my office wall, great smudges left by huge, peasantlike hands. They were the paw marks of George A. Van Nosdall, an autograph and rare-book dealer of doubtful skills and no scruples. The black hands had resisted all assaults with soap and water. Whenever I looked at the wall in front of my desk I recalled with revulsion the fat, angry man who, with palms against the wall behind his back and with jowls aquiver, had expounded to me his anti-Semitic political creed.

For a moment I had listened in amazement to a tirade from a man I already knew to be a forger. My anger had mounted as he continued to rant. Then, in a burst of eloquent profanity that would have awed Falstaff, I told him to get the hell out of my office and never come back.

I first met George A. Van Nosdall in the summer of 1953, when he walked arrogantly into my office and dropped on my desk a Lord Byron letter. "What'll you pay for this?" he asked, without introducing himself. His manner was so brusque and his demeanor so pompous that I suspected he had heisted the letter from some library.

As I swiveled my chair to catch the sunlight on the letter and thus uncover any telltale signs of an erased library stamp, I noticed that the postal markings were not quite "right." A closer look at the handwriting revealed that although the letter was dated in 1812, when the poet was only twenty-four, the handwriting was more like that of his maturity. The lines of the text wove up and down, a characteristic of forgeries by Major George Byron, who claimed to be Lord Byron's bastard son.

"This is a fake by Major Byron," I said. "It's worth ten dollars to me."

"Shrewd! Shrewd!" exclaimed Van Nosdall, mustering a twisted smile, "I like to deal with shrewd men. I'll take the ten dollars."

I was aware, of course, that Van Nosdall had hoped to swindle me. I put him down in my mind as a sharp operator, but I did not then realize that he was also adept in the art of forgery.

Over the next few months I bought

from Van Nosdall quite a few genuine inscribed letters and books, all by living authors. Most of them were addressed to a "Mr. Kouti." Later I discovered that "Kouti" was one of many aliases used by Van Nosdall in his career as an autograph pariah. To his victims, comprising only those authors whose letters and presentation volumes were readily salable, he sent fulsome letters of praise, asking that they brighten his life by inscribing a book to him or sending a signed quotation from their most famous poem or novel. As soon as Van Nosdall received a reply from his "favorite author," it would appear for sale in one of his mimeographed catalogues.

I rarely saw Van Nosdall after the first few months of our acquaintance. Several times he sent me through the mail letters and documents that I branded as fake. Once he offered me a Lincoln forgery that he insisted was genuine. Then there was an Emily Brontë manuscript fragment, for example, on which the ink was scarcely dry. His price was only one hundred dollars, a fraction of its value had it been authentic. Not suspecting that he had forged it himself, I returned it with a jocular note suggesting that he get a new pair of spectacles.

At times Van Nosdall would boast about all the money he had made before the Depression years. "Collectors really spent money then," he would say, "not like these bums today. I can't get a rumble anymore."

Once he bragged that in his youth he was a great dancer. "We fat men can cut quite a figure on the dance floor," he declared.

Van Nosdall was a geyser of anec-dotes. He told me that in his days of glory he had dined and wined with the great bookman Dr. A. S. W. Rosenbach and the noted philographer Walter R. Benjamin. Often drifting off into fantasy, he claimed that the aging Benjamin had begged him to wed his daughter Mary, today the *doyenne* of autograph experts, recognized throughout the world for her skill and knowledge.

Van Nosdall's final success in life came in the early 1950s, when he met George Sylvester Viereck, just out of prison for alleged Nazi activities. Van Nosdall sold on consignment large numbers of letters written to Viereck by Sigmund Freud, a refreshing change from the flood of fakes and letters to Kouti that comprised his inexpensive catalogues.

"I once visited Van Nosdall in his digs," my friend H. Keith Thompson, Jr., has told me. "He lived in a horrible dump in Spanish Harlem, filled with cockroaches and books. When his wife died, he wept hysterically and secreted her body in his railroad flat for five days before the aroma roused his neighbors to action. Yet all the time he was keeping a mistress, Evangeline Ording.

"Van Nosdall taught Evangeline how to beg for autographs by mail, and whenever she conned a celebrity into writing her an interesting letter Van Nosdall popped it into his cheap, mimeographed list."

By the time I'd known Van Nosdall for a year I was almost sure that he was a forger. I viewed with skepticism many of the documents he was selling to credulous collectors. I strongly suspected that some of the fraudulent documents he had offered to me were products of

George A. Van Nosdall. Forgery of a signed, handwritten manuscript of John Howard Payne's "Home, Sweet Home!"

Home, sweet Home!

'Mid pleasures & palaces though we may roam
Be it ever so humble, there's no place like Home!
A charm from the sky seems to hallow us there
Which, seek through the world, is ne'er met with elsewhere

Home, home! sweet, sweet Home!
There's no place like Home!
There's no place like, Home!

An exile from Home, splendour dazzles in vain!—
Oh, give me my lowly thatch'd cottage again!
— The birds singing gaily that came at my call —
Give me them! — and the peace of mind dearer than all!

Home, home! sweet, sweet Home!
There's no place like Home!
There's no place like Home!

John Howard Payne
1850.

his own ingenious pen. But to suspect is one thing; to prove is another. Van Nosdall was now wary of me, and it was several months before I finally found a way to unmask him.

One day he brought in a rare handwritten manuscript of John Howard Payne's famous song, "Home, Sweet Home," signed in full by the poet. It was a superbly executed forgery, although penned on wood-pulp paper, not often used during Payne's lifetime. I pretended to accept it as genuine.

"Just what I've been looking for," I told Van Nosdall. We agreed upon a nominal price, about one fourth of the value of an authentic transcript.

I put the forgery into my personal collection of fakes (where it still remains), and two weeks later I telephoned Van Nosdall. "I've disposed of the 'Home, Sweet Home.' If you ever run across another handwritten copy by Payne, be sure to let me know."

In less time than it takes to say hokus-bogus Van Nosdall sauntered into my office with another Payne forgery, almost identical with the earlier one and on the same kind of paper. I bought the second example for somewhat less than the first. I believe the price was twenty dollars.

Home, Sweet Home!

1

'Mid pleasures and palaces though we may roam
Be it ever so humble, there's no place like home!
A charm from the sky seems to hallow us there
Which, seek through the world, is ne'er met with elsewhere!

Home, home, — sweet, sweet home!
There's no place like home! there's no place like home!

11.

An exile from home, splendor dazzles in vain!
Oh, give me my lowly thatch'd cottage again!
The birds singing gaily, that came at my call! —
Give me them, with the peace of mind dearer than all!

Home, home, — sweet, sweet home!
There's no place like home! there's no place like home!

John Howard Payne./

John Howard Payne. Authentic handwritten manuscript of "Home, Sweet Home!" Payne's own hand is much more fluent than the forger's imitation. Notice the labored appearance of the forged Payne signature compared with the sweeping ease of the poet's own script. Payne invariably put a diagonal after his signature when he wrote the famous song out for admirers.

Now that Van Nosdall had produced a forgery "to order," I had the evidence I wanted. For his part, Van Nosdall was certain he could turn out fakes that would pass muster under my eyes.

It was at this juncture that he decided to divulge his anti-Semitic views, the crowning insult to my intelligence and decency. After I threw him out of my gallery he left behind the two greasy handprints on my wall.

The oily residue of this vulgar Nazi defied all detergents, but I finally met the challenge by giving the entire wall a fresh coat of paint.

And while I was pondering a way to put Van Nosdall behind bars, he died suddenly after wolfing down a whole bowlful of granulated sugar.

10

Lord Byron's Bastard Son

MAJOR GEORGE BYRON

Blow the dust off a letter of Byron or Shelley and what've you got?

A soul-probing epistle by a great English poet or a clever imitation by De Gibler, alias Major Byron?

In the 1840s De Gibler knocked the world of scholarship right off its sedate pins by flooding the market with fascinating letters by Byron and Shelley and Keats. The letters seemed genuine right down to the last dotted *i* and the tiniest curlicue.

De Gibler was a forger both artful and articulate who studied and then beautifully counterfeited the flamboyant style of the great Romantic poets. If he errs in dates and places in his forgeries he makes up for it with a literary skill so convincing that we have half a mind to overlook the mistakes and credit the productions to Byron or Shelley.

In the annals of infamy, De Gibler stands out as one of the few forgers who could not merely counterfeit the handwriting of his subjects with consummate skill but could imitate their literary

style. Even his fabricated postmarks reveal a diabolic ingenuity.

De Gibler was probably born somewhere in the Eastern United States around 1810. Of his origins we know absolutely nothing. He was extremely well educated and spoke five languages. His swarthy complexion, fluency in Spanish, several allusions of his contemporaries and a remark in his spurious autobiography suggest that he may have been a Sephardic Jew. There is even a remote possibility that his real name was De Gibler. Very likely he was born in Philadelphia, a bad seed from one of the great pioneer Jewish families that helped to found America. With his extraordinary linguistic skills it was easy for him to assume a British accent when it suited his purpose.

De Gibler first turned up in the summer of 1843 in Wilkes-Barre, Pennsylvania, a provincial little town famed not for poetic glades but for dark mines of anthracite coal. His entry into the ethereal realm of Byron, Shelley and Keats,

Indeed — I am in despair! — But all may yet be well — — — Good bye! God bless you! — ever yours sincerely

Geo Byron.

Major George Byron, the forger. Conclusion of a handwritten letter signed.

is going to kiss the Pope's toe — He wants a diplomatic situation — and seems likely to get it — with regard to the Title — use your own judgement — "And your petitioner shall ever pray ≈ H. H. Hon

Biron

Major George Byron. Conclusion of a forgery of a handwritten letter of Lord Byron, signed with an unusual signature seldom used by the poet.

Lord Byron. Conclusion of an authentic handwritten letter signed by the poet, also with an uncommon form of his signature.

such a token of remembrance. — I must not forget Mrs Hanson who has often been a mother to me, and as you have always been a friend I beg you to believe me with all sincerity yours

Byron

advance is not usual; I have neither a right nor the wish to insist upon it. Whatever your decision may be, I would humbly solicit the favour of a reply.

I have the honour to be,

Sir,

Your most obedient and humble servant,

George Byron.

P.S. In your reply to my inquiry whether you possessed any Byroniana, you stated that the papers you had, were of little importance. However trivial they may appear to you, I should like to know what they consist of — and perhaps you will be kind enough to acquaint me with their production.

then the sacrosanct gods of English literature, was not auspicious but it was dramatic. He claimed to be the illegitimate son of Lord Byron and dispatched several begging letters to England, one to the then Lord Byron and another to John Murray III, son of the publisher of Byron's poems. De Gibler requested financial aid, claiming that he had gone over his head in buying a farm in the Wyoming Valley. He also asked Murray for a set of Byron's works and a signature of the poet. Neither man responded to his hat-in-hand approach. Their indifference did not deter De Gibler, who by this time had laid out his strategy and plotted the course which was to create mayhem in literary circles.

De Gibler invented a family genealogy, dubbed himself the bastard son of Byron by a Spanish countess and prefaced his new name with the pompous title of "Major." He also started playing the sedulous ape to the handwriting of Byron and Shelley and Keats, for he had now formulated his plan to enrich the

Jan 8. 1814

Dear Sir/

world with some spectacular new letters of these great poets.

Since it costs nothing to accord De Gibler a valueless title, let us from now on call him Major Byron. And let us now allow him to take us adventuring into the fictions of his autobiography. Even more interesting than his own disreputable career was the romantic story he spun for himself. In his mythical identity, his mother was the Countess De Luna, a beautiful Jewess (or possibly Catholic) of the purest Spanish blood with whom the great Lord Byron became enamored on his first visit to Spain. The handsome poet married her in rites of the Catholic church (this does not sound like Byron!) and on his return to England had the marriage disavowed as illegal so that he could carry on his romantic escapades without guilt. The countess gave birth to a son—George Gordon De Luna Byron.

The major fancied himself a Childe Harold, and in one letter described his pilgrimage "over the Orient; from the

Major Byron. Forged letter of Lord Byron. The lines of the letter, and even the individual words, weave up and down, an indication that the forger was concentrating on the formation of the letters in each word rather than on setting down his thoughts.

Major Byron. Second page of a forged handwritten Lord Byron letter, signed. The expressions used are very characteristic of Byron: "I beg leave to conclude by wishing that those sanctimonious judges who throw stones at me, may find a home in a place painted in Michel Angelo's Last Judgement in the Sistine Chapel. . . ."

Major Byron. Conclusion of a forged letter of Lord Byron. The signature is an excellent imitation.

Major Byron. Forged address-leaf of a Lord Byron letter. The postmarks are duplicated with extraordinary skill and can only be detected as forgeries by a careful comparison with authentic postmarks of the same place and time (Milan, Feb., 1820).

City of the Sultan to the Cataracts of the Nile; from Mount Ararat to the Mouth of the Ganges." He visited Byron's grave and in Spain shed tears over the grave of his "mother."

In an amazing "autobiographical" letter to John Murray, he wrote:

If I omit an apology for addressing you, let me hope that a son of the late Lord Byron, whose esteem and friendship you possessed in so eminent a degree, may without apprehension appeal to your kindness, and succeed perhaps in conciliating your good graces.

You will, no doubt, be startled by these news—but of the birth of a son to Lord Byron he, himself, remained ignorant till a short time before his

Major Byron. Forgery of a fabricated and handwritten letter, signed by Lord Byron, to Captain Hay, Pisa, 1822. Notice how the writing is labored and tends to undulate. But the language is deceptively Byronic: "I am more likely to kiss the Pope's toe than to subscribe to liquidate the sum of two thousand pounds for a man with an income of twenty thousand. . . ."

premature death in Greece, and to the world at large family considerations have always kept this fact secret. If I disclose it now to a friend of the late Lord B., it is because my embarrassing circumstances compel me to do so. . . .

Major Byron continues his story with a vague account of his education in Paris:

My heart full of strong and ardent passions, my imagination vivid and uncontrolled, with some knowledge gained from books, and some shrewd sense of my own, but with little self-government and no experience, I set out from Paris to return to Spain. The buoyancy of my youth, the spring vigor of my muscles, and a good deal of imagination, gave me a sort of indescribable passion for adventure from my childhood, which required even the stimulus of danger to satisfy;—and it needed many a hard morsel from the rough hand of the world to quell such a spirit's appetite for excitement.

My only resource at present is like the ostrich in the fable, to shut my eyes against the evils that pursue me, filling up the vacuity of each moment with any circumstances less painful than my own thoughts, and leaving to time—the great patron of the unfortunate—to remove my difficulties, and provide for my wants. Do not, Sir, suppose me to be faint hearted—I am a Byron,—the bar sinister notwithstanding—Civil law cannot change nature.

When the appeals of this self-proclaimed bastard failed to stir the imagination of his correspondents, who, by this time, included Shelley's widow, Mary, author of *Frankenstein,* the major announced that he planned to write a biography of Lord Byron. He advertised for letters by the famed poet. Hundreds poured in. The major did write several installments of the biography, giving personal reminiscences or opinions of Lord Byron's work and life, but he quickly abandoned this useful effort for the speedier profits of selling the autograph letters that had been sent to him, in most cases merely to be copied. When the supply of original letters ran out, Major Byron carried out his plan to forge another supply. Then he added Shelley and Keats to his fabricated

Lord Byron. Authentic handwritten, signed letter to Captain Hay, Pisa, 1822. Byron's own letter does not have the wit and vitality of Major Byron's crafty imitation.

Lord Byron. Last page of an authentic handwritten letter signed by the poet. This is the early handwriting of Byron, most often imitated by Major Byron.

wares. In 1872 the forged Byron letters showed up in London. Some were bought by Byron's own publisher, who was utterly taken in by the adroit imitation of the style and script of the great poet.

Nineteen of Major Byron's forgeries were published in a rare volume, *The Unpublished Letters of Lord Byron* (1872), and half a century later were proclaimed genuine by the eminent critic (and forger!) Thomas J. Wise. And I must reluctantly admit that, when in college, I read the nineteen forged missives to "Dearest L" and was absolutely fetched by them. I even set out to prove, as Murray and Wise had believed, that they were genuine. But I soon piled up enough damning evidence to establish beyond all doubt their spurious nature. I now own a special printing of them in a slender, beautiful little volume, which is a delight to read. Sometimes of a winter night I crowd myself up under the bed covers and peruse these letters. I like to pretend they are not forgeries, because I consider them literature in their own right. For, unless one probes hard into the dates and names and places, the forgeries of Major Byron would trap even the most cautious Byronite.

Oh, the clever scoundrel! When he waxes Byronic one envisions again the handsome, haughty profile, the limp, the flung-back cape. There are in the major's forgeries all the urbanity and arrogance and cynicism that one encounters in the letters of the great poet himself:

I am not all black—indeed rather pie-bald. . . .

I . . . am damned and dunned to death by Christians and creditors, though, God knows, I am bad and poor enough. . . . The child is dead: I do not regret it, though a bastard Byron is better than no Byron.

I am married at last, and mean no disrespect to Lady Byron, who, though she may be a seraph to her friends, and really is, I believe, a good woman, is a devil to me. We have nothing in common except disquiet; and Heaven knows how much ennui.

I am misunderstood, flattered by women, pestered, cursed, hated, reproached, and forgotten to such a degree, that I am most grateful for the night and hail the morning with disappointment.

Rhyming is as easy as punning to one who will allow his thoughts to run more by the associations of sound than of sense. . . . Sometimes in the course of his life, under the influence of love, madness or some other calamity, almost every one is silly enough to sin in rhyme.

Could Lord Byron have put it better?

The numerous Shelley letters forged by Major Byron, who used both his adopted name of Byron and the pseudonym, "Monsieur Memoir" in peddling them to Mary Shelley, were prepared with care and skill and for a while took in the poet's widow. At Puttich and Simpson's auction house in London a group of Major Byron's forgeries of Shelley was put on the block, and Mary was an avid bidder. One letter, which began, "Thus it is—my letters are full of money, whilst my being overflows with unbounded love and elevated thoughts," was picked up by Mary Shelley for sixteen shillings, plus commissions. The most important Shelley letter in the sale, fresh from the dextrous fingers of Major Byron, was a six-page quarto epistle to Mary herself, dated January 11, 1817. "They have filed a Bill to say that I published *Queen Mab,* that I avow myself to be an Atheist, and a Republican, with some other imputations of an infamous nature. . . . I have just heard

Major Byron. Last page of a forged handwritten letter by Percy B. Shelley, with forged address-leaf to Mrs. Shelley, bearing very accurate and deceptive postal markings.

Percy B. Shelley. Conclusion of an authentic handwritten letter, signed. Shelley's script is more uninhibited than Major Byron's imitation. Notice that in his haste Shelley has jettisoned the second *e* from his surname.

Major Byron. Forgery of a handwritten letter signed by Percy B. Shelley. Major Byron's counterfeit of Shelley's script is less successful than his Byron fakes. The almost illegible scribbling, smears and blots so characteristic of the poet's script were never successfully imitated by Major Byron. The major's fabrication is much easier to decipher than Shelley's own hand.

from [William] Godwin that he has evidence that Harriet [Shelley] was unfaithful to me before I left England with you. . . ." This startling letter, which exonerated Mary from all guilt in persuading Shelley to desert his wife Harriet, was obtained for Mary at the biggest price in the sale—six pounds, six shillings.

In 1848 Major Byron, then on one of several trips to his alleged native England, dispatched his wife to visit a British rare-book and autograph dealer,

William White, and over a period of several months White bought from "the Lady Incognita," as he called her, forty-seven Byron forgeries, which White, in turn, sold to John Murray, the publisher, for one hundred and twenty-three pounds and some odd. Major Byron's wife then unloaded on the unsuspecting White a group of spurious Shelley letters and a few faked letters of John Keats. Many of these fabricated letters by the immortal triumvirate later found their way into biographies. The Shelley forg-

literary ordnance of heavy caliber which boomed like a knell of annihilation upon the ear of the period. — Man and nature as they appear through the telescope of Wordsworth, assume no ideal grace, no visionary excellence; but they wear a comeliness which engenders optimism. The age is not yet prepared to appreciate the Poet in his fullness — who in winning accents of sweetly-altered knowledge convinces us that the humblest object which can attract our gaze, though seemingly inanimate, is yet ~~~~~ an instrument of design in the laboratory of the Lord of all. It is an essential part of the Poet's

faith that nothing has been created vainly. The muse of Chaucer thus attests his evidence in the early lispings of our mother-tongue:

"Eternalle God that through thy purveyance, Ledest the worlde by certain governaunce, In idle, as men saine, ye nothing make."

In his own peculiar empire Wordsworth stands pre-eminent. — But however great an admirer of Wordsworth's poetry I may be, I cannot submit to the imputation of having suffered my originality whatever it is — to have been marred by its influence. — If you can come, do

Your sincere friend
J. Keats.

Major Byron. Forgery of the second and third pages of a handwritten letter signed by John Keats. The text is composed with vitality and captures some of the vigor of Keats's prose, but the handwriting lacks the regularity and spontaneity of the poet's script.

Major Byron. Forgery of the first page and address leaf of a letter of John Keats. The address-leaf is executed with great skill (see illustration on p. 262).

Oxford. Sept. 1817

My dear Spencer,

I rejoice that you are become acquainted with Wordsworth — nature's most amiable philosopher. His affluence of imagination, his glowing and impassioned sentiments, the utter sweetness and delicacy of his style — but above all, that delightful enthusiasm, which, worshipping at the shrine of simple and beautiful nature, makes every reader a convert to her principles, — all these qualities give the supremacy to Thos. W... — How multitudinous and motley a host have levelled insult, contempt, and coarse abuse at Wordsworth —

John Keats. First page and address-leaf of a signed, handwritten letter to his sister Fanny, showing authentic postal markings.

John Keats. Authentic signature.

eries were, in fact, so cunningly contrived that they hoodwinked all the scholars, and Moxon published them in a special edition in 1852, for which Robert Browning wrote the preface. It was then accidently discovered that portions of many of the letters [penned by Major Byron] were heisted from printed copies in old periodicals. The coincidence surpassed all credibility, and almost the entire edition was taken up and destroyed.

For a time Major Byron lived in New York, where he ran up so many bills that he finally fled to Cleveland. One of his creditors was a bootmaker who had given him credit under the alias of "Major George Gordon Byron of the British Army." While he was in Cleveland, the major apparently spent most of his time writing begging letters to celebrities and speculating unsuccessfully in real estate. He claimed to own a farm on the Hudson River, about thirty-two miles from New York.

In March, 1886, *The American Antiquarian* printed a capsule account of Major Byron's residence in New York:

> His office at No. 40 Broadway, where he professed to do business, was rather a mythical one, he having simply permission to use part of a room there. He made a show of doing business by exhibiting what he called a "patent fish-tail" in a trough of water.

He used to wear a semi-military uniform, with spurs, and carried a lady's riding whip in his hand. . . . He posed at various times, as a litterateur, a journalist, a diplomatist, a Government agent, an officer of the British army in the East Indies, a British naval officer, an officer of the United States Army, a mining prospector, a broker, a merchant, a spy, an agent for cotton claims, a commission agent, an Oriental traveler, a representative of European mercantile interests, a bookseller, a patent rights agent, a gentleman of means, and an aristocratic exile, expatriated and pensioned on condition that he should never reveal his genealogy.

As all the world knows, Lord Byron was a damnably handsome man. The London beggars even imitated his limp, and a jealous Edward John Trelawney, who looked upon the great poet in death, sneaked a peek at his feet and falsely reported that Byron had *two* club feet. Friends of Major Byron said that he looked like his adopted namesake—"his head, eyes, hair and nose bear a striking resemblance to those of his putative father." But an unbiased witness, the editor of the *New York Evening Mirror,* noted with asperity that "the person claiming to be a 'son of Lord Byron' has the look of a sneak and the manners of a Jeremy Diddler."

If Major Byron did not meet the requisite good looks expected of a bastard son of Byron, he certainly put on a natty appearance for the ladies. New York acquaintances recalled him as a rather short, brisk person "with a Jewish cast of features, an olive complexion, keen eyes, wax mustache and affected military gait." He smoked incessantly, perhaps as an excuse to take out and flash his silver cigarette case which bore the Byron crest. The major carried himself with a superior air and was a skilled raconteur.

Even during his lifetime outrageous and exciting tales were circulated about Major Byron. It was rumored he had perished gallantly in the Civil War, fighting for his "adopted" country. Actually he lived on for two more decades, subsisting on beggary and confidence schemes. He died in London on June 4, 1882.

Thank God for Major Byron! He brought excitement and thrills into the wasting world of scholarship. He infused the auction room with fresh vitality. His frauds and fakes are with us everywhere, in biographies, in collections of letters, in academic tomes. Nobody yet knows the full extent of his literary havoc, for the major's artful imitations of Byron and Shelley still haunt the halls of learning. And, I venture to predict, his rogueries will bedevil collectors and scholars for at least another century.

11

The Man Who Foxed Woodrow Wilson

S. MILLINGTON MILLER

Dr. S. Millington Miller had a fierce passion for American history. He delved deep into Colonial and Revolutionary lore. He poured over scores of dusty old tomes, gathering arcane data and digging out obscure facts that nobody else knew about, until events that took place two or three hundred years ago were very real to him. So real, in fact, that he decided to add to our knowledge of the past with some new "facts."

Dr. Miller's first improvement in history was with a batch of Myles Standish letters, rather naïvely penned, but good enough to fool the scholars at the turn of the century. Collectors gobbled up his pen-and-ink outbursts from Priscilla's unsuccessful suitor at fancy prices— nobody had seen one in years!—and historians swooned over the new data furnished by the fakes.

The staid, untrusting Woodrow Wilson, then professor of jurisprudence and political economy at Princeton, tumbled for Dr. Miller's amateurish products. Wilson was at work on his unreadable five-volume *History of the American People* at the same time that Dr. Miller was grinding out Standishes. It was almost inevitable that Wilson should illustrate one of Dr. Miller's forgeries in his book. And I am sure that Dr. Miller looked with parental pride upon the facsimile reproduced by Wilson in Volume I of his history, published in 1902.

Dr. Miller was born in 1853 and came from a distinguished Philadelphian family. He was graduated from the University of Pennsylvania. Although a medical doctor, he neglected his scalpel for the greater excitement of probing into history and searching for ways to improve our acquaintance with the past. In 1905 he came up with the greatest "historical discovery" of modern times. With the skilled use of two forgeries freshly created by himself, Miller hurled this "factual" grenade into the quiet halls of learning, and the fragmentation from its explosion is still raining down.

The discovery of Dr. Miller was nothing less than "absolute proof" that the Declaration of Independence was really proclaimed first in Mecklenburg

S. Millington Miller. Signed postscript to a letter of Miller sending a Calderon manuscript in which he sets his mark up for a Myles Standish forgery. "I have gotten on the track of *another* Miles Standish letter (I sold the only one I ever had for $500) in the South. If I can get it wh. seems likely I will let you have it for $250. . . ."

County, North Carolina, on May 20, 1775, and that the July 4, 1776, Declaration was an imposition and should be expunged from the history books.

There was, in fact, a local tradition backing up Dr. Miller's "facts." Some congressman from North Carolina had stated, back in 1819, that the patriotic people of Mecklenburg County had severed their relationship with Britain in 1775 and issued the first Declaration of Independence. The Mecklenburg Declaration had supposedly been published in a June issue of the *Cape Fear Mercury,* a local paper, but nobody had ever set eyes on a copy. John Adams and Thomas

Jefferson were both alive in 1819, and for once in their torrid half-century relationship they agreed. They both condemned the congressman's assertion as utterly false. Those who espoused the congressman's claim also spoke of some "resolves" issued by the patriots of Mecklenburg County, but these, if they ever existed, had long ago vanished. In short, there was no tangible evidence of any Mecklenburg Declaration, and this was the situation that Dr. Miller set out to remedy.

In the July 1, 1905, issue of *Collier's,* then one of the most powerful and widely read magazines in the country,

---

A HISTORY OF THE AMERICAN PEOPLE

persons taken aboard in England who were not of their congregation,—and not certain, therefore, to submit without compulsion to be governed by their authority and discipline,—they judged it best to draw up an agree-

ment before going ashore, by which all should bind themselves to accept the authority of their leaders, until, at any rate, they should obtain a grant of lands and of power from the Plymouth Company, upon whose coasts they were thus unexpectedly to be set down. That done, they were ready to make their landing, and

88

FACSIMILE OF A LETTER FROM MYLES STANDISH TO GOVERNOR BRADFORD

S. Millington Miller. Forgery of a handwritten letter signed by Myles Standish to Governor Bradford, illustrated as genuine on page 88 of Woodrow Wilson's *A History of the American People.* The imitation of seventeenth-century handwriting is very amateurish but it was good enough to fool Professor Wilson of Princeton.

Myles Standish. Authentic document signed, 1648, certifying to the election of Governor Bradford. Also signed by William Collier and William Thomas of Plymouth.

there appeared an article about Dr. Miller's discovery with the spectacular title "The True Cradle of Liberty. Independence Bell Rang a Year Earlier in Charlotte than in Philadelphia. By S. Millington Miller, M.D."

Although Dr. Miller's article was rambling and about as comprehensible as a prescription, his point was clear. Miller had ferreted out the missing issue of the *Cape Fear Mercury* (June 3, 1775) that had printed the resolves, and he had "discovered" a letter of John Adams dated in 1819 proving that Adams accepted the resolves as authentic.

The most important of the resolves

were: "that we, the citizens of Mecklenburg County, do hereby dissolve the political bonds which have connected us to the mother country, and hereby absolve ourselves from all allegiance to the British Crown, and abjure all political connection, contact, or association with that nation, who have wantonly tramped on our rights and liberties" and "that we do hereby declare ourselves a free and independent people . . . to the maintenance of which independence we solemnly pledge to each other our mutual cooperation, our lives, our fortunes, and our most sacred honor."

It would appear from these resolves,

supposedly signed by twenty-five North Carolina patriots, that Jefferson did a little cribbing when he composed the Declaration of Independence fourteen months later in Philadelphia.

Dr. Miller's great "find" was instantly acclaimed as a major historic discovery. For a while it appeared that Independence Day would be celebrated nationally on May 20 instead of July 4.

The John Adams letter about the resolves lacks the jolting power, with every word picked for its impact, that characterizes most of the second president's correspondence. Adam's letter, published in *Collier's,* is addressed to Jefferson and reads in part: "How is it possible that this paper should have been concealed from me to this day . . .

you know that if I had possessed it I would have made the Hall of Congress echo and reecho with it fifteen months before your Declaration of Independence. What a poor, ignorant malicious, short-sighted crapulous mass is Tom Paine's Common Sense compared with this paper. Had I known it I would have commented upon it from the day you entered Congress till the fourth of July 1776. The genuine sense of America at that moment was never so well expressed before nor since." The letter concludes with a trite observation in Latin that Adams would have winced at.

Both of Dr. Miller's forgeries were reproduced in *Collier's,* but the photographs were so muddied that it required considerable skill to uncover the evi-

S. Millington Miller. Forged copy of the corrected issue of *The Cape-fear Mercury* (June 3, 1775), which includes the spurious Mecklenburg resolves. This rare gazette was pieced together by Dr. Miller from fragments of other early newspapers. Only three copies of the forgery survive. The plate from which Miller printed it was destroyed in 1911.

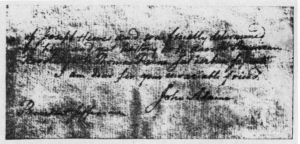

Reduced facsimile of the letter from John Adams to President Thomas Jefferson, in which he expresses surprise and displeasure at not having been apprised until this late date of the Mecklenburg Declaration of Independence

The original of this letter is now in private hands, but was originally in the Randolph Collection of Jefferson Letters, sold by Jefferson Levy, Esq., of Monticello.

TEXT OF THE LETTER

QUINCY, 22d June, 1819

DEAR SIR:—May I enclose you one of the greatest curiosities and one of the deepest mysteries that ever occurred to me; it is in the Essex Register of June the 5th, 1819. It is Entitled from the *Raleigh Register* "Declaration of Independence." How is it possible that this paper should have been concealed from me to this day. Had it been communicated to me in the time of it, I know, if you do not know, that it would have been printed in every Whig newspaper upon the continent, you know that if I had possessed it I would have made the Hall of Congress echo and reecho with it fifteen months before your Declaration of Independence. What a poor ignorant malicious, short-sighted, crapulous mass is Tom Paine's Common sense compared with this paper. Had I known it I would have commented upon it from the day you entered Congress till the fourth of July 1776.

The genuine sense of America at that moment was never so well expressed before nor since. Richard Caswell, William Hooper and Joseph Hewes, the three Representatives of North Carolina in Congress, you know as well as I and you know that the unanimity of the States fully depended on the vote of Joseph Hewes, and was finally determined by him, and yet history is to ascribe American Revolution to Thomas Paine sal verbum sapienti.   I am, dear Sir, your invariable friend,

PRESIDENT JEFFERSON.   JOHN ADAMS.

S. Millington Miller and John Adams. *Top of page.* Forged letter of John Adams by Miller, penned in the fluent, ebullient script of his Revolutionary years but dated 1819. *Right.* John Adams. Handwritten signed letter, written in his later printlike hand, in June, 1815, when he was eighty. The script is quavery and the lines waver.

Quincy June 11. 1815

Dr Rush

"Watchman! What of the Night?" To what hour of the Evening are we advanced? How many hours remain before day break? Have you a repeating Watch that can Strike the hour and the quarter of an hour in the darkest hour of Sablest night?

Rochefaucaud, Condorcet, Robespierre, Brisot, Danton, Orleans Buonaparte, Pitt, Fox, Burk, Alexander, George, Louis's, Charles's, Francis's Fredericks are but Puppets; they are but Bubbles. The real Struggle is not between them. They are no more than Ghaff in the Wind, or than Froth on the Surface of the Sea. The fundamental Conflict is between two Systems of Religion and Governmont.

The War of Religion lasted thirty Years, from 1618 to 1648. Will you date this War from 1775 or from 1793.? If from the latter Period, it has has been only 22 years; eight more are wanting to make thirty. And Question; whether Supurstition or a rational Religion, and whether Absolute Monarchy or mixed representative Government shall prevail, will

dences of forgery. The newspaper was exposed as a fake when Dr. Miller tried to sell it for a huge sum. It turned out to be "manufactured," a sort of patchwork quilt of the printer's art, with the Mecklenburg Declaration pieced together from bits and fragments of real newsprint, then photographed and reproduced from a plate. When the true character of this newspaper was revealed, and some of the incongruities and mistakes pointed out, Dr. Miller promptly "discovered" another one with all the errors corrected.

As for the Adams letter, a glance takes it in as the script of his youth. In 1819 Adams was eighty-four, and his handwriting was labored and printlike. His lines had a tendency to weave a bit, but his signature was still very bold, although quite different from that in Dr. Miller's forgery. Had the date of Adams's letter been fifty years earlier, it might have deceived me for a moment in this reproduction which conceals so many of its defects.

As usual with fakes, the provenance, or source of the items, was impeccable. The rare newspaper, according to Dr. Miller, came from the correspondence of Andrew Stevenson, U. S. Minister to the Court of St. James's and the letter of John Adams was from the Randolph Collection, sold by Jefferson Levy of Monticello.

Although the newspaper was exposed as a fraud seventy-five years ago, I don't believe anyone has ever before condemned the Adams letter. There are still scholars who argue that the Mecklenburg Declaration is authentic. In North Carolina, the date of May 20 is a holiday, annually observed with patriotic celebrations.

After the exposure of his forged newspaper, Dr. Miller vanished from history for many years. Doubtless he was quietly at work producing fakes that, when identified as fabrications, are set down as "the work of an anonymous forger."

In his old age the once-brilliant historian was forced to give up the fine art of forgery and turn to common theft, in which menial work he committed a serious blunder. Dr. Miller obviously felt that his alma mater owed him something for his "contributions" to American history, so he collected the debt in the form of some rare books that he carried out of the university library under his coat. On May 29, 1937, the enfeebled eighty-four-year-old forger, using the alias of Dr. Milton Miller, approached Richard Wormser, a rare-book dealer in New York, with ten volumes from which he had neglected to remove the library markings. Wormser called the police. Dr. Miller was at once arrested. The cops searched his residence and discovered one hundred and seventy-five heisted books. Dr. Miller readily admitted the thefts from the University of Pennsylvania.

Nobody seems to know what hap-

John Adams. This authentic signature, written in 1819, when Adams was eighty-four, is tremulous and very unlike the firm, swiftly signed name of his earlier years.

John Adams

pened to Dr. Miller after his arrest. Perhaps he was released to plot some fresh incursion into American history. Even an old, infirm man, with palsied fingers, is still good for forgeries. How about an exciting letter by Stephen Hopkins, signer of the Declaration of Independence, describing how he hap-pened to sign that immortal document?

For the guidance of octagenarian forgers, here's a facsimile of Hopkins's signature as it appears on the Declaration:

12

He Could Sign Any Name

ARTHUR SUTTON

In the spring of 1976 an unemployed grocery clerk in Rumford, Maine, began peppering the nation with forged signatures of celebrities. These were so adroitly scrawled that half a dozen autograph dealers were delighted to buy them at bargain prices. Collectors all over the country spruced up their collections with brand-new signatures of John F. Kennedy, Marilyn Monroe, W. C. Fields, Adolf Hitler, Picasso, Errol Flynn, Walt Disney, Jacqueline Kennedy Onassis, Charlie Chaplin and even George A. Custer and Sitting Bull.

The forger, Arthur Sutton, a perky young man, was not new to the game of the name. He had been quietly turning out forgeries for three years and had honed his chirographic skills to the point where not even Richard Nixon could tell his own signature from Sutton's imitation. No wonder philographers eagerly bought up every pen scratch that came out of Rumford.

Oddly enough, it was Sutton's first forgery that finally trapped him—but more of that later. In July, 1973, the twenty-three-year-old Arthur, after only six months as a forger, suffered his first setback. Sutton coveted a genuine John F. Kennedy letter in the catalogue of Paul C. Richards, the distinguished Massachusetts dealer. Sutton's cupidity led him into a folly that could have put him behind bars. He wrote to Richards, submitting half a dozen forgeries:

Greetings! I have decided to specialize in autographs of JFK because my funds are limited and I do admire the late President greatly.

In making this decision I have decided to part with a few items that no longer fit into my collection and I was wondering if you could assist me and grant me this special favor.

I wish to *trade* the enclosed material for your JFK letter of May 28, 1953.

Sutton enclosed signed photographs of Sir Winston Churchill and Theodore Roosevelt, signatures of Lincoln and Hitler, a signed print of N. C. Wyeth and a signature of Sitting Bull. Later Sutton wrote me that these forgeries were "not that well done, very early and poorly done."

Sutton concluded his letter to Richards: "I think this is a fair offer, please accept it, for would love to own the Kennedy letter."

In declining Sutton's offer, Richards wrote on July 19, 1973:

In my opinion, most all the items you have sent are forgeries. Please inform me where you obtained the Lincoln and Th. Roosevelt and Sitting Bull items, also the Churchill. In my opinion these are all forgeries, and I wish to know who is perpetrating this fraud. If you have copies of a bill-of-sale for these, please send me copies. Otherwise, I will want a good explanation of how they came into your possession. I am holding the material here pending your satisfactory response to this letter.

Richards's answer to Sutton was an ominous warning of what was to happen three years later, but Arthur met the thinly veiled accusation with a swift denial, eloquent but specious:

Dear Mr. Richards,

Your letter of July 19 comes to me as a great shock, as you know I am a good customer of yours and would never think of cheating you, nor would I ever want to be cheated (which it seems now I have been royally cheated by some no good lousy con-artist.)

Now relating to the fake material.

On Sat. April 14, 1973 I received an unexpected visit from a Mr. George Murphy (at least that was the name he gave and which is on the bill of sale also) of Littletown, New Hampshire (he did have N.H. licence plates on his car.) He said he had read my name and address in "Manuscripts" [a collector's publication] and since he was so close he thought he would drop in and offer me a few autographs which he had for sale. He was so sincere and very knowledgeable on autographs that I figured he knew the real from phony.

He offered me about 25 items which he carried in a folder he brought with him, and I purchased 6 items.

Cut signatures of Lincoln, Sitting Bull, Remington

Signed portraits of Churchill, T. Roosevelt, Wyeth for a total of $225.00, not including the Hitler signature which I had acquired from a local collector.

I am now ashamed to say that I fell for the oldest trick in the books, the prices he was asking were so much lower than the dealer prices that I couldn't pass them up. I spent a good part of my mad money on these, but I had hoped to sell them and make a good size profit.

Enclosed is the bill of sale he gave me. I swear that I did not intend to cheat you, for I completely beleived they were genuine, but I am grateful to you for informing me of their phoniness before I purchased more items from this junk dealer . . .

I am going to the authorities here in my town to see what can be done. What would you suggest I do with the forgeries? Keep them in case they locate this man? (I feel like destroying them so I don't have to look at them again and also so they don't trick anybody else.)

Sincerely

ARTHUR SUTTON

Sutton's letter of protest, larded with unnecessary details, did not deceive Richards, who answered:

July 25th 1973

Dear Mr. Sutton:

I am in receipt of your letter of explanation.

Frankly, I do not believe either your letter or the bill-of-sale. I have heard from two of my colleagues that you have offered them material of a spurious nature, thus establishing a pattern.

In view of these facts, I do not wish to receive any further communication from you. I am returning herewith the material you sent.

Sincerely yours,

PAUL C. RICHARDS

The hint was clear. Sutton should lay down his pen and go into retirement. But he had, meanwhile, sold a forged handwritten John F. Kennedy letter to Dr. Jay Steinberg for one hundred dollars. It was, Sutton later admitted, the first forgery he ever created, around January of 1973.

For a while Sutton accepted the forced layoff from his ink pots and lived quietly in the old family home in the town of Rumford where he was born on November 22, 1950. There was little in Sutton's youth that suggested his future career as a forger. He attended a Catholic parochial school and was graduated from Stephens High School in 1969. Arthur was a normal boy who enjoyed swiping apples from old man Hanson's back yard, building a tree house with his father's good lumber and paneling, and swimming in the town's drinking water. He and his friends once spread thousands of ripe chokecherries over the track-and-field course used by the local high-school girls.

But Arthur was always intrigued by pen and ink and the things he could do with them. He drew sketches of famous people. Sketches, and signatures. After his rebuff by Paul Richards, Sutton kept a low profile, but he continued to practice the fine art of forgery. His method was to copy the facsimiles that illustrated the Charles Hamilton autograph-auction catalogues until he could scribble them freehand with every curlique and flourish in place. He would fill a large sheet with signatures, then cut out the best one for sale. Gingerly at first, then with increasing abandon, he began flooding the market with bogus signatures of his famous contemporaries. Stan Laurel, Eleanor Roosevelt, Al Jolson, Judy Garland, Betty Grable, Fay Wray, Otto Skorzeny, John Carradine, Picasso, Bela Lugosi, Lyndon Johnson—the list was almost without end. And the signatures of all of them executed with ex-

Richard Nixon. Authentic signature.

Arthur Sutton. Forged signature of Nixon on a portion of a newspaper.

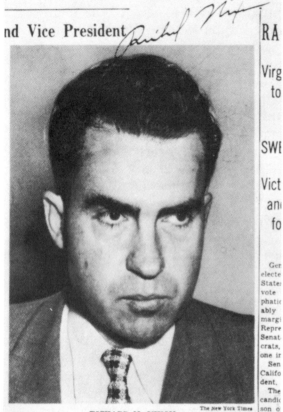

nd Vice President

RA

Virg
to

SWI

Vict
an
fo

Ger
electe
State:
vote
phatic
ably
margi
Repre
Senat
crats,
one ir
Sen
Califo
dent,
The
candic
son o

RICHARD M. NIXON

The New York Times

W. C. Fields. Authentic signature.

Arthur Sutton. Forgery of a W. C. Fields signature.

traordinary skill. In fact, Sutton was so pleased with his Custer and John F. Kennedy that he put them in his own private collection.

On April 15, 1976, a distinguished collector and entrepreneur, Aubrey Mayhew, who will be recalled as the man who bought the Texas Book Depository Building in Dallas, from a window of which Oswald shot Kennedy, showed up in my gallery with a holograph Kennedy letter. A glance at it brought a flush of anger to my face.

"Where the devil did you get this?" I asked.

Aubrey was startled. "Anything wrong with it?"

"It's a forgery." I turned the letter over in my hands. "About two years old. The trail is fresh on this one. Let's see if we can't catch the fabricator."

Mayhew wrote out a statement at my request that the letter had come from Dr. Jay Steinberg, who had, he told Mayhew, bought it from one Arthur Sutton. This was the first time I had ever heard Sutton's name, even though he had been on my mailing list for several years.

A few inquiries among philographers brought me by return mail several dozen examples of Sutton's recent work as well as copies of his letters offering the counterfeit wares.

Within a month I had a huge dossier on Sutton with nearly fifty forgeries from his versatile pen, all of them brilliantly executed.

I reported the forgeries to the United States postal authorities, who refused to take any action.

Oct, 1976

Dear sir.

    Dear sir, please find enclosed an item from my collection which is for sale. In your add you stated your interests whee "Autographs - Historical Americana", I do hope that "Indian" signatures are included.

① Sitting Bull - noted Indian (Sioux) leader very rare, pencilled signature on a small (2 x 4") slip of paper. fine cond. Very difficult Western autograph to obtain. Mounted (can be removed) to a nice 8x10 B+W print (modern) of Sitting Bull, circa 1881.
        - $275.00

Arthur Sutton. Handwritten signed letter, offering a forged signature of Sitting Bull to an autograph dealer.

Thank You
Sincerely
Arthur Sutton
540 Pine St.
Rumford, Maine
04276

Arthur Sutton. Forged signature of Sitting Bull.

Sitting Bull. Authentic signature.

Arthur Sutton.

Postal Inspector Calvin N. Smith, a supersleuth.

Then I appealed to a United States attorney who owed me a favor, and within forty-eight hours I had the full cooperation of Calvin N. Smith, a clever and persistent postal inspector from Manchester, New Hampshire.

"We've got to nab him red-handed," said Inspector Smith.

My friend Neale Lanigan, Jr., a prominent autograph dealer from Fairview Village, Pennsylvania, suggested: "Why don't you run a want ad in some magazine that Sutton reads? If he answers the ad he will send the forgeries through the mail to Inspector Smith."

It was a smart ploy. I composed the following ad, which the inspector ran in a little journal called *The Autograph News:*

URGENTLY NEEDED FOR MY PRIVATE COLLECTION: SIGNATURES OR SIGNED PHOTOS OF HITLER, EISENHOWER, LYNDON JOHNSON, GEN. GEORGE CUSTER AND CHARLES A. LINDBERGH. C. N. SMITH, BOX 4797, MANCHESTER, NH 03108

The advertisement appeared in the July, 1976, issue and by July 11, 1976, Sutton had put his foot in the trap. To the inspector he wrote:

Dear C. N. Smith,

Read your ad in the "Autograph News" and thought I would offer you some items from my own collection, which I hope you will like.

I do hope you will like the L.B.J. item as I am offering my autographs at very reasonable prices compaired to dealers as I really need the money right now, being unemployed.

I would not receive any more if I was to sell them to dealers so I thought I would pass the savings along to a fellow collector.

With the letter, Sutton enclosed a forged Lyndon Johnson priced at twelve dollars, adding that he had available a George A. Custer signature at fifty dollars, a Hitler at thirty-five and a John F. Kennedy at seventy-five.

In congratulating Smith on his initial success, I wrote: "May I suggest that you now send for the George A. Custer? Custer's signature is difficult to forge, and there is also the problem of duplicating the ink of his period, so that in

Arthur Sutton. Forged signature of Adolf Hitler on a Nazi-stamped postcard.

Arthur Sutton. Forgery of an Adolf Hitler signature.

Adolf Hitler. Authentic signature from a document.

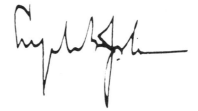

Arthur Sutton. Forged signature of Lyndon B. Johnson.

Lyndon B. Johnson. Authentic signature.

Arthur Sutton. Forged signature of General George A. Custer.

George A. Custer. Authentic signature.

court the evidence of forgery could be proved beyond any doubt."

Smith continued to gather evidence until, on October 19, 1976, I wrote to him: "If you decide to get a warrant for the arrest of Sutton, and a search warrant for his residence, would it be feasible for me to be with you and the police at the time of arrest so that I can identify forgeries?"

Arthur Sutton. Forged signature of John F. Kennedy.

John F. Kennedy. Authentic signature.

Arthur Sutton. Forged signature of Dwight D. Eisenhower.

Dwight D. Eisenhower. Authentic signature.

The inspector decided that my presence was not required. On November 16 he picked up Sutton at the house of a girl friend, who was also an autograph collector and had amassed a collection of movie stars' and astronauts' signatures valued at over two thousand dollars merely by writing to celebrities.

Sutton immediately confessed and offered to make full restitution.

He was indicted by a Portland, Maine, grand jury on December 3, 1976, on twelve counts of mail fraud.

In December I lunched with the assistant United States attorney, John Wlodkowski, and told him: "Sutton has been very cooperative in every way. It does not seem to me that it would serve any purpose to send him to prison. As the original complainant, I'd like to see him get a suspended sentence."

Wlodkowski promised to convey my thoughts to the judge, and on January 6, 1977, Sutton was allowed to plead guilty to only one count. The other counts were dropped and the judge suspended sentence for one year with the understanding that Sutton would make restitution.

Sutton wrote to me and announced that he had quit the forgery racket forever. His *apologia* was very similar to those he sent to his victims:

January 3, 1977

Dear Mr. Hamilton:

It troubles me greatly to have to write this letter to you sir, but what I have done has me so upset and worried, that I must let you know my feelings concerning the matter of my forgeries.

I have always had the greatest respect for you and love for this fabulous hobby, since 1970 when I first started a collection. I really enjoyed mail bidding and purchasing items from your catalogs.

I am not going to make excuses to you sir for what I have done, but I do offer my sincere apologies for any damage incured to this great hobby because of my forgeries.

I can not tell you how badly I truly feel and which I have felt since this whole mess started. I am *glad* I have been *caught* and can promise not only to you, but to all the other dealers and collectors that I will never forge any autographs ever again, and that all previous forgeries in my possession have been destroyed.

I am selling what few valuable items I have and am slowly paying back every cent I have stolen, as best as I can remember, even though I am still unemployed at present. I have sent payments to 4 dealers as of the above date.

I would really appreciate your understanding in this matter. Thank you.

Sincerely

ARTHUR SUTTON

This letter closed the case. But now I am going to let Arthur Sutton in on a little secret: *It is the forgeries and fakes that give piquancy and excitement to the chase. Without them philography would be a pretty dull pursuit.*

13

History's Most Brazen Faker

CLIFFORD IRVING

To forge a 230,000-word "autobiography" of a man still alive (Howard Hughes) and sell it to a top publisher (McGraw-Hill) for a vast sum of money ($750,000) was the incredible feat performed by the most audacious forger of this or any century (Clifford Irving).

Betwixt the eight parentheses in the preceding sentence lies a bizarre tale of fakery and intrigue that began in December, 1970, on the little Spanish island of Ibiza and ended in a prison cell at Allenwood, Pennsylvania.

There have been other daring forgers in history. George Psalmanazaar posed as an Oriental pagan and invented a whole history of the island of Formosa that for a while fooled the most astute scholars in Europe. Thomas Chatterton created a host of clever poems allegedly written by a fifteenth-century monk, Thomas Rowley, and took in even the wary Horace Walpole with his bogus earlie Englysshe. William Henry Ireland fabricated letters of many Elizabethans and "discovered" an unknown manuscript play of Shakespeare that was

unmasked as a forgery only when hooted off the stage at Drury Lane. But not one of these nervy rascals had the chutspah to fake an entire manuscript by a living victim.

Clifford Irving was born in New York City on November 5, 1930. No doubt he acquired his chirographic skills from his artist father, Jay Irving, creator of a cartoon strip called "Potsy," a delightful Sunday comic about a genial, rotund cop. In school Irving made the most of his good looks, worked at his studies now and then and developed a dilettantish interest in the "new" literature of the variety admired by college students and imitated by fledgling authors. After college Irving turned to hack writing as a career and wrote two not-very-successful novels and a biography of an artist friend who specialized in forgeries, *Fake!* In 1967 Irving married his third wife, Edith Sommer, an artist, and the newlyweds set up housekeeping in Ibiza, where, in the fall of 1970, the forty-year-old Irving found himself disconsolate, discontented, flirting with

Clifford Irving.

Howard Hughes.

failure—a character in search of an exciting plot.

Irving found just the scenario he wanted. Act One was to gather tall tales about Howard Hughes, the most famous recluse of modern times, the man who had been lover, aviator, inventor, financier and health nut, and weave them into a spurious autobiography. A close friend of Irving's, Dick Suskind, would do most of the research for one-fourth of the take. Irving secretly obtained a typescript of an unpublished Hughes biography written by Noah Dietrich, a top Hughes aide, with the help of a seasoned reporter, Jim Phelan. Out of this intimate biography Irving pumped some startling fresh details. To these details he added more facts and anec-

dotes gathered from news clippings, and then colored and amplified all the events with his own rampant imagination.

Act Two of the scenario, in which Clifford Irving was to play the star role, involved selling this marvelous potpourri, most of it in question-and-answer form, to Irving's publisher, McGraw-Hill. One of the scenes in this second act was the toughest part of the whole drama—forging notes by Hughes in the margin of the manuscript and a few letters to Irving from Hughes that would clinch the deal with McGraw-Hill. Just when he needed help the most, *Life* magazine came to his aid by publishing a lengthy handwritten Hughes letter that provided a perfect guide for the beginning forger. Irving knew how to mind his p's and q's and within a short time had mastered Hughes's script. He fabricated three holograph letters from Hughes, the first acknowledging the receipt of his book *Fake!,* the second a brief friendly note and the third praising Irving's integrity and adding: "It would not suit me to die without having certain misconceptions cleared up and without having stated the truth about my life. The immorality you speak of does not interest me, not in this world. I believe in obligations. . . . I would be grateful if you would let me know when and how you wish to undertake the writing of the biography you proposed."

McGraw-Hill struck at the bait, and Irving quickly produced a signed contract from Howard Hughes. While haggling went on over the total amount of the advance, McGraw-Hill forked over a one-hundred-thousand-dollar check payable to H. R. Hughes. It was a matter of great importance to Irving that the check be made out to H. R. Hughes, not Howard R. Hughes, because Irving's willowy wife Edith was going to pose as Helga R. Hughes and deposit the check in a Swiss bank account. Which is precisely what she did.

In negotiating a blood-letting contract with McGraw-Hill Irving showed nerves of triple-brass. He told his publishers: "Hughes insists upon a prepub advance of eight hundred and fifty thousand." He showed them a freshly forged letter

Howard Hughes. First page of an authentic handwritten letter to Chester Davis and Bill Gay, published in *Life*. This letter served as a model for Clifford Irving's brilliant Hughes forgeries.

> Dear Chester and Bill—
>
> I do not understand why the problem of Mahew is not yet fully settled, and why this bad publicity seems to continue. It could hurt our company's valuable properties in Nevada, and also the entire state.
>
> You told me that, if I called Governor Laxalt and District Attorney George Franklin, it would put an end to this problem.
>
> I made these calls, and I do not understand why this very damaging publicity should continue merely because the property constituted board of directors of Hughes Tool Company decided, for reasons they considered just, to terminate all relationship with Mahew and Hooper.

11-17-71

Mr. Harold McGraw
McGraw Hill
New York, N.Y.

Dear Mr. McGraw —

The facts placed before me I find astonishing. I do not understand, in the first place, why it is not possible for your publishing house in possession of a legitimate contract between myself and Mr. Clifford Irving and between yourselves and Mr. Irving, for the publication of my autobiography, cannot deal firmly and forcefully with other publishers who which are asserting fraudulent claims to the rights which I have granted to Mr. Irving and Mr

Clifford Irving. First page of a forged Howard Hughes letter to Harold McGraw of McGraw-Hill. The imitation is almost flawless, capturing not only Hughes's handwriting but his atrabilious disposition.

from the billionaire authorizing Irving to "offer my autobiography for sale to another publisher" if McGraw-Hill didn't come up with the cash. When McGraw-Hill hemmed a little, Irving produced a refund check for $100,000 "signed" by Hughes, explaining: "Hughes says to take your advance back if you won't meet his demands." McGraw-Hill finally raised the ante to $750,000 and "Hughes" accepted. Irving had played a masterful poker game and got away with his biggest pot.

When Irving handed over the finished manuscript of around one thousand pages the publishers were delighted. Here was the great man of mystery in bedroom slippers! It was Hughes himself speaking. Especially the long technical diatribes about aircraft. The intimate anecdotes. The meretricious amours. The savage business philosophy. It was with pride and certainty that McGraw-Hill announced to the press the biggest publishing coup of the decade.

A lot of reporters were skeptical at the news. Hughes had been silent for so many years that it was hard to believe that he had at last dictated an autobiography. His aversion to publicity was

Clifford Irving. Signature (genuine).

Howard Hughes. Signature (genuine).

legendary, and this candid stripping of his very soul was certain to put him in the limelight. There were also rumors that Hughes was dead, and dead men tell no tales. The Hughes Tool Company, controller of the Hughes empire, heatedly denied the authenticity of the book.

To silence the allegations of fraud McGraw-Hill consulted a handwriting expert who declared that the scribbling of Hughes in the letters and in the margins of the typed manuscript was authentic.

Then the one thing, the only thing, that Irving feared happened. Howard Hughes broke his silence for the first time in fourteen years and telephoned a reporter: "The book is a phony and Clifford Irving is a phony," said the billionaire. "I never met him and I never wrote any autobiography."

Life magazine had bought first magazine rights, and it now demanded that McGraw-Hill consult the world-famous handwriting experts Osborn, Osborn and Osborn to determine once and for all the authenticity of the handwriting attributed to Hughes.

Under pressure, the publisher called in the firm. Paul Osborn and his brother Russell gave the handwriting a very careful scrutiny. They compared it with examples known to be genuine. They examined the ink lines. They looked closely at the dots on the i's and the crosses on the t's. They probed into the script for telltale signs of a tremor or an erasure. Then they delivered their report.

"Both the specimen and questioned documents reveal great speed and fluency of writing," read their analysis. "Yet the questioned documents accurately reflect in every detail the genuine forms and habit variations thereof which make up the basic handwriting identity of the author of the specimen documents. Moreover, in spite of the prodigious quantity of writing contained in the questioned documents, careful study has failed to reveal any features which raise the slightest question as to the common identity of all the specimens and questioned signatures and continuous writing. These basic factors . . . make it impossible . . . that anyone other than the writer of the specimens could have written the questioned signatures and continuous writing."

In the light of subsequent developments, it is easy to criticize the Osborns for their mistake; but as a handwriting expert I must concede that Irving's forgeries of Howard Hughes were masterfully executed. Irving's artistic talents did not fail him when he picked up his felt-tipped pen, for he captured the eccentricities of Hughes's script as adroitly as he caught the oddities of his personality in the "autobiography."

Act Three of this wild scenario was one which the protagonist had not planned. While his wife was in Zurich getting the boodle in Swiss francs, seven newsmen gathered to hear the real Howard Hughes talk to them through an electronic box. There was no mistaking the famous aviator's trembling voice as he condemned the fake autobiography and denounced the forger. For a while Irving stuck to his story. He chatted knowingly about all the interviews he'd had with Hughes. He joked with the hoards of reporters who pursued him and invited them to his apartment, where his wife regaled them with wine. He had had a wild fling with a Baroness Nina Van Pallandt, a singer, which delighted the press. He faced the television cameras with a confident smile. Then, in the end, he pleaded guilty to forgery and went off to prison.

Irving's diabolically accurate imitation of Hughes's style of speech and handwriting leads us to the inevitable question. Suppose Irving had forged the autobiography of some person who was not alive to speak up and denounce him? Rudolph Valentino or Warren G. Harding, for example. What a scandalous and exhilarating document!

I am not presuming to offer any suggestions to Clifford Irving. He is a man of extraordinary talents and will make his own way in the world.

14

The Poet Who Forged Robert Frost

THOMAS McNAMARA

"The most interesting case I ever handled," said Inspector Calvin N. Smith of the Robert Frost caper. "Right from the start I knew it was going to be exciting. It had all the ingredients of a melodrama. Here was a poet named Thomas McNamara who lectured on flying saucers, gave public readings of his poetry and was secretly conducting a mail-order operation in forgeries with his girl friend as a shill."

Thomas McNamara, as the inspector soon found out, was a genius at imitating the script of Robert Frost and many other poets. He began his secret life as a forger early in 1970. On May 8 of that year he wrote to a prominent New York rare-book and autograph dealer offering typescripts signed by William Carlos Williams, one of them a corrected short story, "Use of Force," for which the forger asked one hundred and twenty-five dollars. "These are not souvenir copies," wrote McNamara, who described himself as "Professor of Creative Writing," "but were part of a literary manuscript. I own the only copy of the story. . . ." In the same letter, McNamara announced his plans "to liquidate fully signed typescripts of Archibald MacLeish, Langston Hughes, John Hall Wheelock, Richard Eberhart, Richard Wilbur, Padraic Colum, Robert Hillyer and Oscar Williams."

After an exchange of several letters, the New York dealer wrote: "Herewith our check in the sum of $125.00 in payment of the corrected typsescript of THE USE OF FORCE."

No further correspondence between them ensued until August 22, 1973, when McNamara, writing from Belknap College in Center Harbor, New Hampshire, and using the title "Dean, The School of Fine Arts," offered a volume containing two handwritten poems by Robert Frost "appraised at 1,400.00." The dealer complained about the high price, adding: "I thought you had given or sold your Frost material to Plymouth." Three years later the dealer bought ten forged William Carlos Williams signed typescripts for two hundred and five dollars, but declined a

Love Song

Sweep the house clean,

hang fresh curtains

in the windows

put on a new dress

and come with me!

The elm is scattering

its little loaves

of sweet smells

from a white sky!

Who shall hear of us

in the time to come ?

Let him say there was

a burst of fragrance

from black branches.

William Carlos Williams
9 Ridge Road
Rutherford, N.J.

Thomas McNamara. Forgery of a typed poem signed "William Carlos Williams," with a correction in Williams's hand. So quavery and infirm was Williams's own script (he had suffered several strokes) that his handwriting was temptingly easy for a forger to duplicate. "Love Song" is reprinted courtesy of New Directions, publisher of *The Collected Earlier Poems* of William Carlos Williams. Copyright 1938 by New Directions.

William Carlos Williams. Authentic signature in old age.

further purchase of ten Williams type-scripts in June, 1977.

The persistent forger, who kept meticulous records in a small notebook, a copy of which is in my possession, now approached another dealer and on September 5, 1975, unloaded a collection of ten typescripts signed by Langston Hughes in the familiar green ink at twenty-five dollars each and two handwritten poems of Robert Frost in blue ink at one hundred dollars each. He quickly followed up this sale on November 3, 1975, by selling the same dealer five Langston Hughes signed typescripts and two manuscript poems signed by Robert Frost at a total of three hundred and seventy-five dollars.

Emboldened by success, McNamara now approached the Carnegie Book Shop in New York and on March 10, 1976, mailed it a large collection of twenty-six forgeries on approval. David Kirshenbaum, the proprietor, recognized the wares as fakes and promptly returned the whole group.

The work of Thomas McNamara was brought to my attention in April, 1977, by a New York philographer who placed before me a collection of Robert Frost manuscript poems, along with typescripts signed by Langston Hughes and William Carlos Williams and holograph letters by Millay, William Dean Howells and others.

"Are they okay?" he asked.

"All forgeries," I told him. But the Frost fakes were truly remarkable. They were the best I'd ever seen, even better than those of the notorious Florida forger of Frost and Lindbergh (whom I

NEGRO DANCERS

" Me an' ma baby's
Got two mo' ways,

Two mo' ways to do de Cherleston!

   Da, da
   Da, da, da!

Two mo' ways to do de Charleston!"

White folks laugh!
White folks, pray!

Me an' ma baby's got two mo ways.

Langston Hughes

Thomas McNamara. Forgery of a typed poem signed by Langston Hughes. The signature of Hughes, as was his custom, was written in green ink. Except for a little shakiness, visible especially in the first bar of the *H* and the lower loop of the *g,* this is an excellent imitation.

Langston Hughes. Authentic signature from a letter.

The poem as Hughes actually wrote it is as follows:

   Negro Dancers

"Me an' ma baby's
Got two mo' ways
Two mo' ways to do de Charleston!
   Da, da,
   Da, da, da!
Two mo' ways to do de Charleston!"

Soft light on the tables,
Music gay,
Brown-skin steppers
In a cabaret.

White folks, laugh!
White folks, pray!

"Me an' ma baby's
   Got two mo' ways,
Two mo ways to do de
   Charleston!"

Rose Mary
Edna St V. Millay

For the sake of some things
That be now no more—
I will strew rushes
On my chamber floor.
I will plant bergamot
At my kitchen door.

For the sake of dim things
That were once so plain
I will set a barrel
Out to catch the rain
I will hang an iron pot
On an iron crane,

Thomas McNamara. Forgery of the first page of a handwritten poem signed by Edna St. Vincent Millay. An extremely poor imitation.

Edna St. Vincent Millay. Conclusion of an authentic signed, handwritten letter. Notice that her script bears little or no similarity to McNamara's fabrication.

hope to send to prison one of these days).

With the forgeries was a letter from a woman offering these manuscripts from the collection of her "granddad," and explaining that they were all "certified" by Thomas E. McNamara of Ashland, New Hampshire.

"Leave the manuscripts with me," I told the dealer. "Let me see if I can stop the forger."

My first thought was that Arthur Sutton, who lived not far from Ashland and whom I had exposed as a forger a year previously, and whose career is described in an earlier chapter, had decided to augment his grocery clerk's income by going back into the forgery racket. But I was puzzled because Sutton specialized in signatures, and the forgeries in front of me were complete manuscripts.

I quickly concluded that they were the work of an entirely new forger, and I wrote on April 21, 1977, to Inspector Calvin Smith, of Manchester, New Hampshire, who had worked with me to effect the arrest of Sutton, and told him about the Frosts and other fakes, sending photocopies of the forgeries and the woman's letter, adding that "if the forger of these manuscripts is not stopped, his work will soon be all over the country."

Inspector Smith was extremely cooperative and at once made inquiries into the activities of the woman and McNamara. "They are very close friends," he told me over the telephone, "and evidently they are working together on producing and selling the forgeries."

Smith dug deeper and came up with some more facts. McNamara, in his forties, had taught a course in Frost's poetry and been a "professor" at Antioch's branch in Ashland and curator of the Frost collection at Plymouth State College. The woman worked in Suzanne's Kitchen in Ashland, and she and McNamara had imported poets for readings in the restaurant. McNamara himself wrote verse and had read samples of his own work.

At Plymouth State College McNamara was still recalled for his ebullient personality. He had been appointed curator of the George H. Browne collection of Robert Frost, an assemblage of rare

books and letters by the poet that he had personally obtained from the donor. Although the only college degree McNamara ever got was a Bachelor of Science from Springfield College in Massachusetts, he claimed to have a Master of Arts degree from Wayne State and donned the title of "professor." He also invented a story about how the manuscripts of his poems were treasured in the Firestone Library at Princeton University. The librarian there later said he had never heard of McNamara. Associates who knew McNamara said that he had a big ego and was extremely ambitious. Despite his popularity with the students he was dismissed at the end of

Thomas McNamara. Forgery of a handwritten letter signed by William Dean Howells about his hope to be Frost's "friend and mentor." Written in a stilted, stumbling English of which Howells was incapable. The forged handwriting is spastic and not characteristic of Howell's craggy script.

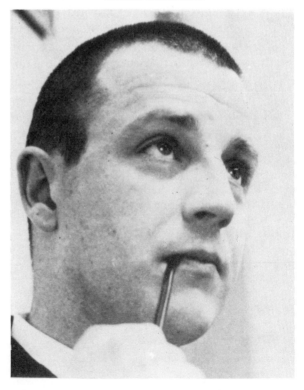

"I sing in March to if
the bird lays
And hope a May, and
do not know.

W. D. Howells.
Columbus, Ohio, 1860.
Kittery Point, Me., 1905.

William Dean Howells. Authentic handwritten poem, penned and signed for a collector forty-five years after it was originally written.

June, 1969. An investigation showed that some of the valuable Frost-inscribed books in his custody had vanished. McNamara's explanation: "The new curator must have lost them."

McNamara doted on titles and distinctions, and in an article he provided for *The Record Citizen* of Plymouth, New Hampshire, on March 9, 1977, the "professor" rattled off an impressive list of vanity publications which had featured biographies of him:

McNamara is listed in Heims Athletic Hall of Fame, the Directory of American Scholars, the Dictionary of International Biography, Who's Who in American Literature, the International Who's Who in Poetry, Who's Who in the East, Outstanding Educators of America, the Centennial Edition of the Dictionary of International Biography; he is also listed in Community Leaders and Noteworthy Americans, in the International Who's Who in Community Service, in the International Who's Who of Intellectuals, in the International Who's Who of World

Authors, and in the North American Register of Profiles.

And now McNamara comes to the ultimate in biographies, the climactic achievement for a man of distinction:

The World Edition of the International Profiles is "strictly limited to one thousand selected individuals who by their outstanding service to their fellow man achieved international recognition and acclaim." McNamara is being recognized for his outstanding achievement in areas of writing, service to community and country and for his dedicated service to education. The World Register is the highest honor that can be paid to

Thomas McNamara.

a contemporary citizen of the world. Mr. McNamara is one of less than forty Americans selected to be so highly honored for his achievements.

It would seem difficult after this plethora of laudatory biographies to add any garnishment, but McNamara also points out, in this same article, that two of his many books of verse (all published by vanity presses) have attained unusual distinction. *To Lucy from Dreamland and Other Poems* was a Pulitzer Prize nominee, and *Wild with the Scent of Flowers and Other Poems* was a national Book Award nominee.

As the case against McNamara unfolded, I acquired a small sheaf of his poems, introspective free verse in which the writer created vignettes and profiles, always in search of some inner meaning that seemed to elude him. All the poems were signed "Thomas Edward Francis" (McNamara's given names), and were penned in a script remarkably like that of Robert Frost. Was it possible, I wondered, that McNamara looked upon himself as a reincarnation of Frost? The iambs and trochees that Frost doted on

were absent, but McNamara showed the same intellectual curiosity as his mentor.

While McNamara was immersed in his poetry recitations, Inspector Smith and I were getting ready to put the noose around his neck.

Suddenly I was shocked by the dealer who had turned the forgeries over to me for action. "I've got to have them back, with all the correspondence," he said. "McNamara says he'll sue me if I don't return his papers. He says he'll get the postal authorities after me."

When my powers of persuasion proved useless against his cowardice, I gave the papers back to him, and on July 14, 1977, I wrote to Inspector Smith that the whole case had blown up. "So we have no evidence left. McNamara is now apparently at liberty to peddle his forgeries through the United States mails."

Previously I had suggested to the inspector that he use the same trick that had proved so successful in the Sutton case: run an ad in an autograph journal asking for manuscripts of Frost and

Thomas McNamara. Final lines of a handwritten poem signed with his pen name, comprising his first given name and two middle names. Written in a quaint neologistic dialect, these lines are difficult to understand and apparently refer to obscure incidents in his own life. McNamara's script bears a remarkable similarity to Frost's and is perhaps an unconscious imitation.

Robert Frost. Authentic signature.

Williams for his "personal collection." The inspector ran the ad and McNamara struck at the lure.

"I am writing you regarding the collection of modern literary authors presently available through the Vansandts," replied McNamara on July 8, 1977. "I am now handling the sale of the items."

With McNamara's letter came a list of Frost manuscript poems, plus typescripts signed by Williams and Hughes, all available for sale, each with a "certificate of authentication."

The inspector wrote to me on July 20: "I intend to make a couple of small purchases . . . I will send them to you . . . I would be quite lost without your expert opinion."

The manuscripts which Inspector Smith sent for my examination were forgeries, and I was again amazed by McNamara's superb imitations of Frost. They lacked the customary personalized inscriptions which Frost invariably put at the bottom of the poems he copied out for admirers, but in all other respects they were masterfully executed.

At this point I got in touch with Paul C. Richards, the noted Frost expert, and Kenneth W. Rendell, the distinguished Massachusetts dealer, and solicited their cooperation. Both were familiar with McNamara's work. Richards had previously been offered by McNamara—and had returned—some forged poems of Frost and Williams. He was enthusiastic in his offer of cooperation.

On September 9, 1977, I wrote to Inspector Smith and asked if we did not now have enough evidence "to close the iron door on McNamara."

The inspector agreed. Armed with search warrants, he raided the apartment of McNamara's girl friend. While he found only one forgery, a framed poem of Frost hanging on her wall, he turned up a quantity of illegal drugs. He placed the woman under arrest, and she was subsequently released on one hundred and fifty dollars' bail. At McNamara's residence the inspector struck a rich vein of forgeries. He seized one hundred and seventy-eight documents, including sixty-three framed examples of Frost, plus forgeries of Whitman, Poe (whose middle name, Allan, McNamara had misspelled!), Williams and Hughes.

The "professor" was furious and indignant at his arrest. As Smith removed one framed item from the wall, McNamara caustically observed: "I was with Frost when he wrote that one."

The impounded Frost poems were beautifully framed with early photographs of the poet. One of the fakes, "Stopping by Woods," was so skillfully executed that McNamara had marked it "not for sale," deciding that so perfect a creation belonged in his own collection.

All of the framed items bore authentications and huge, dazzling paper seals on the back. McNamara's favorite fake was Frost's celebrated verse about the joke God played on him.

With the forgeries, the inspector found a large supply of pens and colored inks, including blue ink that matched the Frost forgeries and green ink that matched the Langston Hughes forgeries.

At the time of his arrest, and even after his release on bail, McNamara was a lecturer on flying saucers with the New

Certificate of Authentication

I Verify the Following Document is Authentic

LOVE SONG BY WILLIAM CARLOS WILLIAMS

TYPESCRIPT WITH FULL SIGNATURE)CIRCA 1960–1

[signature]

Signature

AUG 24 1977

Date

10141

Registration Number

Original "Certificate of Authentication" signed by McNamara at lower left, for his forged, signed typescript of William Carlos Williams's "Love Song." A flashy document, it is printed in blue with a red seal embossed "One of a kind originals/Certified document/Ashland, New Hampshire."

One Step Backward Taken

Not only sands and gravels
Were once more on their travels,
But gulping muddy gallons
Great boulders off their balance
Bumped heads together dully
And set off down the gully.
Whole capes caked off in slices
I felt my standpoint shaken
In the universal crisis.
But with one step backward taken
I saved myself from going.
A world torn loose went by me
Then the rain stopped and the blowing
And the sun came out to dry me.

Robert Frost

To William Burton Stitt

Robert Frost. Handwritten signed transcript of his celebrated poem "One Step Backward Taken." *

One Step Backward Taken

Not only sands and gravels
Were once more on their travels,
But gulping muddy gallons
Great boulders off their balance
Bumped heads together dully
And set off down the gully.
Whole capes caked off in slices
I fell

Thomas McNamara. Incomplete forgery, apparently a tracing, of the first portion of Frost's poem, found among McNamara's papers at the time of his arrest.

*All examples used by permission of the estate of Robert Frost.

Registered Certificate of Authentication
United States of America

THIS DOCUMENT IS certified AS AUTHENTIC, AND IT BEARS THE NUMBER(S) OF REGISTRATION ON THE REVERSE BOTTOM OF EACH DOCUMENT. THIS CERTIFICATE AND SEAL ATTESTS TO THE AUTHENTICITY AND THE REGISTRATION OF THE DOCUMENT.

LOVE SONG BY WILLIAM CARLOS WILLIAMS

10141
Registration Number(s)

AUG 24 1977
Date Certified

Signature

Another "Registered Certificate of Authentication," signed at lower left by Thomas McNamara, for his forged, signed typescript of William Carlos Williams's "Love Song."

Hampshire Department of Recreation. A lengthy article in the *New Hampshire Sunday Times* on March 26, 1978, pictured the poet as he peered "skyward in search of additional evidence of extra-terrestrial visitors from a wooded area in Penacook." The article summarized McNamara's ideas:

"We've been too fictionalized and Hollywoodized in our beliefs about extra-terrestrial beings," says the Penacook poet, who also lectures on "psychic phenomena."

"We think of them as sinister forces out to do violence to us."

However, McNamara tells his audiences, he believes the alien visitors may actually hold the key to the survival of the human race.

The beings are benign, he believes, and he openly counsels his audience to share his confidence.

"There is nothing ever to fear, be-

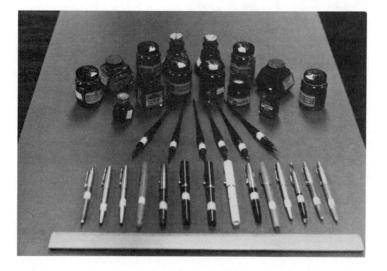

Collection of fourteen bottles of colored inks and twenty pens discovered in McNamara's possession when he was arrested. A typical "forger's arsenal." This array of inks and pens made it easier for McNamara to imitate the handwriting of Robert Frost (thick-nibbed pen in blue ink) and Langston Hughes (medium-nibbed pen in bright green ink). All these items bear government exhibit numbers.

cause an alien has never hurt a person," he announces near the close of his slide show and presentation.

"Mankind is on the threshold of a sensational change," he concludes. "Are you ready for it?"

My wife, Diane, and I flew up to Manchester, New Hampshire, on December 6, 1977, to meet the inspector and examine the huge quantity of forgeries and other papers he had taken from McNamara. Every document was a fake, and there were scores of them, plus a large table heaped high with framed Frost poems. There was a notebook of blue-lined paper in which were drafts by McNamara, imitating Frost's handwriting. Many of the framed forgeries of Frost were written on similar lined paper. Diane suggested that we take apart a framed item and see if the blue-lined

To the Thawing Wind

Come with rain O loud Southwester!
Bring the singer, bring the nester.
Give the buried flower a dream.
Make the settled snow-bank steam.
Find the brown beneath the white.
But whate'er you do tonight
Bathe my window, make it flow,
Melt it as the ice will go.
Melt the glass, and leave the sticks
Like a hermit's crucifix
Burst into my narrow stall.
Swing the picture on the wall.
Run the rattling pages o'er,
Scatter poems on the floor.
Turn the poet out of door.

Robert Frost

Thomas McNamara. Forgery of a handwritten poem signed by Robert Frost. The writing is spread out more than Frost's, but the imitation is excellent and extremely deceptive.

Men left her a ship to sink;
They can leave her a hut as well,
And be but more free to think
For the one more cast off shell.

Robert Frost

Robert Frost. Authentic signed, handwritten quatrain. The lines and words are more compressed than those in McNamara's fake.

Thomas McNamara. Forgery of Robert Frost's famous poem "Some Say the World Will End in Fire." A brilliantly executed fabrication that would deceive almost anyone except a Frost expert.

Some say the world will end in fire,
Some say in ice
From what I've tasted of desire,
I hold with those who favor fire
But if it had to perish twice,
I think I know enough of hate
To say that for destruction ice
Is also great
And would suffice.

Robert Frost

paper aligned with that in McNamara's working notebook.

"An exact match!" exclaimed Inspector Smith, as he placed the manuscript poem from the frame into the precise spot in the notebook from which it was torn.

That evening we had dinner with the inspector, a tall, slender, soft-spoken man in his fifties.

I asked him what the forgers were like.

"McNamara is arrogant and self-confident. He refuses to admit anything and won't say where he got the manuscripts. His records show that he received over four thousand dollars for the fakes he sold. Most of them were peddled, unwittingly, by the Raven Antique Shop. His girl friend is so spaced out on narcotics that I doubt if we will want to prosecute her."

Paul C. Richards, the world's leading expert on Frost, also examined the collection and pronounced every item a forgery.

McNamara, released on bail, denounced Richards as a "self-proclaimed" expert. I was not privileged to hear his remarks about me, but I understand they were vehement and in the same vein.

In January, 1978, both McNamara and his girl friend pleaded "not guilty" and were released on one thousand dollars' bail.

McNamara was so hostile and uncooperative that I wrote Inspector Smith outlining why I believed he should be sent to prison. I asked the inspector to give a copy of my letter to the judge.

Before the scheduled trial, at which Paul Richards and I were to testify, McNamara changed his plea. On July 19, 1978, he appeared before the judge and said: "I was so grossly negligent as to be culpable."

The judge did not accept this gobbledy-gook, but said: "You have to plead guilty or not guilty."

McNamara and his lawyer withdrew

and shortly returned. The "professor" pleaded guilty to six counts of selling forgeries through the United States mails.

Chemical tests in Washington, meanwhile, had proved conclusively that the ink used in the William Carlos Williams forgeries was not manufactured until a year after he died.

McNamara was sentenced to a year in federal prison by Judge Hugh Bownes of Boston.

The forgeries of McNamara in government custody were ordered destroyed by United States Attorney William Shaheen. But there are some still around in private hands, and I recommend that dealers and collectors look very carefully at all typescripts signed by Langston Hughes and William Carlos Williams as well as manuscript poems by Robert Frost that are not individually inscribed to a collector in the bottom left corner.

If you should discover in your collection a bogus Frost, do not be dismayed but remember that the forger himself so admired his own handicraft that he kept one especially adroit forgery for his private collection and gave his sweetheart a framed fake to display on her wall.

Robert Frost. Authentic signed manuscript poem.

15

He Got Fooled by His Own Forgery

OWEN D. YOUNG

The rags-to-riches story of Owen D. Young is right out of Horatio Alger. Not a single ingredient is missing. There was the tough early life on the squalid little farm and the struggle against poverty, the slow rise through hard work and a bit of luck, the menial post in a lawyer's office and, finally, the big break that started our hero on the road to phenomenal success. With this difference: none of Alger's farm boys succeeded like Owen D. Young. He became an awesome power in the banking world and one of the richest men in America.

Young organized and was chairman of the Radio Corporation of America. He was chairman of the board of directors of the General Electric Company and a director of the Federal Reserve Bank of New York, General Motors Corporation, the International General Electric Company and so on. He was an intimate of Woodrow Wilson and one of the great rare-book and -manuscript collectors of America.

Young was born October 27, 1874, on a little farm at Van Hornesville, New

York. There was not much in his early life except sweaty hard work, the usual chores that started before dawn and lasted until sunset. But one day Owen ventured into town, where, in a "cool and shady courtroom," he saw several lawyers at work. He asked himself: "Is it possible that men really get a living in this pleasant way?" Young decided to become a lawyer, and despite a constant shortage of funds he managed to get through St. Lawrence and into the law school at Boston University. While at college he lived in a garret that cost two dollars and a half a week. He spent only forty cents a day for food and "extras." There were holes in his shoes and he was often hungry, but he was finally graduated in 1896.

Young got a job as a scrivener with Charles H. Tyler in Boston, copying legal documents at ten dollars a week. Two years later he got married. His salary was then only fifty dollars a month. Money was tough to get. There was a depression in 1898 and, as one observer put it, "Boston was bankrupt."

February 9, 1933.

Signature of Owen D. Young.

Years later, in a rare moment of confidence, Young revealed to the great bookman Dr. A. S. W. Rosenbach one of the dark secrets of his life. In retailing Young's story in his famous memoirs, *Books and Bidders,* Rosenbach mixed the facts to conceal Young's identity. He even gave him a shock of white hair. But there was no mistaking his graphic portrait of the great financier:

"I cast my bread upon the waters, and it came back to me after many days!"

"What do you mean by that?" I asked the tall white-haired man who sat opposite me in his luxurious library. The room was an enormous one, and thousands of fine books lined the walls from floor to ceiling. My friend seemed in a confidential mood, and I expected to hear something startling. This Gothic room, with its early Spanish religious sculptures, had the very atmosphere of a confessional. My companion had had a somewhat weird career, and as I watched him through the heavy smoke of our cigars I recalled many strange stories of his youth. Once he had been a lawyer's clerk, but now he was a director in many banks, with financial interests all over the world. The variegated stages by which he had risen to such eminence, not only in business but as a collector of pictures and books, were not always clear to the friends of his later years.

He told me that he had been so poor as a boy he had often known hunger; that, as a scrivener in the lawyer's office, he had eked out a most pitiable existence copying deeds and other legal documents. In 1885 he happened to read in the newspapers of famous auction sales of autographs in London, and of the first arrival in this country of representatives of the English book houses. . . . My friend was fascinated, and as he had no capital to invest in great rarities himself, he thought he would make a few. He determined to try his hand at imitation.

Just about that period there was an

awakened interest in the ill-fated Major André, who had suffered death as a British informer. In his grimy boarding house on Grand Street my friend practiced imitating André's handwriting. He finally manufactured a splendid letter in which Major André wrote to General Washington requesting that he be shot as a soldier and not hanged as a spy. As he described his youthful fabrication his mouth lighted with a smile of pleasure, and he confessed that he had been very proud of this forgery; it had been a work of art! He finally actually sold this pseudo-André letter for $650! Those were the days when unpedigreed rarities were more easily disposed of, as there were not so many autograph sharks around as there are to-day.

Thirty years elapsed. My friend had grown in riches and in reputation. Now he was a noted collector; forgotten were the peccadillos of his youth. In 1915, during the Great War, he noticed the advertisement of a sale in London containing an André letter. He cabled an unlimited bid, as was now his custom. The letter was bought for him for £280. A few weeks later, upon opening the package which he received from the custom house, the inclosed autograph letter looked familiar to him. A closer scrutiny revealed the fact that he had bought back, at three times what he had received for it, his own fabrication!

Owen D. Young was one of Rosenbach's favorite clients, buying rarities at high prices and spending his money lavishly for precious autograph letters and rare books.

Young had a darkly mysterious face and a quiet charm, plus a prodigious knowledge of history and literature. He was an ideal client and a perfect drinking companion for the doctor. Young began with heavy purchases of Dickens and Thackeray, then bought one hundred and forty-six Hawthorne letters and a bundle of Mark Twain's correspondence. As General Electric shot up in the market so did Young's purchases, and when Young sprang for a rare *Canterbury Tales* at $25,500 Rosenbach jettisoned a portrait of Pizarro scheduled for reproduction in *Books and Bidders* and replaced it with one of Owen D. Young.

The market crash of 1929 found Young in hock to Rosenbach for hundreds of thousands of dollars. Eight years later much of the account was still unpaid and Owen D. Young was ready to part with his great collection. In 1941 he decided to fuse it with the famed Berg material in the New York Public Library. There were fifteen thousand rarities, including Young's forged letter of John André.

Aware that the André letter was a fake but not realizing that Owen D. Young had forged it, the Berg collection displayed it in 1972 in an exhibit entitled "Documents Famous & Infamous." But there remains an unanswered question. Why didn't Young destroy this incriminating evidence of his youthful folly?

Maybe because he was secretly proud of his creation. It is a clever and very deceptive forgery. Or, more likely, he kept it for sentimental reasons, a memento of the first "big money" he ever earned—more than a year's salary for a scrap of paper!

Owen D. Young. First page of a forgery of a handwritten letter from Major John André to George Washington, asking that Washington allow him to be shot as a soldier and not hanged as a spy, a request Washington refused.

Owen D. Young. Second page of Young's forgery of Major John André's letter. An ebullient attempt to imitate André's hand. The signature has an extra *e* and the accent is *grave* instead of *aigu.*

Tappan the 1st October 1780

Sir

Buoy'd above the Terror of Death by the Consciousness of a Life devoted to honorable pursuits and stained with no Action that can give me Remorse, I trust the request I make to your Excellency at this Serious period and which is to soften my last moments will not be rejected.

Sympathy towards a Soldier will surely induce Your Excellency and

John André. First page of his original signed, handwritten letter to Washington, October 1, 1780, asking that he be shot as a soldier and not hanged as a spy.

I have the honour to be

Your Excellency's Most obedient and most humble Servant

John André Adj Gen to the Brit: Arm

John André. Last page of his famous letter to Washington of October 1, 1780. André's signature was cut off by some vandal and later replaced.

John André. Authentic signature.

16

Some Scribbling Scalawags

The knocker suddenly dropped his voice to a dramatic whisper and leaned forward. "How would you like to own the greatest American inscribed book in existence?"

"Tell me more," I said. The man to whom I spoke was one of the most skilled in his trade and had picked up more rarities knocking on doors than any knocker I'd ever met.

"There's this rich guy in Philly," said the knocker. "Rich, and with clout. I hear he's got nickels and dimes and quarters struck in gold, just for him, by the mint in Philly. His name's Balizzio.

"Well, Balizzio's got a great collection of books inscribed by presidents—every single one, even the hard-to-getters like Zachary Taylor and Andy Johnson. But the jewel—you won't believe this!—is a copy of the plays of some old Greek writer inscribed by Cornwallis to Washington, with Washington's signature in it."

The knocker paused to let the impact of his words sink in. Mine was certainly the fastest intellectual osmosis on rec-

ord, because by the time his five-second pause was over I had my coat on and my checkbook in my pocket. I wanted this presentation book from the defeated to the victor more than I had ever wanted anything in my life.

The knocker, Gene Delafield, called Balizzio to let him know we were on our way.

As we walked down the sumptuous corridor that led to Balizzio's library, I noticed a framed Lincoln photograph with a forged signature. Balizzio had taken the old volume out of its elaborate and expensive leather slip case and placed it dramatically in the very center of his huge library table. The binding was battered and worn, unlike most of the books in Washington's library, and the old tome had about it the apologetic air of a mendicant. I had a strange foreboding and a bowline in my stomach as I approached it.

A glance at the inscriptions confirmed my suspicions. Valued by the owner at ten thousand dollars, the book bore blatant forgeries of Cornwallis's and Washington's handwriting. It lacked Washington's book-plate, as do most faked books from his library. Then I examined the collection of forty or fifty books, all allegedly from the libraries of our presidents. The commoner books, such as those of Wilson, Coolidge, Hoover and the two Roosevelts, were authentically signed, but more than half the volumes sported fraudulent signatures, some of them obviously fabricated in the same ink and the same handwriting and on the same day by the same forger, even though they purported to be signed by presidents who had lived more than a century apart.

After I refused to buy the collection, Balizzio said: "I suppose you are going to tell everybody that my collection is made up of fakes. I've got a lot of money in it and you could easily ruin its sale."

I said: "I have no further interest in what you do with these turkeys."

Several years after I turned down this collection, I got a letter from a great library in Texas, asking my opinion on a collection of presidential books which they had just acquired. They enclosed photocopies of the inscriptions. It was the same group of tatterdemalions, volume for volume, that I had examined in Philadelphia. How the library got the collection I don't know, but the agent for the library at the time was a man of tasteless arrogance and abysmal ignorance who had made a fortune out of his cutely bastardized initials, a glib tongue and a fat upper lip habitually curled in scorn. I often wondered whether he had stuck his client with these preposterous fakes.

Forgers like to write famous names in old books. For a few dollars the forger can pick up a two-hundred-year-old volume, usually a cheap religious tract or a late edition of some popular author, and thus have a ready-made prop to which he can add a valuable signature. During my long career I've been offered at least a dozen books "signed" by Button Gwinnett and Thomas Lynch, Jr., whose rare signatures command many thousands of dollars. Literally scores of old law books that allegedly belonged to Lincoln and several dozen volumes of essays or poetry with the forged name of George Washington, who probably never read anything except the *Farmer's Almanac,* have come my way.

Not long ago I was offered a sumptuously encased Bible, supposedly from Jefferson's library and signed by the great Virginian. It was a large, heavy book, but the file of credentials which accompanied it, authentications, notarizations, validations, provenances and I-swear-to-Gods signed by alleged previous owners, was bigger and thicker than the Bible itself. Any rare signed book or document that comes with such a pile of guarantees is almost certain to be a fake, and this volume was no exception. The imitation of Jefferson's signature was very crude, and the forger hadn't even bothered to learn the secret method by which Jefferson protected the books in his library. You may recall that in the early days of printing, the signatures, or page gatherings, of all books were marked with tiny printed letters of the alphabet at the bottom of every sixteenth or thirty-secondth page to guide the binder. The first signature was coded *A,* the second *B* and so on. Jefferson identified his books by writing a tiny *T* in front of the signature *I* (there was no *J* in the Latin alphabet) and a tiny *I* after the signature *T.*

Thomas Jefferson. Authentic handwritten initial *T* preceding the printed page signature *I* (bottom left) in a book from Jefferson's library. Most books from Jefferson's library bear this secret ownership code. The word *REVIEW* at the lower right is known as a *catchword* and leads the reader to the same word at the top of the following page.

(65)

rity. When this shall be done, the government can be changed and modelled on republican principles, as may become neceſſary and uſeful.

By the Conſtitution it is provided, that " Nul ne peut être empêche de dire, écrire, imprimer et publier ſa penſée " No one is to be impeached for expreſſing, writing or printing his thoughts.

THIS proviſion is abſolutely neceſſary to a free country, but very hazardous in a revolutionary ſtate. The ſame idea is recognized in all the American conſtitutions : but they were not formed whilſt the independence of the country was at hazard. The printers in favour of the claims of Great-Britain, had, in the time of the revolutionary war, no ſtanding in united America, excepting within the lines of the Britiſh army. Our committee of correſpondence, our county, and colonial conventions, were the authors of the domociliary viſits, and took care of the unfriendly printers and writers, until our governments were formed ; and then, laws duly made, prohibited, under the moſt ſevere penalties, the writing, printing, or ſpeaking, any thing againſt the independence of the United States, or in favour of the claims of the Britiſh King upon the American colonies.

HAD this been omitted, our country would have teemed with preſſes devoted to the Britiſh crown, and with artful mercenary writers, even native Americans, to diſtract our counſels, and to divide and diſunite our people.

———————✧———————

Twenty years ago my brother Bruce, on the lookout for rare manuscripts in France, turned up a Franklin document in the collection of a wealthy doctor in Paris. The mere news of its discovery exhilarated me, for it was the hitherto unknown original manuscript of *The Rules and Regulations of the Philadelphia Chess Club"* entirely in Franklin's hand and bearing his bold signature. From a photostatic copy, the document appeared to be authentic, and I was delighted when my brother persuaded the owner to send it to me.

Within a few days I was examining an excellent forgery. Aside from its technical defects, which were numerous, the parchment document was not mentioned in Franklin's *Autobiography,* nor was there any mention in Franklin's book on the chess club, nor of the secretary of the club, one Stephen Gorham. No more than a second was needed to determine the spurious nature of the *Rules.* The ink, the parchment, the writing, the signature—indeed, the whole of the document—proclaimed its true character. The French doctor accepted its return with good grace.

Two years ago one of America's most prominent philographers sat in my gallery and suddenly turned to me, announcing triumphantly: "I've just bought the finest Franklin document I've seen in years."

"What is it?" I asked.

"Nothing less than the original *Rules and Regulations of the Philadelphia Chess Club."*

Now, I can never remember a face or a telephone number, but I rarely forget a document, and my mind instantly

Forgery of a map of the Battle of Bunker Hill, dated May 4, 1775, about six weeks before the battle, suggesting that Clinton had planned the assault on the American fortifications far in advance. The signature of Clinton in the lower right is an extremely poor imitation and bears no similarity to Sir Henry's own swashbuckling and almost illegible scrawl. There are other forgeries similar to this on the philographic market, usually dolled up in elaborate and costly slip cases or sumptuous bindings.

bridged the nearly two decades since I had looked at the Franklin forgery. I gave my astonished visitor a full description of it, adding: "It is signed also by Stephen Gorham, is it not? And you know, Gorham is a Massachusetts name. There were no Gorhams in Philadelphia."

With a speed and dexterity that amazed me, my elderly visitor leaped to the telephone, called the bank and stopped payment on a check just issued to the owner of the forgery.

Sometimes when a forger gloms on to a good thing, he turns out a dozen or more examples for his credulous victims. Back in July, 1927, when Americana was booming in London, the British dealer Francis Edwards, of High Street, Marylebone, got stuck with a forgery of the British plan for the Battle of Bunker Hill. The noted bibliophile A. Edward Newton, in his collection of essays, *This Book-Collecting Game,* tells the tale just as he got it from Edwards. A mysterious stranger, on whom Newton appends the makeshift moniker of Crawford, approached Edwards with a list of very valuable books that Crawford's friend, an elderly clergyman in Melton Mowbray, wished to sell. As an afterthought Crawford whipped out a parchment map of Bunker Hill, doubtless the product of an American forger. While

Edwards was still hypnotized by the list of rare books, Crawford scored with the fake map. Here's the story as Edwards told it to Newton:

"Another matter, Mr. Edwards. I quite forgot. In going over some old papers that have been in my family since I don't know when, I came across a drawing of an old map which looks to me quite interesting: it seems to be a plan of a battle of some kind. It is signed 'H. Clinton, Major General,' and it is dated May 4, 1775," whereupon he handed Edwards a slightly torn and somewhat discolored plan of the Battle of Bunker Hill! By this time, with his mind still on the books, Edwards had his mind prepared for anything. Did Mr. Crawford wish to sell it? He did. And for how much? Mr. Crawford did not know. What would Mr. Edwards say to thirty guineas? Automatically Edwards's idea was twenty pounds—that would be quite satisfactory to Mr. Crawford. Mr. Edwards took from his pocket four five-pound notes—they would be better for Mr. Crawford's purpose than Mr. Edwards's check; he had a few small purchases to make—and Crawford departed.

Ten minutes later Mr. Edwards's manager came in and was shown the map. "What do you think of it?" said Edwards. "It looks too good to me; what did you pay for it?" "Twenty pounds." "Not enough—or too much." "That's what I think," said Edwards. "Put it away; it's a fake. Don't sell it: it's not worth a damn." A few days later the whole story came out.

The kind stranger, the friend of the old clergyman in Melton Mowbray, had a dozen such friends in different parts of England and in one day had disposed of a like number of such maps, all practically identical and all clumsy forgeries; but in order to work the ruse successfully the mind of the victim had to be carefully diverted from the fake map by the story of an old clergyman and his books. Mr. Edwards was the only bookseller I met who admitted being stung; all the others to whom I talked told me that one of their rivals had been the victim—the speaker, fortunately, had escaped by having his suspicions aroused.

This interesting forgery might have eluded exposure had not the forger overestimated the intelligence of his victims. The Battle of Bunker Hill, known to academicians as the Battle of Breed's Hill, was, as every schoolboy quickly forgets, fought on June 17, 1775, but this map was dated May 4, 1775. One critic noted that the map "is exposed by the date of May 4, 1775, which antedates the battle by six weeks," forgetting, perhaps, that battle plans are nearly always drawn up weeks in advance. There are still copies of this fascinating manuscript map in circulation, masquerading as originals.

Malefactors in pen and ink trip up for many reasons, but a unique blunder is visible in a forgery owned by the New York Public Library—Custer's last message, penned in desperation at the Little Big Horn to Major Reno: "For gods sake send help I am surrounded and cant break through I have only 40 troopers

left and cant hold out another minute. . . ." The message rattles on for
another three sentences. Custer was certainly guilty of an egregious military
blunder in attacking the Indians, who he
knew outnumbered him, but he would
never have compounded this error by
sending a flatulent, disjointed and unsyn-
tactical appeal for help. The forger, confident that the message would speak for
itself, added a few "blood stains" and
bullet holes, but apparently made no
effort to imitate Custer's handwriting.
Now, the really remarkable thing about
this document is that it was presumably
folded twice by the messenger of defeat
but has *only three holes* in it where it
was struck by a bullet. The missile
penetrated three of the folds but not the
fourth! Millionaire industrialist Owen
D. Young (for whose own career as a
forger see pp. 185–89) bought this blatantly spurious relic (as genuine) for
three hundred and fifty dollars and had
it enshrined in a silk-backed, velvet-
mounted levant case at an additional
cost of fifty dollars. The original message

Forgery of a handwritten Custer note from the
battlefield of the Little Big Horn. Notice the three
holes, indicating that the Indian bullet penetrated
three folds of the document but not the fourth!

George A. Custer. Authentic handwritten note,
signed.

of Custer, a masterpiece of brevity—"Big village. Come quick. Bring packs."—is preserved in the archives at West Point Military Academy.

Speaking of preposterous but delectable forgeries recalls to mind the witchcraft documents "signed" by Cotton Mather, of which there seem to be numerous copies and variants on the market. The last one to show up was offered by the world's biggest auction house but was withdrawn when its authenticity was questioned. It was an order for the execution of Martha Carrier as a witch, dated August 2, 1692: "Ye are herebye goven orders—to have ye wich Martha Carrier . . . conveighed to the green in the village of Salem—in Essex—in Massts—and cause said Martha to hange by her necke untill daid. . . ."

I recall another Mather order in which, carried away by his imagination, the forger had composed in faltering seventeenth-century English a death warrant for a witch and then placed upon it an astonishing juxtaposition of signatures. Not only Mather's (double its usual size) but those of Governor William Phips, William Stoughton, Increase Mather, the slightly demented president of Harvard, and King Philip, the noted Indian leader who could neither read nor write and had been slain sixteen years earlier. The Mather forgeries may easily be recognized because they are on thick, heavy paper and are stained with coffee, which lies in ripples over the page. Sometimes when I long for a cup of java, and there is none to be had, I reflect angrily on the awful waste

of about two cups per document perpetrated by the Mather forger.

Cast your eyes over the text of the latest Mather fake to come my way and you will see what can be accomplished by a rampant imagination:

Whereas Susana Martin—Wich—hath beene tride by this courte—settinge in a special session in the Meetinge howse in Salem . . . tryinge Wich Craff and hath been founden Giltie . . . of the crimes here in set fourth . . . she hath beene founde Giltie of holdinge diabolical sacramentes and aiding and abetinge Wiches and the causin of akes and paines to her kin and kindrede . . . she had killede some 40 odd fowles and severale swine and she had a devils teate on her left legg—and she did kutt the Indian Wench Pituba with an axx and many other things—all which is again the lawes of this province. . . . Therefore . . . at the houre of highe Sun—on 19th July 1692—ye shalt remove said Susana Martin outen the goal and safely conveighe her to the galowes on Exocution hill in the village of Salem and said Susana Martin—Wich—shall hange by her necke untill she is daid. . . .

Favorite targets of forgers are the presidents, and there is no president who has not, at one time or another, been the mark of the nimble-fingered gentry. Important war documents of Franklin D. Roosevelt on which the ink was barely dry were sold at auction several years ago for high prices. Fakes of George Washing-

Forgery of an order to execute a witch, Salem, 1692. Heavily stained with coffee, this bogus document bears forged signatures (lower right) of William Stoughton, Cotton Mather, Robert Calef and Samuel Sewall. Just above the seal at the lower left is the "mark" of King Philip.

William Stoughton. Authentic signature.

Cotton Mather. Authentic signature.

Robert Calef. Authentic signature.

King Philip. Authentic "mark."

Samuel Sewall. Authentic signature.

ton, most of them so badly executed that they are more risible than menacing, are offered to me every month. Rare documents of William Henry Harrison, signed during his one-month tenure of office, are so valuable they constantly tempt forgers. Even fakes of Coolidge, whose genuine letters are so abundant you could paper the whole State of Vermont with them, seem to attract fakers. But the prime target for inkpot villainy in recent years is John F. Kennedy, whose letters and signed books fetch astonishingly high prices.

In October, 1973, I was offered a whole sheaf of Kennedy papers, holograph notes for speeches and a few very interesting sketches. From a collector I learned something of their provenance. They originated in McLain, Virginia, in 1970, and were offered for sale by a man who "claimed to be friends with the Kennedy children, specifically RFK's children and told me the items were given him out of friendship. Besides the handwritten speeches there was a letter of RFK's to a congressman with a forged endorsement of JFK's at the bottom of the letter and an additional forged endorsement of RFK's below that. Also in the collection were two unsigned doodles . . . done by JFK.

"Several months later while on a short visit to the Thieves Market in Alexandria, Virginia, I was again offered the very same items by an antique toy dealer. I told the toy dealer that I believed the autographs were forged and that he should withdraw them from the market or send them to you for your opinion. He obviously did neither."

In July, 1974, a vendor mailed me two sketches of John F. Kennedy on scrimshaw. As usual with forgeries, they were accompanied by authentications, the first one of which was by Hans-Bernd Lubeck of the National Antiquitats-handler-Hat in Bohn. It was an impressive warrantee with several flashy seals, stating the pictures "were drawn by Mr. President John F. Kennedy of Amerika. This determination was reached after examining the ink. . . ." Present with the forgeries was a notarized statement by the owner that "these pictures, being personal gifts to me from President and Mrs. Kennedy, are hereby certified genuine due to their execution by Mr. Kennedy during November 1963." In another document, adorned with ribbons and a seal, the owner certified that "I assisted the Kennedy staff with personal and interpretation duties, and met the Kennedy family. . . . These two drawings were presented as a rememberance of this trip. . . . I do hereby certify that these drawings are true and genuine." A final statement issued by Paul Sichert in Hanover/Linden warranted that the drawings "being submitted to handwriting examinations, records, and historical data are hereby certified genuine by this organization."

The signature of Kennedy on the drawing on page 228 was based on the facsimile signature on the official engraving issued at Kennedy's inaugural. It is a curious signature, incidentally, and very unlike the signatures of Kennedy two years later in 1963.

The late Samuel Loveman, a seedily

dressed bookman who operated the Bodley Head Bookshop in New York City and who claimed to be one of Hart Crane's lovers, also dabbled in forgery. Most of his little tricks were innocuous. He got a supply of Crane's bookplates and pasted them in volumes likely to have been owned by the poet. Avoid them. Nearly every catalogue Loveman issued was filled with fabulous "bargains"—books signed by Melville, Mark Twain or Hawthorne—a whole galaxy of great authors, all priced at ten to twenty-five dollars each. The signatures were in pencil and were not, of course, genuine; but it was exciting to study his catalogue and pretend that such bargains really existed. Original sketches by Gauguin and Picasso abounded at ridiculously low prices. I owe many hours of innocent pleasure to Loveman. He was a poet of sorts and published several volumes of verse and, like many another who flirted with the Muses, died in a cheap nursing home. May the gods be kind to his spirit and put but few ink pots and pens on the chains it drags.

There are many active forgers today. In most cases I know their names. They have thus far eluded arrest, but I am always ready, with a little provocation and some fresh data, to go all out to catch them. Right now I am laying for the Florida forger who specializes in Robert Frost manuscript poems and Charles A. Lindbergh first-day covers. There is also a Canadian forger at work on Lindbergh, and if I can get the evidence I am searching for, he will find that the border between his country and mine offers sparse protection.

Then there's the scalawag in Alabama who is turning out "signed" photographs of Marilyn Monroe, Brigitt Bardot and Jayne Mansfield. And the New Jersey man who has pumped a lot of fake Hitler and other Nazi autographs on the market. Maybe he didn't forge them, as he claimed when I confronted him eye-to-eye with the evidence, but I am keeping a dossier on him, all the same. His is, in fact, one of a whole file drawer full of dossiers, any one of which could suddenly become alive by a mere telephone call from me to the police bunco squad or the United States postal inspector's office.

Practice sheet of a Washington forger. Judging from the quality of these imitations, the forger needed a great deal more practice before marketing his work.

Boston
June 1st 1778

Respected Gen!

Would you please
hand the bearer Mr Pearsons
my "Letters of Euier"
You are probably aware
that I left them at your house
when I called last November
With regards to thyself and spouse.
Your friend

Saml. Morris Sec'y.   *G Washington*

Forgery of a George Washington letter. An amateurish effort, reproduced in actual size, typical of many inept fakes that come on the philographic market and are peddled by uninformed antiques dealers or sold at country auctions.

George Washington. Authentic
signature, actual size.

Dear Brother Haveng Soe good an opper
tunity by Mr Frankleny I Could
Lett Slipe I inquier by all oppertuni
from you & am glad to hear you
& my Sister & Mrs Downman & his
Lady keeps your healths soe well
I some tims hear you intend in verg
ma once more I should be proud
to See you I have known a great
Seal of trouble Sinc I See you thear
was no end to my troble while
George was in the army butt he
has now given it up pray Give
my kind love to my Sister & Cozen
Downman & I am Dear Brother
your Loving and
                              affectinate Sister
July the 26 1759   Mary Washington

FORGERY
MS. & A.
NYPL

Forgery of a handwritten letter signed by Washington's mother, Mary. A rather skilled fake, possibly based upon an original letter of Mary Washington.

affectinat humble Servant
Mary Washington

Mary Washington. Authentic handwriting and signature.

Mount Vernon, Dec 23rd 1799

Mr J. H. Sears

Kind friend Mr John Dawson is here this morning and I will send by him the spring lancet that my husband was bled with the time of his death as he has said so often that he wanted you to have it and to keep it so long as you may live. And then give it to one of your sons and let him do like wise, this is the request of your troubled friend I will close hoping you will get the lancet comes as you may make convenient,

Your Friend.

Martha Washington

Forgery of a Martha Washington letter, authenticating a spring lancet allegedly used to bleed Washington during his final illness. Washington died only nine days before the date of this curious letter, in which little effort was made to imitate Martha's script. The lancet, *above*, was encased in an elaborate velvet box together with the "authentication."

Martha Washington. Authentic signature. Martha's writing and spelling was so atrocious that her husband frequently wrote and signed letters for her.

Many and pointed orders have been issued against that unmeaning and abominable custom of swearing, notwithstanding which, with much regret the General observes that it prevails, if possible, more than ever. His feelings are continually wounded by the oaths and imprecations of the soldiers whenever he is in hearing of them. The name of that Being from whose bountiful goodness we are permitted to exist and enjoy the comforts of life is incessantly imprecated and profaned in a manner as wanton as it is shocking. For the sake therefore of religion, decency, and order the General hopes and trusts that officers of every rank will use their influence and authority to check a vice which is as unprofitable as it is wicked and shameful. If officers would make it an invariable rule to reprimand and, if that does not do, punish soldiers for offences of this kind, it could not fail of having the desired effect.

G. Washington

Forgery of a handwritten order signed by George Washington. An inept imitation that utterly fails to capture the beauty and sweep of Washington's curvaceous script.

George Washington. Authentic handwriting and signature.

WASHINGTON AND HIS FORGERS

Mount Vernon 27th Octn 1798

G. Washington

George Washington. Authentic signature and date.

George Washington. Authentic signature and subscription.

*I am — Dear Sir
Your Obedt. Hble Serv*

G. Washington

Your very H.ble Servant
G. Washington

Charles Weisberg forgery.

Your most Obed.t Serv.t
G. Washington

Robert Spring forgery.

G. Washington

Unidentified forgery.

G. Washington
Com.?

Joseph Cosey forgery.

Forgery of a handwritten letter signed by Benjamin Franklin, Passy, 1778. A skillful counterfeit of Franklin's script and mode of expression, marred by the forger's failure to size the old paper so that the modern ink would not feather. The feathering of ink is one of the most obvious marks of a modern fake on old chain-lined paper.

Benjamin Franklin. Authentic signature.

Forgery of a signed, handwritten Lafayette letter in French. The writing is far more legible than Lafayette's and does not quite capture the "feel" of his script.

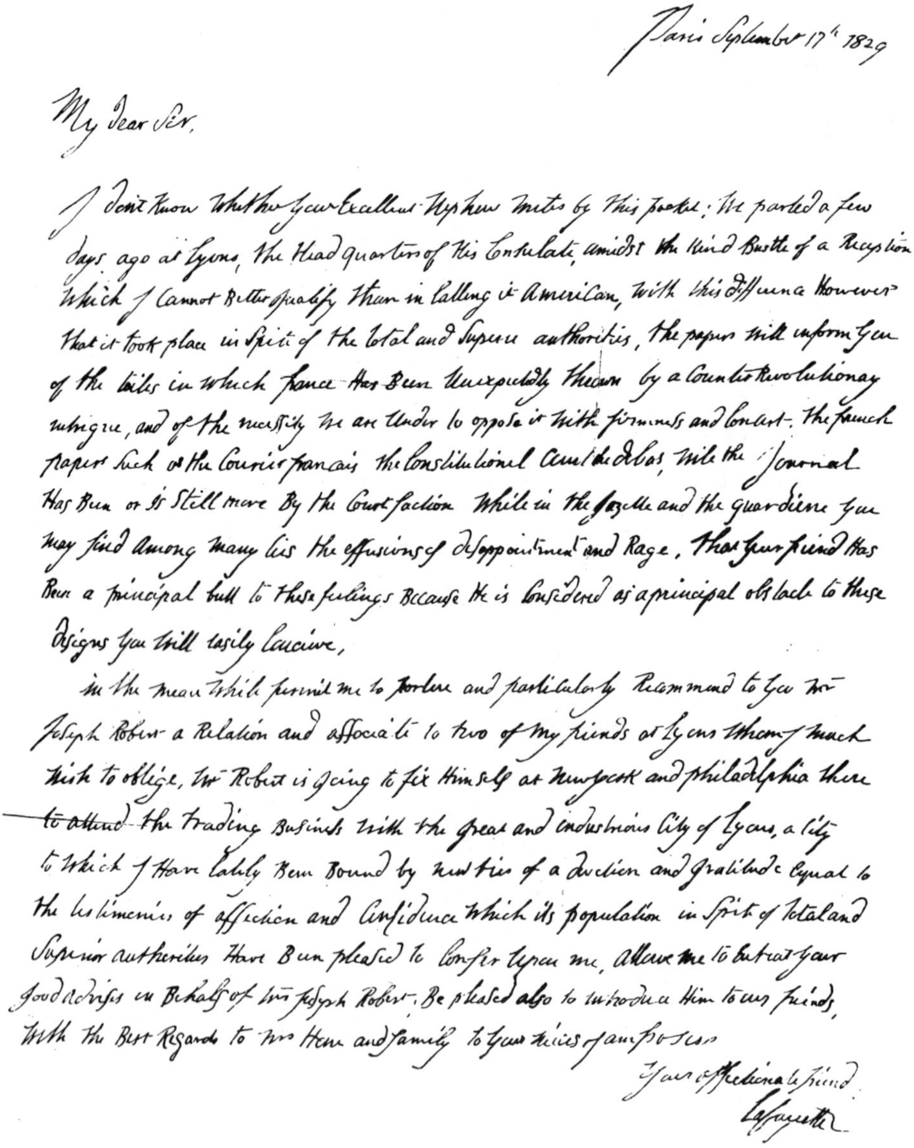

Paris September 17th 1829

My Dear Sir,

I don't know whether your Excellent Nephew writes by this packet: we parted a few days ago at Lyons, the Head Quarters of his Consulate, amidst the kind Bustle of a Reception which I cannot better qualify than in calling it American, with this difference however that it took place in spite of the Local and Superior authorities, the papers will inform you of the crisis in which France has been unexpectedly thrown by a Counter Revolutionary intrigue, and of the necessity we are under to oppose it with firmness and concert. The French papers such as the Courier français the Constitutionel and the Debats, while the Journal has been or is still more by the Court faction while in the Gazette and the Quotidienne you may find among many lies the effusions of disappointment and Rage. That your friend has been a principal butt to these feelings because he is considered as a principal obstacle to these designs you will easily conceive,

in the mean while permit me to introduce and particularly Recommend to you Mr Joseph Robert a Relation and associate to two of my friends at Lyons whom I much wish to oblige, Mr Robert is going to fix himself at New York and Philadelphia there ~~to attend~~ the trading business with the great and industrious City of Lyons, a City to which I have lately been bound by new ties of a devotion and gratitude equal to the testimonies of affection and Confidence which its population in spite of Local and Superior authorities have been pleased to confer upon me, allow me to entreat your good advices in behalf of Mr Joseph Robert. Be pleased also to introduce him to our friends, with the best Regards to Mrs Hone and family to your niece I am yours

Your affectionate friend
Lafayette

Forgery of a handwritten, signed Lafayette letter in English. The penmanship is shaky and seems drawn rather than written. It's possible that this fake is by Robert Spring, as it shows the care and attention he gave to details yet lacks chirographic virtuosity.

Lafayette. Authentic signed, hand-written note in French.

Lafayette. Authentic signed, handwritten letter in English.

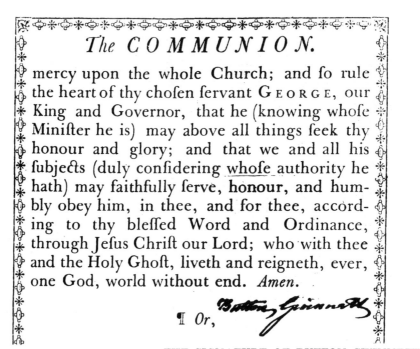

THE SIGNATURE OF BUTTON GWINNETT

210 GWINNETT, BUTTON. A leaf from the Book of Common Prayer, with the autograph of the Signer from Georgia.

THE CORNERSTONE AUTOGRAPH OF THE SIGNERS OF THE DECLARATION OF INDEPENDENCE. Written on the upper half of leaf T2 of the Baskerville 1760 edition of the Book of Common Prayer.

With a certificate of authenticity by Albert D. Osborn, reading as follows: "*After a careful comparison of this signature on this half sheet of paper with the genuine signatures of Button Gwinnett, it is my best judgment that this is a genuine signature of Button Gwinnett . . .*"

Together with other related documents and photos.

Button Gwinnett. Authentic signature from the Declaration of Independence.

Forgery of Button Gwinnett's signature on the page of an old prayer book, with a description of the volume from the June 25, 1938, sale of the American Art Association in New York. This fake, done with great care by a skilled forger, was authenticated by the noted expert Albert D. Osborn and, if genuine, would have sold for many thousands of dollars. Some of the defects are the downward curl of the *n* in *Button* and the crowding together of the first and second names. In the case of an extremely valuable signature, when the determination of authenticity hangs upon small details with only two words to go on, a single tiny mistake can condemn a forgery.

Forgery of a Button Gwinnett signature (third line from top) in an authentic old account book, about 1770. Notice that in "canceling" the name with a large *X* the forger was careful not to put the criss-cross cancellation through his forgery of Gwinnett's signature.

Forgery of a rare handwritten letter signed by Thomas Lynch, Jr., signer of the Declaration of Independence. Only one authentic handwritten Lynch letter is known to exist. In 1860 a forger named James W. Turner of Washington, D.C., turned out several holograph Lynch letters that he offered for sale at twenty-five dollars each, at that time a very high price for an autograph. This is possibly one of his products.

Forgery of a signature of Thomas Lynch, Jr., similar to the examples cut from Lynch's books.

Thomas Lynch, Jr. Conclusion of a signed, handwritten letter to George Washington, 1777. Lynch's own script is not so legible as that of the forger, who has erred on the side of clarity, a common fault with the scalawags who fake historical and literary documents.

Forgery of a Daniel Boone signature on an authentic document, 1799. It is a common practice of forgers to add a rare signature to an authentic old paper, usually as a witness or partner in a venture.

Daniel Boone. Authentic signature on a letter, 1782. Boone's autographs are rare and valuable and frequently tempt forgers.

Warshington November 28th 1831

I hereby appoint William Donnelly to be Keeper of the ——— Light House ——— at Sapelo Island Ga ——— The duties of which Office he will perform until further notice

Andrew Jackson

By the President

Louis McLane

Secretary of the Treasury

Forgery of a document signed by President Andrew Jackson, 1831, with the countersignature of Louis McLane.

Andrew Jackson. Authentic signature as president.

Louis McLane. Authentic signature.

Forgery of Zachary Taylor's signature from a fabricated document. The signature is shaky and too rounded to be an accurate imitation, but the forger has caught the thick, heavy strokes characteristic of Taylor's writing.

Zachary Taylor. Authentic signature.

Forgery of a handwritten note signed by William Henry Harrison as president. Harrison was president for only one month and was ill in bed for most of that period. His autographs as president are of great rarity and command enormous prices. The forger of this note has cleverly placed it on a genuine letter cover addressed to the president, but there is no way to date the cover. The flourish on the terminal *n* of Harrison's name betrays the forger's touch.

Forgery of Winfield Scott's signature from a faked document of the Mexican War period. Probably by the same forger as the Zachary Taylor, but not as accurate or as deceptive as the Taylor.

Winfield Scott. Authentic handwriting and signature.

Forgery of a signature of William Henry Harrison on a letter dated March 22, 1841, during Harrison's one month as president. If genuine this letter would be valued at many thousands of dollars. An excellent forgery of Harrison, but at this period, only about a week before his death, Harrison's illness was far advanced, and he wrote only with great difficulty and in a very quavery hand.

William Henry Harrison. Authentic signature as president.

New York City,
June 14th 1883.

Dear Sir:

Your letter of the 13th of May, inclosed to me by General Longstreet in which you ask a few words from me in regard to my estimate of the late Honorable Alexander A. Stevens, reached my office during my absence in the west. Since that time I have

Henry W. Cleveland. First page of a forged handwritten U. S. Grant letter, addressed to Cleveland. An excellent imitation of Grant's script. Cleveland will be recalled as the forger whose clever fabrications of Lincoln (1867) took in most of his contemporaries and were printed by Lincoln's secretaries in their standard biography of Lincoln. This forgery was probably executed about 1886.

afraid to speak his honest convictions without regard to whether they would be popularly received or not. To the day of his death I retained the high estimate of his life and character that I had formed before I knew him, increased by a personal acquaintance.

Very Truly Yours

U. S. Grant

Rev. H. W. Cleveland
Atlanta Ga

Henry W. Cleveland. Last page of a forged handwritten letter signed by U. S. Grant. The main defect in this forgery is Cleveland's inability to improvise the concise and vigorous style of Grant, which Mark Twain compared to Caesar's swift, powerful prose. Note that the flourish which crosses the *t* in Grant's signature is slightly tremulous. The letter, a eulogy of Confederate Vice President Alexander H. Stephens, alludes to Stephens as "Alexander *A. Stevens*" and later as both *Stevens* and *Stephens,* a spelling blunder of which Grant was incapable.

U. S. Grant. Last two pages of an authentic signed, handwritten letter.

U.S.S. SANTA FE

January 22, 1907.

My dear Mr. Secretary:

    In reference to Bagoon's two letters of the 13th and 16th, which are returned herewith, I need hardly add to what I said this morning. There can be no talk of a protectorate by us . Our business is to establish peace and order on a satisfactory basis, start the new Govenment, and then leave the Island; though of course it might be advisable for some little time that some of our troops should stay in the Islands to steady things. I will not even consider the plan of a protectorate, or any plan which would imply our breaking our explicit promise because of which we were able to prevent a war of devistation last fall. The good faith of the United States is a mighty valuable asset and must not be impaired.

          Sincerely yours,

          Theodore Roosevelt.

          THEODORE ROOSEVELT.

Hon. Wm. H. Taft,
Secretary of War.

NAVY DEPARTMENT
U. S. S. SANTA FE

San Francisco, Calif.

OFFICIAL BUSINESS

Forgery of a letter signed by Theodore Roosevelt to William Howard Taft, January 22, 1907. The forger obviously acquired some authentic, official rubber stamps, plus some early stationery of the U.S.S. *Santa Fe,* and then created a group of Theodore Roosevelt letters, many with important contents. This is one of more than a dozen such letters. The signature on this, as on the other forgeries, is a very poor imitation.

THE HOUSE No. 118 North 12th Street is hereby let to and taken by Mr. E. A. Poe from Richmond, Virginia for one month and thereafter, from month to month — until either party shall have given One months notice to the other before the end of any quarter at the rent of Twenty — dollars per month

Philadelphia, April 1, 18 38

Edgar Allan Poe
James Pedder

Forgery of a partly printed document signed by Edgar Allan Poe. This document was written and signed in tobacco juice.

Edgar Allan Poe. Handwritten signed stanza from "The Raven."

And the Raven, never flitting, still is sitting — still is sitting
On the pallid bust of Pallas just above my chamber door;
And his eyes have all the seeming of a demon's that is dreaming,
And the lamp-light o'er him streaming throws his shadow on the floor;
And my soul from out that shadow that lies floating on the floor
            Shall be lifted —— nevermore.

Edgar A. Poe.

Forgery of a handwritten letter signed by Mark Twain, 1876. If the writing did not betray this fake, which it certainly does, the stumbling expressions and punctured prose would give it away.

Always acknowledge a fault
frankly. This will throw those
in authority off their guard
& give you opportunity to commit more.

Yr truly
Saml L Clemens
Mark Twain

July '77.

Mark Twain. Authentic handwritten quotation,
signed, 1875.

Hartford, Feb. 26.

Gentlemen:
I am not so sit-
uated as to be able to
sell the Jumping Frog,
because I am just on
the point of issuing it
in book form through
my publishers here
along with all
my sketches complete
Very Truly Yrs.
Saml L. Clemens
Mess. Warren Choate & Co
Washington.

Mark Twain. Authentic signed, handwritten letter, about 1875.

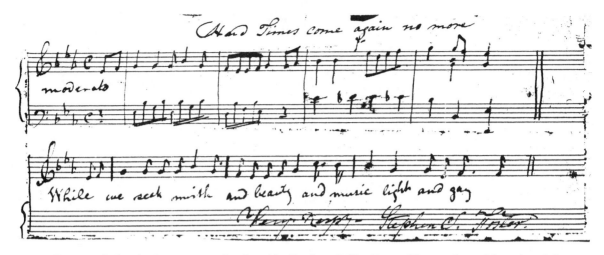

Forgery of a handwritten manuscript signed by Stephen Collins Foster. The words are labored, and the lines of the text weave up and down, indicating the forger's intense concentration on the formation of words or even individual letters of words. There is no matching between the musical notes and the words, which shows that the forger was not acquainted with music. The words and signature lack the liquidity and fluency of Foster's beautiful script. It is possible that this forgery was done by Charles Weisberg, who is said to have sold many of his fakes to the Foster Hall Collection at the University of Pittsburgh. The curator of the Foster Hall Collection, Fletcher Hodges, Jr., opined in a letter dated July 21, 1961, that "The words on this score are written in Stephen Foster's own hand" and "The music itself is not in Stephen's hand," adding, "I am at a loss to explain this situation. . . ."

Stephen Collins Foster. Authentic handwritten manuscript. Notice Foster's beautiful cursive script and the swift, precise way he forms his musical notes. The words are skillfully coordinated with the musical notes.

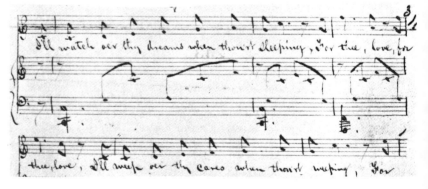

Stephen Collins Foster. Authentic signature. This example is not as flamboyant and handsome as his usual signature.

Stopping by Woods on a Snowy Evening
Whose woods these are I think I know.
His house is in the village though.
He will not see me stopping here
To watch his woods fill up with snow

My little horse must think it queer
To stop without a farmhouse near
Between the woods and frozen lake
The darkest evening of the year

He gives his harness bells a shake
To ask if there is some mistake
The only other sound's the sweep
Of easy wind and downy flake.

The woods are lovely dark and deep.
But I have promises to keep,
And miles to go before I sleep—
And miles to go before I sleep.

Robert Frost

Florida forger. Freehand fabrication of Frost's celebrated poem "Stopping by Woods on a Snowy Evening." A skillful forgery by a man who specializes in faking Frost and Lindbergh. There is little to fault in this superb imitation. It would be easy to point out that the words and lines in the fake should be spaced a little farther apart, but the fact is that Frost himself often crowds his words and lines.

Stopping by Woods on a Snowy Evening
Whose woods these are I think I know.
His house is in the village though.
He will not see me stopping here
To watch his woods fill up with snow.

My little horse must think it queer
To stop without a farmhouse near
Between the woods and frozen lake
The darkest evening of the year.

He gives the harness bells a shake
To ask if there is some mistake.
The only other sound's the sweep
Of easy wind and downy flake.

The woods are lovely dark and deep.
But I have promises to keep,
And miles to go before I sleep
And miles to go before I sleep.

Robert Frost

For Louise Nicholl.

Robert Frost. Authentic handwritten manuscript, signed, of "Stopping by Woods on a Snowy Evening." Note the personlized touch at the lower left, characteristic of nearly all the poems which the poet copied out for admirers.

Forgery of Charles A. Lindbergh's signature on an
airmail cover.

Another Lindbergh forgery, on a commemorative
cover.

Forgery of Charles A. Lindbergh's signature on a first-day cover.

Charles A. Lindbergh. Authentic signature.

Forgery of Charles A. Lindbergh's signature on an airmail cover. A very poor imitation. The script is too large and the letters of the signature are incorrectly formed.

Charles A. Lindbergh. Authentic signature.

ADOLF HITLER
PRIVATKANZLEI

BERLIN W 35
FRIEDRICH-WILHELMSTR.13
FERNRUF: 12 76 01

DEN 9.Mai.1937

TAGEBUCH-Nr. AZD/378
BEI RÜCKFRAGEN UNBEDINGT ANZUGEBEN

Doktor Hugo Eckener !
    Die Art der Geschehniße in den letzten zwei Tagen macht es
unumgänglich, daß Sie sofort nach Berlin kommen.
    Ihre Anwesenheit ist erforderlich bei der Besprechung einer
gründlichen Untersuchung, die anlässlich der Explosion des Luft-
schiffs Hindenburg eingelitet werden soll.
    Es handelt sich um den Tod, den Ihr Nachfolger, Kapitän
Ernst Lehmann, in diesem unerklärlichen, tragischen Unglück gefun-
den hat.

Der Führer und Reichskanzler

ADOLF HITLER
PRIVATKANZLEI

BERLIN W 35
FRIEDRICH-WILHELMSTR.13
FERNRUF: 12 76 01

DEN 13.Mai 1937

TAGEBUCH-Nr. AZD/495
BEI RÜCKFRAGEN UNBEDINGT ANZUGEBEN

Sehr geehrte Frau Kapitän Lehmann !

    Im Namen des Deutschen Volkes drück ich Ihnen tiefstes
Beileid darüber aus, daß eine so ausgezeichnete Laufbahn wie
die des Kapitäns Lehmann nach so vielen vorangegangenen, für
das Vaterland bestandenen Gefahren zu Ende kommen mußte.

Der Führer und Reichskanzler

Two forgeries of letters signed by Adolf Hitler. The forger first fabricated Hitler's signature, then *printed* it simultaneously with Hitler's personal letterhead on many sheets of paper, later filling in the text between the letterhead and the signature. He could write as many different texts as he had printed sheets. An unusual method of forgery. This fake may have originated in New Jersey.

Adolf Hitler. Authentic signature.

Forgery of a drawing and signature of John F. Kennedy. The signature, which purports to be from 1963, is in fact an imitation of the facsimile signature used on the inaugural program. By 1963 Kennedy's signature had altered dramatically and was totally different from the signature on this fake.

John F. Kennedy. Authentic signature, 1963.

and of the Independence of the United States the One Hundred and Eighty-seventh.

By the President:

Sincerely,

John F. Kennedy. Authentic signature, 1963.

Forgery of some holograph notes and a sketch by
John F. Kennedy. A crude effort.

Authentic handwriting of Kennedy as president.

17

Frivolous Fakes

Once in a while a forger uses his art to perk up a listless world. Edgar Allan Poe fabricated a few delectable epistles in his essay on autography, including one that ridiculed the redundant prose of a literary competitor. "I am exceedingly and excessively sorry that it is out of my power to comply with your rational and reasonable request," began a letter created by Poe and attributed to his rival. It might have amused and delighted Poe to know that only twenty-eight years after his death another poet, unable to get his verses published, pulled a Chatterton and forged an "original" poem by Poe. The poet was James Whitcomb Riley. On July 23, 1877, Riley proposed his hoax to the editor of the Kokomo [Indiana] dispatch:

>   . . . This idea has been haunting me:—I will prepare a poem—carefully imitating the style of some popular American poet deceased, and you may *"give it to the world for the first time"* thro' the columns of your paper,—prefacing it, in some ingenious man-

ner, with the assertion that the *original* M.S. was found in the album of an old lady living in your town— and in the handwriting of the poet imitated—together with signature etc. etc.—You can fix the story. . . . If we succeed . . . we will then . . . bust our literary bladder before a bewildered and enlightened world. . . .

>   Should you fall in with the plan, write me at once, and I will prepare and send the poem in time for your issue of this week. . . .

The editor, J. O. Henderson, approved Riley's scheme: ". . . Your idea is a capital one and is cunningly conceived. I assure you that I 'tumble' to it with eagerness. . . ."

Riley composed a four-stanza poem called "Leonainie," in the gloomy and mystical style of Poe. Riley then "discovered" the poem, which, after wide publicity and many printings, was (to satisfy doubters) forged in pen and ink into an old book by Riley's friend Samuel Richards. The forgery does not look much like Poe's handwriting, but it apparently put the quietus on at least a few critics.

Riley's poem was a pretty awful bit of verse, like many of Poe's own morbid excursions into alliteration and assonance. In a fascinating article on Riley published in *Manuscripts* (Spring, 1965), William R. Cagle, Lilly librarian at Indiana University, told the story behind Riley's poem and quoted the poem in full. A single saccharine stanza will suffice here:

Leonainie. Angels named her,
And they took the light
Of the laughing stars and framed her
In a smile of white:
And they made her hair of gloomy
Midnight, and her eyes of bloomy
Moonshine, and they brought her to me
In the solemn night.

The soporific rhymes continue with more pathetic fallacies and infelicitous metaphors ending when "God smiled" and "my Leonainie drifted from me like a dream."

Riley's dribble of doggerel won wide acclaim, and Edmund Clarence Stedman,

Forgery of Riley's faked poem by Poe, written on a blank leaf in an old book by Riley's friend Samuel Richards. Despite the show-through and the fading of the ink, it is possible to discern the inferior quality of the forgery, which fails utterly to capture the exquisite beauty of Poe's script.

And the Raven, never flitting, still is sitting — still is sitting
On the pallid bust of Pallas just above my chamber door,
And his eyes have all the seeming of a demon that is dreaming,
And the lamp-light o'er him streaming throws his shadow on
the floor,
And my soul from out that shadow that lies floating on the floor
Shall be lifted — nevermore.

Edgar Allan Poe. Authentic signed, handwritten stanza from "The Raven."

who never learned to distinguish jingles from poetry, gave it such accolades that Riley promptly announced his authorship and was launched on a poetic career that eventually netted him over three million dollars.

The puckish poet of childhood, Eugene Field, was an expert at calligraphy and often uncovered "ancient manuscripts," verses which he wrote himself in imitation of Middle English. These he printed with mock seriousness in *The Chicago News.* Both the script and the language were convincing enough to deceive many amateur scholars. Field pulled off his most ambitious hoax in 1888, when he "turned up" a parchment folio that purported to be a manuscript volume discovered by Colonel John C. Shadwell, "a wealthy and aristocratic contractor," while laying sewer pipes in the cellar of a deserted old residence at 1423 Michigan Street, Chicago, an address that would have put the house somewhere in Lake Michigan. The colonel presented "The Shadwell Folio" to "The Ballad and Broadside Society of Cook County, Illinois, for the Discovery of Ancient Manuscripts and for the Dissemination of Culture (limited)." The society at once adopted a series of resolutions commemorating the gift, including, "That we hail with pride these indisputable proofs that our refinement and culture had an ancestry, and that our present civilization did not spring, as ribald scoffers have alleged, mushroom-like from the sties and wallows of the prairies." In reviewing the spurious folio in his column, Field pointed out that not all the poems in the old parch-

A brace of facetious forgers. Eugene Field (seated) and James Whitcomb Riley.

ment volume were "purely local; quite a number treat of historical subjects." One of his own favorites was "The Alliaunce," which affords "a pleasant glimpse of the rare old time." The first and last stanzas read:

Come hither, gossip, let us sit
　　beneath this plaisaunt vine;
I fain wolde counsel thee a bit
　　whiles that we sip our wine.

•

Sic stout and brave a sone as mine
  I lay youle never see
And theres nae huskier wench than
    thine—
  Saye, neighbor, shall it bee?

Other poems in "The Shadwell Folio"
included "Ye Crewel Sassinger Mill,"
"The Texas Steere," "A Vallentine,"
"Ailsie, My Bairn," "Ye Morris Daunce,"

"Ye Battaile Aux Dames," "How Trewe
Love Won Ye Battel" and "Lollaby."

Among the pleasant and harmless
forgeries of the world are handwritten
messages from the spirit world, penned
by mediums who presumably contact
the dead. I once owned a splendid one-
page sheet bearing "spirit signatures" of
Washington, Jefferson, Hancock, Madison, Monroe and others, with a man-

Eugene Field. A quaint imitation, "The Alliaunce," by the poet, of an early English ballad.

Emancipation! Emancipation! Emancipation!

G.[?]*Washington.*

Th. Jefferson.

John Hancock.

Steph. Hopkins.

H. Clay.

Dan¹ Webster.

John Adams.

John Quincy Adams.

James Madison.

James Monroe.

Andrew Jackson.

Roger Sherman

uscript note, "From the 5th Sphere. G. Foster, Medium." A number of other such quaint impositions on mortal credulity have come my way in the past. It would appear that once a person becomes disembodied, his penmanship suffers a change into something rich and strange. Spirit signatures are usually tremulous and very unlike the writer's script in his mortal state.

One of the most hilarious fakes ever produced by mortal impudence was the

number 1 moomuch Street
Penalloy
September forth 1820

Sur
Wil you playe reed this.
Here as been found
heer a curus boc with
a ole buk in it wore
tuk by me an mi mate
bil Winch wile we wus
trouling of the corlby
hed it is rote on in ole
leters an got pitchers in
it that as ships as wudnot
sale an we cannt tel wot
it is the thule maister
he say as it is very
ole an beelonged to
culumbuss an is is loys

an as discovered merika
but we dunt num on
us Hole wiff eddecashun
an wee thinz ze ze larbin
but mester zumon thats
our Karpenter say as for no
all abot them thinks an
we treat us fare i have
send the think to you be
the have an me an tone
make wud bee parktiler
obliged if you wud tel
us wot if is if it is went
anuthink pleas send us a
triffle for it
I remane
Jonas Cokes
for Mister Elyacht Stok
Lundun—

Humorous forgery of a handwritten letter by one Jonas Cokes, alleged discoverer of Columbus's lost logbook. Cokes, in this first page of his letter, describes how "it were tuk by me an mi mate bil Winch wile we was trowling. . . ."

Second page of Jonas Cokes's letter about finding Columbus's lost logbook.

duplicate logbook of Columbus's first voyage, pitched into the sea in the hope it would be washed safely ashore, so the story goes, during a raging storm which threatened to capsize the tiny *Santa Maria*. The logbook was picked up a great many years later by a trawling fisherman, who wrote: "There as been found heer a curus box with a old buk in it it were tuk by me wile we was trowling. . . ."

Encrusted with seashells, this ancient document, entitled "My secrete Log Boke," was conveniently adorned with modern illustrations and penned in a bastard Elizabethan English. Columbus must have written a number of "duplicates," because this odd forgery turns up

Parchment cover of the "Log Boke" of Columbus, bearing an imitation of his signature and covered with glued-on shells and kelp.

Christopher Columbus. Authentic signature.

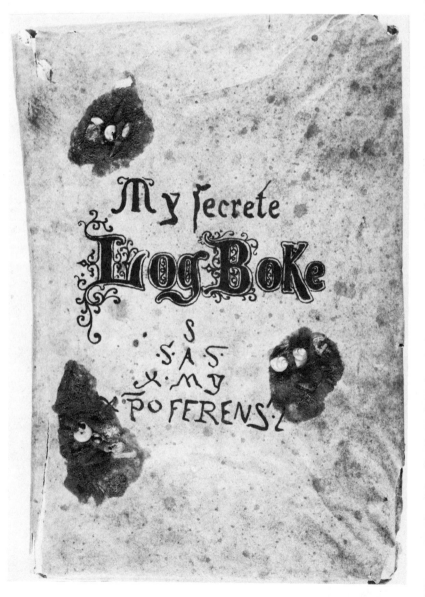

Two illustrated pages from the humorous Columbus logbook, meticulously printed in an imitation of Elizabethan English.

DOÑA ISABEL POR GRACIA DE DIOS REINA DE CASTILLA Y LEON ETCETE A DON CRISTÓBAL COLON DE GÉNOVA

Muy Señor Nuefo. Debe affigarnos mucho q intentábades defarnos fin faberlo Nos; fin embargo de q hazíamos favor tãto á vos como á vuefa emprefa. Eftábamos pues ya para acordaros los medios neceffarios a vuefa emprefa; y concedidas todas las condiciones eftipuladas por vos. Pues para evitar la opoficion de Nuefo juzgado y de las Cortes; aun eftábamos para empeñar las joyas de Nuefa corona á fin de procuraros los dichos medios. Pero nuefo teforo Don Luis de Sant Angel Nos ha afirmado; q él mifmo ya ha recogido los medios para aquefta emprefa. Por lo cual os acordamos los medios neceffarios nombrándoos Nuefo Virey Almirante y Eftañador general de todas las iftas y paifes q ferán defcubiertos por vos difpute á cien leguas á poniente de las Açores y del Cabo verde junto cõ el Xino de los recibos q aportarán las nuevas vias de comercio; afí para vos como para vuefos defcendientes. Todo aquefto os acordamos bajo de Nuefa palabra de Reyna y con Nuefo fello real.

Granada á trece de abril de MCCCCXCI.

Humorous forgery of a letter of Queen Isabella the Catholic to Columbus, written in modern Spanish and offering to pawn her jewels to raise money for his expedition.

Queen Isabella. Authentic signature, "Yo la reyna" (I the Queen), on a portion of a genuine document of her reign.

every now and then and is always treasured by its owners as a conversation piece. Usually accompanying the logbook is a letter to Columbus from Queen Isabella, penned in modern Spanish, in which the queen offers to pawn her jewels to raise money for Columbus's expedition. Dated 1492, this quaint epistle bears a handsome ornamental initial and an impressive seal.

It is always great fun to fool an expert, and Dr. Randolph G. Adams, head of the famed Clements Library at the University of Michigan, was once the target for a forgery so preposterous that it moved into the realm of the believable. Adams was one of the smartest literary detectives of his era, forever prying into new plots to disrupt scholarship. His mind and his tongue were equally sharp. Once, at a cocktail party of the sort which all sensible men avoid, Adams was tailed by an admiring dowager, who, at every bon mot uttered by the great man, exclaimed: "Oh, professor!" At last the peppery historian could tolerate this unwanted adulation no longer. He turned to his adoring pursuer and snapped: "Madam, a *professor* is a guy who plays the piano in a whorehouse." To fox this clever scholar was the pleasant task undertaken by Adams's assistant, Howard H. Peckham, then at work on his monumental biography of the Ottawa chieftain, Pontiac.

Aware that Adams's knowledge of the Ottawa tongue was limited to one word, Pontiac's Indian name Obwandiyag, Peckham devised an elaborate prank. He recalls:

Around the Clements Library we had bits of blank eighteenth-century paper, and I owned a printing press that was a couple of steps above a toy. I don't know how I happened to think of trying to print a bookplate for Chief Pontiac in the Ottawa language. I called my colleague the late Emerson Greenman, at the Museum of Anthropology, and asked him what the translation of "his book" or "ex libris" would be in Ottawa. Greenman was a specialist in the Indians of Michigan, but he was stumped. However, he called me back and said he had worked over a couple of words that could be translated "from his bookcase." That was good enough for me. I explained that I was going to fool Adams, who would probably call him after he saw my product.

So far, so good. I printed a few bookplates on authentic paper. "Ogima" is the Ottawa word for chief. The next step was taken when Forest H. Sweet, the autograph dealer from Battle Creek, called on Adams, as he did frequently. I showed the hoax to Sweet and asked him simply to show it to Adams as something he had found in some old Michigan papers he had bought, and ask Adams to tell him what it was.

Sweet tossed the bookplate on Adams's desk with a brief word of explanation. Adams studied it, held it up to the light to see the chain lines in the paper, and told Sweet it had something to do with Pontiac. He asked me if I knew what the words

Authentic Ojibway pictographs with translations, showing how the Indians sent messages to attend a religious powwow.

 medicine house

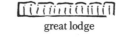 great lodge

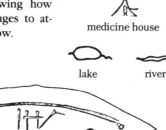 wigwam; woods

lake river canoe come Great Spirit

Howard Peckham.

Forgery of an American Indian (Ojibway) clay tablet "found" in Montcalm County, Michigan. The inscriptions evidently portray the flood, Noah's ark and the landing on Mount Ararat. This curious and romantic fake was doubtless inspired by the theory, advanced more than a hundred years ago, that there is a "great flood" myth in the religious lore of all peoples of every continent.

Pontiac's bookplate.

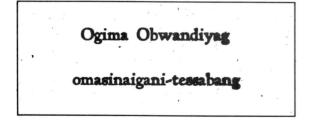

Ogima Obwandiyag

omasinaigani-tessabang

meant. I said I thought Ogima meant chief, but I didn't know the other words.

"It must be something a Detroit trader had printed for him," I suggested. "Why don't you call Greenman. He knows Ottawa and Chippewa."

Adams picked up the phone and got Greenman. He spelled out the words for him. There was a long pause while Greenman presumably was looking for a dictionary, then he gave Adams the translation.

"My God!" Adams exploded. "It's his bookplate!"

Sweet couldn't keep a straight face as Adams hung up. I began to laugh, too. Adams looked at us suspiciously.

"It's not unique," I said and held up another one. The jig was up and Adams began to enjoy it, too.

Six years later, in 1950, the Pontiac forgery achieved what Howard Peckham modestly calls "a dubious fame" when it was exhibited in a collection of fakes at the Library of Congress.

One of the most artful of amateur forgers was Mark Twain.* He knew the worth of minute details and never copped out on the fine points. And he could mimic any script, humble or elegant. You may recall the scene in *Tom Sawyer* where Tom and Huck Finn accidentally witness the moonlight murder of Dr. Robinson by Injun Joe. The two frightened boys took a blood oath to hold secret their knowledge of the murder. Tom pulled a fragment of red keel from his pocket and scrawled on a pine shingle a fearsome contract, afterward signed by each youth in his own blood.

Mark Twain was fascinated by chirography and could, when he wished, indite an epistle in Spencerian flourishes. I once saw a letter by the youthful Twain to Longfellow written in so sweet and flowing a hand that it looked like a penmanship exercise on copper plate. The humorist had dressed up his rugged,

Mark Twain. Blood-oath scrawled in red chalk by Tom Sawyer.

"Huck Finn and Tom Sawyer swears they will keep mum about this and they wish they may drop down dead in their tracks if they ever tell and Rot."

---

*Pages 241–44 contain material from *The Adventures of Tom Sawyer* and *Roughing It* by Mark Twain. Reprinted by permission of Harper & Row, Publishers, Inc.

Mark Twain (S. L. Clemens).

everyday scrawl to pay obeisance to the great poet. In *Roughing It* Mark provided an elegant frame in his Sunday-go-to-meeting script for a crude Indian mark that, observed the humorist, "looked like a cross that had been drunk a year."

The zenith of Twain's pen-and-ink spoofing came in 1871, when he created a Horace Greeley letter, actually an inspired burlesque of a note written to Twain by the peppery editor. Greeley's handwriting was already renowned for its illegibility. One rival editor had quipped: "If Belshazzar had seen Greeley's handwriting on the wall he would have been a good deal more frightened than he was." And there's an old tale still current among grizzled reporters that Greeley once scribbled a curt message to an employee discharging him for incompetence and the man afterward used the note as a letter of recommendation.

In May, 1871, while in the midst of writing *Roughing It,* Twain received an unsolicited letter from Greeley. The editor's baffling script delighted Twain, and he promptly invented a fresh episode for his book-in-progress that included a spurious Greeley letter. Twain's imitation, reproduced in facsimile in his book, captured perfectly the spastic lunacy of Horace's hen scratches.

Here is a summary of Twain's yarn

Mark Twain. Humorous forgery of the "mark" of Wah-ho-no-pah, an Indian. Note the handsome script in which Twain penned the Indian's name.

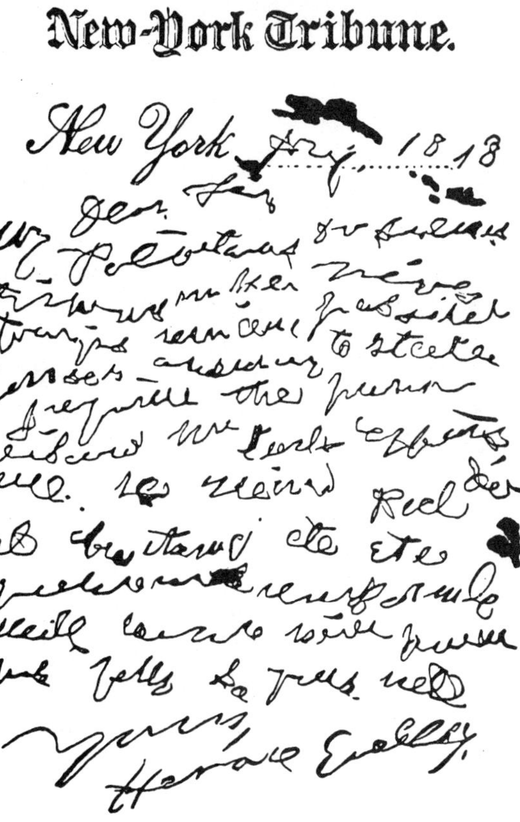
New-York Tribune.

Mark Twain. Humorous forgery of a Horace Greeley letter.

about the Greeley letter: During his travels Twain ran into a preacher from Michigan who said he had held a correspondence with Greeley that was "the talk of the world." It appears that a widow from Kansas had a son who was obsessed by turnips. He ate and talked and studied turnips until "the bloom forsook his cheek," at which point the widow appealed to the minister for aid. The reverend wrote for advice to Greeley and received a reply that he found very difficult to decipher. But he finally made it out:

Polygamy dissembles majesty; extracts redeem polarity; causes hither-

Horace Greeley. Authentic signed, handwritten letter to Mark Twain, New York, May, 1871. This curious letter, addressed to "Mark," served as a model and inspiration for Twain's famous spoof of Greeley's handwriting in *Roughing It* (1871). Horace's letter reads: "Mark: Sir, You are mistaken as to my criticisms on your farming. I never publicly made any, while you have undertaken to tell the exact cost per pint of my potatoes and cabbages, truly enough the inspiration of genius. If you will really betake yourself to farming, or even to telling what you know about it, rather than that you don't know about mine, I will not only refrain from disparaging criticism, but will give you my blessing."

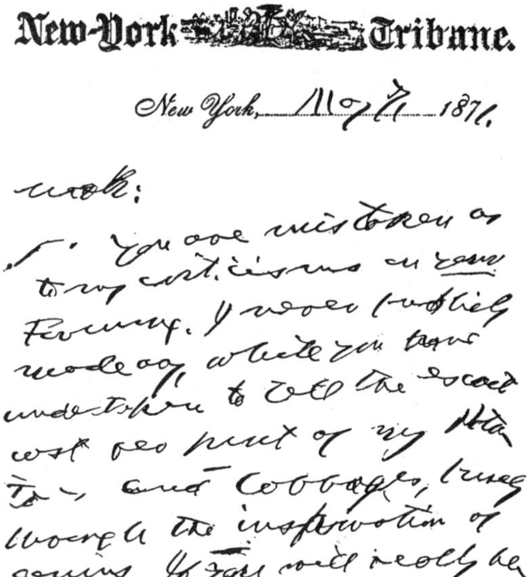
New-York Tribune.

New York,

to exist. Ovations pursue wisdom, or warts inherit and condemn. Boston, botany, cakes, felony undertakes, but who shall allay? We fear not.

Yrxwly,

HEVACE EVEELOJ.

However, after more thought, the clergyman worked the letter over again the following morning, and although the language was still eccentric and avoided the issue, it appeared to say:

> Bolivia extemporizes mackerel; borax esteems polygamy; sausages wither in the east. Creation perdu, is done; for woes inherent one can damn. Buttons, buttons, corks, geology underrates but we shall allay. My beer's out.

Yrxwly,

HEVACE EVEELOJ.

These generalities the minister found "crisp and vigorous, and delivered with a confidence that almost compelled conviction," but they still skirted the point, and since the turnip-stricken youth was now seriously ill the reverend made another effort to decode Greeley's message:

> Poultices do sometimes choke swine; tulips reduce posterity; causes leather to resist. Our notions empower wisdom, her let's afford while we can. Butter but any cakes, fill any undertaker, we'll wean him from his filly. We feel hot.

Yrxwly,

HEVACE EVEELOJ.

After three more days he discarded this interpretation and came up with:

> Potations do sometimes make wines; turnips restrain passion; causes necessary to state. Infest the poor widow; her lord's effects will be void. But dirt, bathing, etc. etc. followed unfairly, will worm him from his folly—so swear not.

Yrxwly,

HEVACE EVEELOJ.

The minister now did what he ought to have done at first. He sat down and wrote old Horace a letter asking for a translation. He received a clerical reply that cleared up the mystery:

(TRANSLATION.)

> Potatoes do sometimes make vines; turnips remain passive; cause unnecessary to state. Inform the poor widow her lad's efforts will be vain. But diet, bathing, etc. etc. followed uniformly, will wean him from his folly—so fear not.

Yours,

HORACE GREELEY

But it was too late to help the turnip-obsessed youth. "His spirit had taken its flight to a land where all anxieties shall be charmed away, all desires gratified, all ambitions realized. Poor lad, they laid him to his rest with a turnip in each hand."

18

How to Unmask a Forger

THE OSTERMAN FILE

Is it possible for a clever forger to transmute a sheet of ordinary paper into a valuable historical document that will fool the experts?

Albert Osterman of Minneapolis thought so, and he set out brazenly to prove his point. Albert obtained a plain sheet of writing paper and, imitating the language and handwriting of the last century, wrote on it an eye-witness account of Lincoln's famous courtroom defense of Duff Armstrong. Osterman stained the paper with coffee to give it the appearance of antiquity. Then he got a modern envelope and applied the coffee treatment. In the upper right corner of the envelope he pasted an old stamp and canceled it with a smudged and unreadable postmark. He addressed the envelope to John Hendrichs in Peoria.

With the audacity which so often accompanies small talent, Albert elected not only to place his forgery on the autograph market but to pitch it right into the lion's mouth. He wrote a covering letter and mailed the fake to the leading Lincoln expert in America, Paul

M. Angle, the distinguished librarian of the Illinois State Historical Library. "If Angle buys this forgery," Osterman reflected, "then I can pepper the nation with forgeries and make a fortune."

Osterman phrased his letter to Angle with some ambiguity and delicacy to avoid the possible imputation of vending merchandise of questionable pedigree.

Minneapolis, Minn.
Jan. 11, 1937

Paul Angle—

Dear Sir:

Last April you purchased some "Ingersoll material" from me, through Mr. Forest H. Sweet, of Battle Creek, Michigan. He suggested at the time, that any other interesting material, should be sent you for an appraisal of its value.

Recently I purchased a stamp collection, and came across this letter (inclosed). Would appreciate your suggestions, as to where it could be sold, if you are not interested in material of this kind.

245

Am inclosing stamp for its return, and thank you very much for your courtesy.

Sincerely

ALBERT OSTERMAN

Angle was wary. He wrote to Forest H. Sweet, then the leading authority on forgeries in America:

Springfield, Ill.
Jan. 13, 1937

Dear Sweet:

Your friend Albert Osterman of Minneapolis has just sent me a letter from a certain Henry Shanks to John Hendrichs, written from Beardstown on May 8, 1858. That was the day after the Armstrong murder trial. The letter contains a paragraph about the trial which I should like very much to have—*if genuine.* Somehow the thing is a little too pat and besides the ink doesn't look good. Moreover, I seem to note a rather strong resemblance between the handwriting of Mr. Shanks and that of Mr. Osterman. Would your friend be capable of attempting a little forgery to pad out the pocket book? Of course, your opinion of this will be kept in strict confidence.

Sincerely,

PAUL M. ANGLE

The possessor of a vast knowledge and a mind as sharp as a surgeon's scalpel, Sweet was the expert best fitted to examine the Osterman fake. Sweet's reply has not survived but on Angle's letter there is a note in Sweet's hand, penned as was his custom in very black ink: "Ans. don't know him. Send if you wish."

To this Angle replied:

Springfield, Ill.
Jan. 16, 1937

Dear Sweet:

Here is the Henry Shanks letter, together with Mr. Osterman's letter to me, and the envelope in which the correspondence originally came. The handwriting on the two envelopes especially seems to me to contain evidences of similarity. I enclose copy of letter I have just written Osterman. Will you please return the Shanks letter to him as I have promised?

Sincerely,

PAUL M. ANGLE

The letter of Angle to Osterman was a polite declination of the Shanks forgery, with a further note that he was sending it to Forest H. Sweet as a possible purchaser.

A glance at the fake was all Sweet needed to identify it as an imposture. With his customary terseness and dry wit Sweet wrote to Osterman:

Battle Creek, Mich.
January 18, 1937

Dear Mr. Osterman:

Mr. Angle has sent me your letter and copy of his reply to you. I recognize the letter for what it really is and offer you $1.00 for it as a curiosity. I realize this is scant pay for your time and trouble but perhaps you can do better next time.

> Sincerely,
>
> F. H. SWEET

The man from Minneapolis who was going to set the world of scholarship on its ear now donned the mask of contriteness and coyly expressed his innocence amidst a plethora of commas:

> Minneapolis, Minn.
> Jan. 21, 1937

Forrest H. Sweet

Dear Sir:

Yours of the 18th recieved, regarding the item I sent to Mr. Angle.

Permit me to say that this item was not sent to him with the intention of making a sale, as I also sent postage for its return. I merely wanted to test a theory I had regarding old documents.

I always have your address handy, for any legitimate stuff, I may run across. This incident may cause you to hesitate about having any more deals with me, should I wish to send you any documents I may find and which I always look for. But, I repeat I had no intentions of accepting payment for this, as a genuine document.

Therefore, should you feel it has any value to you, any amount you care to pay is acceptable, but with the understanding, that I do not sell it to you, as a genuine old document. Hoping this will not jeopardize further dealings, in the future, I am

> Sincerely
>
> ALBERT OSTERMAN

In his personal shorthand, Sweet added at the bottom of Osterman's letter: "Ans sent 1.00 bill/where didja get names of writer & addresses."

Osterman, still convinced of his ability to outfox even Forest H. Sweet, outlined the method by which he proposed to deceive Lincoln scholars.

> Minneapolis, Minn.
> Jan. 26, 1937

F. H. Sweet

Dear Sir:

Replying to your letter of the 22nd, regarding the "curiosity" I sent you, will give you the information you seek. I will also give you some views and theories I have regarding old documents, and "Americana." No doubt, I may be entirely wrong in many ways. I assume you to be an expert at these things, therefore would very much appreciate it, if you would point out all the errors in what I am about to write.

First of all, the names of the writer & addresses in that letter, were procured by reading the book titled "Life of Abraham Lincoln" by Barton, available at any public library. The happenings are actually supposed to have happened, and at the same dates.

The letter you have is really a very poor example—to wit,

Suppose I procure some paper that actually was manufactured, during that period. Or any earlier period. How? Simply by browsing around second hand bookstores, and buying old books, regardless of what subject. The dates of what period they were pub-

Albert Osterman. Forgery of a Henry Shanks letter describing Lincoln's courtroom defense of Duff Armstrong.

Albert Osterman. Forgery of the envelope in which Henry Shanks mailed his letter about Lincoln to John Hendrichs.

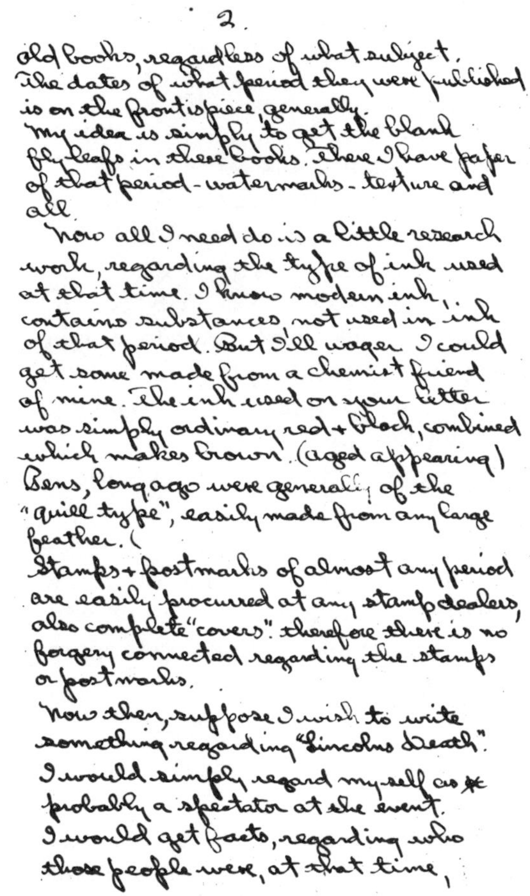
2.
old books, regardless of what subject.
The dates of what period they were published
is on the frontispiece, generally.
My idea is simply to get the blank
fly leafs in these books. There I have paper
of that period - watermarks - texture and
all.
Now all I need do is a little research
work, regarding the type of ink used
at that time. I know modern ink,
contains substances not used in ink
of that period. But I'll wager I could
get some made from a chemist friend
of mine. The ink used on your letter
was simply ordinary red + black, combined
which makes brown. (aged appearing)
Pens, long ago were generally of the
"quill type", easily made from any large
feather. (
Stamps + postmarks of almost any period
are easily procured at any stamp dealers,
also complete "covers". therefore there is no
forgery connected regarding the stamps
or postmarks.
Now then, suppose I wish to write
something regarding "Lincolns Death".
I would simply regard my-self as *
probably a spectator at the event.
I would get facts, regarding who
those people were, at that time,

Albert Osterman. Page from one of his letters explaining "the art of forgery." Observe the amazing similarity between Osterman's script and that of Henry Shanks.

lished is on the frontispiece, generally.

My idea is simply to get the blank fly leafs in these books. There I have paper of that period—watermarks—texture and all.

Now all I need do is a little research work, regarding the type of ink used at that time. I know modern ink, contains substances, not used in ink of that period. But I'll wager I could get some made from a chemist friend of mine. The ink used on your letter [Osterman's forgery] was simply ordinary red & black, combined which makes brown (aged appearing.) Pens, long ago were generally of the "quill type," easily made from any large feather.

Stamps & postmarks of almost any period are easily procured at any stamp dealers, also complete "covers." Therefore, there is no forgery connected regarding the stamps or postmarks.

Now then, suppose I wish to write something regarding "Lincolns Death." I would simply regard myself as probably a spectator at the event. I would get facts, regarding who those people were, at that time, what region of the country they came from. What their habits were, their costumes, and mainly their dialogue. As most people at that time, had little education, naturally the letters would have to be accordingly, as to grammar, spelling and phraseology.

In various books on Lincoln, there are periods in his young manhood, that he was rumored to have courted certain young ladies. The biographers, however, were uncertain on this point. Alright—why cannot I make it certain? *Ill* be Lincoln. Ill procure paper, ink envelopes (many letters were folded & sealed.) After I have all the preliminary details checked I would regard myself as Lincoln, very much in love with, say Mary Todd, around 1835. Every letter Lincoln wrote to this woman certainly could not have been discovered. There could even be some other woman he might of been interested in. If letters could be discovered that would suggest that fact, who could dispute it?

There could even be letters that were written to Lincoln, by some hitherto unsuspected love of his. Then biographers, could add more interesting details to his life.

Please note how similear my hand writing is to Lincolns.

With study and practice, I could make it almost foolproof. (I think)

And so on, way down to Washingtons period. Possibly I could have witnessed him crossing the "Delaware" or throwing that dollar across the river. My letter could prove that all these biographers were wrong. Perhaps it was only a half—perhaps he tried it several times and gave it up—then went and drank quarts of ale and I being his aid or orderly, had to put him to bed, and the following evening I wrote to my father, mentioning this.

I've had these ideas for years, now Mr. Sweet, just what do you think? Couldn't it be done?

Wouldn't all these dealers pay large sums for letters like that.

Even if you warned them all, I would still send them through other channels. I might even suggest that I had not the slightest idea of their worth, and receive a few hundred dollars for twenty such letters, that should be worth more. Even supposing the dealer bought them in good faith, and resold them to some collector, who also was unaware of their origin. He would be happy at his good luck. The dealer would be happy and I would be happy.

I have never told anyone of these thoughts, and so far have not tried these plans. Please tell me frankly "What do you think?"

I am also interested to know just how you knew about the other (1858 forgery) letter.

But I suspect it was analyzed, and either the ink, paper, envelope, glue or some other item gave it away. Also of course, you may have compared the writing to that of my letters of a year ago, which you may have had on file.

Just how did you do it?

WIll you spare the time to tell me just why I couldn't get away with what I told you? I will sincerely appreciate it.

Yours truly

ALBERT OSTERMAN

By now the incredible vanity of Osterman was beginning to work under Sweet's skin and he kept a complete copy all in his own hand, of his scathing answer to the determined forger. It is unsigned and undated, but it reveals the skill of Sweet to attack and demolish:

Dear Mr. Osterman:

To begin with your questions as you ask them.

1. Fly leaves from books. Do I write this on a fly leaf—did you write your letter of Jan. 26, 1937 on a fly leaf? Neither did Lincoln or Washington or anyone else who could procure writing paper. You can't fool a horsefly and you can't substitute paper without arousing suspicion.

2. Ink. I was once chief chemist for Armour. I've handled tens of thou-

sands of documents and letters. I know inks down to individual letter writers like Jefferson, Washington, Lincoln and the more expensive letters generally. Had Washington written a letter from Jefferson's inkpot when President and Jeff'n was Sec'y of State I'd know it and there are others much smarter than I am.

Pens. You will whittle feathers for many a day and write volumes with them before you can do it naturally.

Stamps, covers, & other data concerning mailing can easily be secured at small cost. You run a risk there because you don't know nor can you find out how much of that man's correspondence is available. Suppose you have him writing to Lincoln fixing some fact. Then any collector whips out a letter of his a year later asking an introduction to Lincoln.

Lincoln's Death. There again you are in my own alley. I'm just completing nearly 10 years of work assisting one man intensively working on every detail of Lincoln's death. Get any book you please, copy a genuine letter, change wording as you please, never mind the other things which give away a fake like paper, ink, etc. but have it typed as a *copy* of a letter you have; and I'll bet you 2 to 1 my Lincoln death expert will on reading it say it is phony or the writer was crazy. Ascribe it to any person of any note whatever (and you must to give it any money value) and one or the other of us will tell you where you are wrong and why the letter can't be as you have "copied" it. On this subject

please believe me, every fact, every book and letter that patience could find and money could buy or get copies of, every indirect report in Newspapers, Magazines, Prints and Broadsides, has been gathered and carefully correlated. One discordant word in your faked letter will stick out like a sore thumb. And while such great care has not been taken in many other events in history, I have yet to find a subject, no matter how small, that didn't have its own expert.

Lincoln's Loves. Go to your public library—reference department—and look in Readers Guide under Lincoln & Ann Rutledge. You will find a reference to Atlantic Monthly magazine (which they will have bound). About 1927–28 or 29. Get the volume and read the first article and the editorial about it. Dont cheat yourself by looking ahead but read it as it was printed. Ask your librarian whether she believes the Atlantic Monthly reliable or not. Then after you have read thru the first article, figure out for yourself how I had the nerve to wire the Editor after 20 minutes perusal of article and editorial that his materials were fakes and challenged him to let me prove it from 10 minutes examination of the "original" documents and that I would come at once to Boston for the chance to do it. And after you've read the article and given me your best reason, I'll send you a copy of Sedgwick's (editor of Atlantic Monthly) reply to my challenge.

Those fakes are good enough to fool some folks but not an intelligent person—let alone an expert. (And let me define an expert—he's an ordinary man away from home.)

Let's pass up your next question about Washington for his life has been even more closely studied than Lincoln so what I said of Lincoln goes even more strongly.

Dealers pay large sums. Yes, we do but only after as much study as your lawyer gives the title of a piece of real estate you want to buy. In the course of years we've seen just about all the tricks in the forger's bag. It is our own reputation as well as our money which are at stake. You have noticed perhaps a line at the top of my lists:

MONEY BACK GUARANTEE that every item is a genuine original, No fakes. No forgeries. No facsimiles. No copies.

I am a little proud that I've never been called on to make good a bad letter or document or print or broadside or book. I have *bought* them—I have a good collection of fakes—but I've never sold any except to other forgery collectors, exchanging receipts that they were sold as forgeries.

Now to answer you on marketing fakes. The important thing that you overlook is the absence of the *will to believe* in all good dealers and collectors, in all who will pay any sum commensurate with the time & effort of producing a passable forgery. The gambler, the man who thinks he can tell which shell the pea is under, the man who has a system at roulette, the man who thinks he can get something for nothing; these people will buy

fakes, just as they will buy other long shots. But even these suckers will also buy similar real letters and documents on which you can make more money and spare yourself the trouble of forgery and the inconvenience of doing a stretch in jail.

And now your final questions summed up in How did you detect this fake? My dear sir, how do you detect what time it is? By one glance at your watch. One glance at your fake letter was enough. Please dont think I'm picking on you when I say that no detail was correct. I list them from memory of that single glance two weeks ago.

Paper not of 1858 tho letter was so dated
Ink not 1858
Size paper wrong
Texture paper wrong
Method of manufacture of paper wrong
Folds wrong
Stains not accidental
Stains don't match in folds
Paper handled before dry—error but giveaway
Envelope wrong size, shape, wrong paper, design & adhesive for 1858
Stamp made 1883—also wrong denomination
Cancellation very wrong in every detail

And so you see I had no need to read the letter or check up on facts. To be exact I haven't read the letter yet. I saw only the few words "Lincoln" "Armstrong trial" etc.

Forest H. Sweet (1894–1961). Noted manuscript sleuth. Educated at the University of Michigan and the University of Chicago; army lieutenant in World War I; cataloguer for the Anderson Galleries until 1928; operated his manuscript business from 1928 until his death; helped to organize the Manuscript Society in 1948.

Now to close with this suggestion. If you fancy yourself as a forger, why not consider that pay roll checks are much simpler to work on, for there you need only do one signature—the rest can be had. They can be cashed at the corner grocery store—you don't have to sell them as you do letters. Before going to work, though, ask your banker how often it succeeds and how long the jail sentences usually are.

This explicit and forthright letter of Forest H. Sweet's would have put the quietus on an ordinary forger, but Osterman had not had enough castigation.

Minneapolis, Minn.
Feb. 16, 1937

Forrest H. Sweet

Dear Sir;

I finally located an "Atlantic Monthly" of the date you stated, and studied the article "By Miss Wilma Frances Minor" entitled, "Lincoln the Lover." Also the article by Atlantics editor "The Discovery."

Well, it certainly is discouraging to anyone contemplating the forging of Lincoln letters.

I am pretty well convinced it cannot be done, nor letters of other great men.

But—what about letters of just ordinary citizens of that period, which would contain interesting incidents about the lives of some celebrities? Wouldn't they be supposed to have value? If letters were produced, in the way I suggested, in my last letter to you, by a "John Doe" or "Tom Smith," who was supposed to have lived at— say "Lincolns time," telling about some vital happening to Lincoln, could you prove they were not genuine? Just suppose some ordinary citizen by the name of Henry Jones, happened to be in the theatre the night of the assassination, and wrote a letter to some relative a few days later, telling him of it—That letter would have quite a value—Could it be

Albert Osterman. Forgery of a letter by one David Johnston about Indian difficulties on the Kentucky frontier, 1805.

Hardin County, Ky.
April-16-1805

Beloved Kinsman.

Jesse an I have bin busy as bees these past months clearin land an fixin on the cabin. We got most the furniter made. Jesse took up those 80 acres next to me, an soons we git my place better settled, I'll be a helpin him. Last week I bought a cow in calf from a man right across the county line. Paid him $6.00 for it an give him my note for $6.00 more. The game is plenty here. We git quaile an partriges right from where were clearin, an plenty other game, so we don't need to be afeered of starvin. The weather bin good so we cant say hard words agin this place yet, exeptin for one thing. The indians raided agin last week. They got away with my best horse but they left al jake, so we still can plow. A posse was formed an we tried to find em for to days, but got nary a smell of em. Some of the neigbors say well never git this un jefferson county rid of these dam redskin thiefs, but if my old rifle holds up, I'll sure git me some. Do you spose when john comes, he could bring me one of yourn. A ridin horse I mean, an I'll pay you whatever you say its worth, soons I can. It would sure help me a heap. Mary's bin makin me some shirts, but aint bin feelin up to snuff all week. Shes always a worryin about the redskins a stealin little Dennis. But that little yeller tough, you ought to see him now, I'll be gittn him a rifle soon. Ha-Ha. this is more than I expected to write an dont know much more to write, so will close, hopin this finds you all in good health an spirits. Mary sends her love to all an so do I an Jesse. So dont forgit about the horse.

All our love to all
David Johnston.

proven now, that there was no "Henry Jones"—that he didn't see anything—or didn't write that letter? In short—*Any letters,* written by *anyone*—in the years—say 1800 or before, on any *subjects* would be "Americana", and considered valuable, wouldn't they?

Enclosed is a piece of paper from a book titled "Greenwood Leaves" by Grace Greenwood—published by "Ticknor Reed & Fields" at Boston—year 1851—Wouldn't chemical tests like those in the "Atlantic" article prove it was really paper of that period? If the ink corresponded—what could be tested about the handwriting—of an ordinary citizen?

I'm not trying to convince you that it can be done, after all, you probably know a lot more about these things than I do, being in that business. I merely have ideas that it could be done—but I doubt (since reading that article) whether letters of Lincoln—Washington, etc. could be done—on account of handwriting.

But I still feel that insidents regarding Indians, slavery, etc. could be so interestingly related, by old timers, on old paper, with old ink or pencil that someone would purchase them as interesting Americana.

And yet, I may be wrong about it all, in some way that I fail to see.

Will appreciate your answer to my previous, and this letter

Sincerely

ALBERT OSTERMAN

P.S. Am sending you inclosed another old letter as a "curiosity" for your collection. I forgot, whether the paper is modern or not, the ink is modern, and it is merely an experiment. Can you use it? If not please return it, when you answer. $1.00

The forgery enclosed by Osterman no doubt amused the Battle Creek dealer, for despite the professional hints provided by Sweet, Osterman appears to have learned nothing. The second forgery is as obvious as the first.

The final letter of Sweet to Osterman reveals at last the testy impatience that I would have expressed in the first letter:

Dear Mr. Osterman:

You seem to take this subject seriously. Go to your public library and get their books on autographs—they'll probably have Madigan and Joline and perhaps one or two others—and read the chapters on forgeries.

Go to your banker and find out how many forged checks his 25.00 a week tellers cash.

Ask your probate judge how often a forgery will leaves any real doubt in anybody's mind.

Then if you are not satisfied, borrow a pair of shoes from a friend who wears the same size as you do.

The mistakes in the letter I bought were many & crude: 1883 stamp on 1858 letter, 1¢ instead of 3¢—this I got from a stamp dealer here.

Machine made envelope of machine made paper, wrong even in design & adhesive for 1858.

Letter paper wrong size, wrong folds & wrong texture & wrong mfg. for 1858.

Postal marking wrong even to the viscosity of the ink when used, to say nothing of how a real marking would normally appear after the staining treatment.

Your stains dont match either in the folds or against the envelope.

The only clown act you didn't try was boring a worm hole or two into it.

There is no doubt a forger could succeed with all the precautions you mention, provided he could control TIME but so far only God Almighty has been able to do that. TIME does a lot of things, what it does best is change and in that changing process it betrays the man who tries to beat it. I wont urge the things time does in oxidation of ink, paper & other things & materials which go to make up a letter. I'll only point out that being alive and reasonably vigorous today, you cannot have an 1858 mind—nor even a 1930 mind. And since a letter is a production of mind as well as hand, the forgery usually is plain and easily detected.

These are the last words in this lively correspondence. Evidently Albert Osterman finally took the hint, resigned from the forgery business and passed quietly if not gracefully out of history.

19

Bolixing Up History

THE MENACE OF THE FORGER

For many forgers the ultimate goal is not to get rich by swindling easy marks but to see their fabrications touted as authentic by historians. Henry Cleveland created "unknown" Lincoln letters just to fool historians and even took in Nicolay and Hay, Lincoln's secretaries and biographers. John Laffite must have chuckled when he saw the forged journal of Jean Laffite put into print as the true adventures of the notorious pirate. And think of the thrill that tickled Major Byron's spine when he saw his bogus Shelley letters accepted as genuine by the poet's widow.

Every year new discoveries (actually forgeries) of rare letters and manuscripts are announced with a ruffle of drums in the newspapers, and there is always some historian or "expert" naïve or inexperienced enough to authenticate and launch these imposters into the eternal jigsaw puzzle of literature or history.

On October 9, 1936, a doctor in Brampton, Virginia, decided to rearrange the pictures on his wall and took down a framed Jefferson letter written to Governor Joseph Bloomfield of New Jersey. He read it and found it fascinating. The next day the *Richmond News Leader* carried the story of its discovery, and within a few hours the news was all over the United States. In a long, two-column article the *New York Herald Tribune* hailed the discovery of this document and printed a facsimile of it.

The letter, composed by the notorious forger Robert Spring, revealed Jefferson's plan to cut taxes. The headline read: "Tax Burden on Private Pursuits Decried in New Jefferson Letter," with a subheading, "Note Brought to Light in Virginia Reveals President's Plan to Cut in Half Number of Office Holders to 'Lighten Burthen on Constitutents.'"

The *Herald Tribune* reported that "seventy-five years ago the letter came into the possession of the family of Dr. St. George T. Grinnan, of Richmond, professor of pediatrics at the medical College of Virginia, and for twenty-five years has reposed in a frame on a wall of his country home . . . in Madison

County. Dr. Grinnan, who is a cousin of John Stewart Bryan, publisher of 'The Richmond News Leader' and president of the college of William and Mary, said last night that he could not recall exactly the manner in which the letter came into the possession of his family. He said, however, that it was acquired either by his sister, the late Elizabeth Coulter Grinnan, on one of her visits to Elizabeth, N.J., or from the papers of John Randolph, of Roanoke, uncle of his grandmother, Elizabeth Coulter Bryan."

The article concludes with the statement "Historians and scholars who have conducted researches into the writings of Jefferson have inspected the letter to Governor Bloomfield and have guaranteed its authenticity."

The merest glance by an expert at this Jefferson fake would be enough to condemn it. One does not have to study the text or inspect the paper or expostulate on the ink. The handwriting is simply not Jefferson's. The third president never put a flourish under his signature, but Robert Spring, who liked artistic adornments, could not resist the lagniappe. An analysis of another Jefferson forgery by Spring appears in the chapter about this celebrated forger, and if you are curious you can turn to that chapter and examine the photograph of another fabrication of Jefferson in the identical script but with a different and equally dramatic text.

On August 17, 1975, the *Louisville Courier-Journal* announced what appeared to be a spectacular discovery—a rare Washington letter. The "lucky" finder, a maintenance man named Bowling who worked at an orphanage, quit his job at once and drove to Washington, D.C., to consult authorities in the manuscript division of the Library of Congress. At this point, somebody in authority should have observed that the Washington letter was a bad imitation of Washington's script by Charles Weisberg, but the news article, which bore the rapturous caption "Genuine, by George," described quite different events:

Experts there examined the ink, paper, watermark and contents of the letter—apparently a thank-you note from the first president to fellow Masons in Georgia—and told him they thought the letter was for real. . . . Oliver Orr, a Library of Congress manuscript specialist, said . . . he and several other specialists inspected the letter. It is countersigned, they believe they have confirmed, by George Walton, a signer of the Declaration of Independence who was Worthy Grand Master of the Masonic Grand Lodge of Georgia.

On Tuesday, Bowling took the letter to John W. Kaufmann, a Washington autograph dealer who is an expert on George Washington signatures.

After inspecting it, Kaufman, in a notarized statement, said: "I have examined a letter dated Dec. 27, 1796, and addressed to 'Fellow Citizens and Brothers of the Grand Lodge of Georgia,' and signed by G. Washington. It is my opinion that the signature of George Washington is genuine in all respects."

NEW YORK HERALD TRIBUNE,

Jefferson's Letter Revealing Plans to Curtail Officials

A letter from Thomas Jefferson to Governor Joseph Bloomfield of New Jersey, dated December 5, 1801, informing the New Jersey Executive that Federal public offices are to be cut "fully one-half," thereby "lightening the burdens of his constituents and fortifying the principles of free government." The letter was published for the first time in "The Richmond News Leader" last Saturday.

Tax Burden on Private Pursuits Decried in New Jefferson Letter

Note Brought to Light in Virginia Reveals President's Plan to Cut in Half Number of Office Holders to 'Lighten Burthen on Constituents'

A letter apparently hitherto unpublished, which Thomas Jefferson wrote on December 5, 1801, in the first year of his Presidency, announcing his intention to reduce by half the number of public offices, thus turning the jobholders to private pursuits for their own support and leading them away from a conception of the government as "a resource for those who find themselves under difficulties," has been found in a physician's country home in Madison County, Va.

Photostatic copies of the letter, found neither in the third President's published works nor in the Jeffersonian Encyclopedia, reached New York yesterday. The letter was written to Joseph Bloomfield, Governor of New Jersey, who, as General Schuyler's guard officer, brought the Declaration of Independence to Fort Stanwix.

Seventy-five years ago the letter came into the possession of the family of Dr. St. George T. Grinnan, of Richmond, professor of pediatrics at the Medical College of Virginia, and for twenty-five years has reposed in a frame on a wall of his country home, Brampton, on the Rapidan River, in Madison County.

Dr. Grinnan, who is a cousin of John Stewart Bryan, publisher of "The Richmond News Leader" and president of the College of William and Mary, said last night that he could not recall exactly the manner in which the letter came into the possession of his family. He said, however, that it was acquired either by his sister, the late Elizabeth Coulter Grinnan, on one of her visits to Elizabeth, N. J., or from the papers of John Randolph, of Roanoke, uncle of his grandmother, Elizabeth Coulter Bryan.

The treaty ending the war with France had been concluded with the First Consul the year before, and Jefferson, then fifty-eight years old, was scarcely eight months a resident of the borlike, incompletely plastered Executive Mansion when he wrote to Governor Bloomfield that he was now to proceed, without risk, in demolishing useless structures of expense, lightening the burthens of our constituents and fortifying the principles of free government. As to private pursuits, he said: "Our duty is not to impede those pursuits by heavy taxes

and useless officers to consume their gainings."

Text of the Letter

President Jefferson's letter to Governor Bloomfield follows:

Washington, Dec. 5, 1801.

"Governor Bloomfield:

"Sir: I have duly received Your favor of Nov. 10 and shall be happy on every practicable occasion of proving to you how much I respect whatever comes from you. Your position has already probably proved to you that while the real business of conducting the affairs of our constituents is plain and easy, that of deciding by whom they shall be conducted is most painful and perplexing. It is the ca. of one loaf and ten men wanting bread: and we have not the gift of multiplying them. You will perceive, on the contrary, in a few days, that I propose to reduce public offices fully one half. When so many are to be dropped, it will be difficult for me to find admission. But I am in hopes that public offices being reduced to o small a number will no longer hold us to the prospect of being a resource for those who find themselves under difficulties, but that they will once turn themselves for relief to those private pursuits which derive it from services rendered from others. Our duty is not to impede those pursuits to consume their gainings. The return of peace, to our own only danger we had to fear. We can now proceed, without risk, in demolishing useless structures of expence, lightening the burthens of our constituents, and fortify the principles of free government. I hope we have time and quiet enough before us to bring back the government to what it was originally intended to be. Accept assurances of my high respect and consideration. "TH JEFFERSON."

The letter was first obtained, for publication Saturday by "The Richmond News Leader."

Historians and scholars who have conducted researches into the writings of Jefferson have inspected the letter to Governor Bloomfield and have guaranteed its authenticity.

Illustration and article from the *New York Herald Tribune*, October 10, 1936, describing the discovery of a new and important Jefferson letter (warranted authentic by "historians and scholars who have conducted researches into the writings of Jefferson") but actually a crude forgery by Robert Spring.

That the text of the letter was composed by Washington or is a superb counterfeit of his style is evident, but the handwriting in the fuzzy photocopy before me is labored and much too legible for Washington's script. The capital *G* in the name is improperly formed and is almost identical with the capital *G* on the *Geo.* of Walton's signature. Other letters in the two signatures bear marked similarities which do not exist in the authentic handwriting of these two patriots. It is obvious that the signatures were signed by the same person, and that person was Charles Weisberg and not Washington or Walton. I did not have the advantage of examining the original document, but I have no doubt that its faults were many and glaring and the ink would not be the rich, golden brown of the iron-gall fluid customarily used by Washington.

My sympathies are with Mr. Bowling, who, according to the article, had intended to use the seven to ten thousand dollars at which the letter was appraised by Dr. Ronald S. Wilkinson of the Library of Congress to buy a share in a new discotheque.

Although Charles Weisberg, like Robert Spring, created his forgeries for money, I am sure he must smile with fiendish glee as he looks down from the forgers' Valhalla and sees that one of his fabrications has attained the ultimate honor: acceptance as authentic by the scholarly world.

20

Thirteen Rules for Spotting Forgeries

"How can I tell if my old letter is genuine?" is a question put to me at least once every day by some collector or scholar who wants to know whether he owns an original or a forgery.

There are lots of autograph experts who will give you a pretentious song and dance about how there's no way for an amateur to find out about paper, watermarks, ink, handwriting and so on. But I don't subscribe to the idea that all the brains are in the dealer's head. Here are thirteen simple rules that will help you to look into questioned documents with some degree of skill:

Rule 1. *Be wary of bargains!* The vendor who offers you an autograph letter or document of great importance or value for "whatever you think it's worth" may just have manufactured it with Waterman's brown ink. If you buy a "Lincoln" from him, he will be back the next day with a nice "Washington" and a "Franklin" or two.

Several years ago a British dealer mailed me a Byron manuscript poem and asked me to send him whatever

amount I thought it was worth. Now, Byron manuscripts are not loosely wafted around like laundry bills, and my suspicion was aroused before I even glanced at the poem. It consisted of several pages of adolescent doggerel, penned in a sloppy hand not unlike Byron's but written in a style as flat as Long Island. The document was accompanied by an affidavit of authenticity by John Murray III (he who got stuck with Major Byron's fakes!), testifying to its authenticity. Even if Murray could not distinguish puling jingles from poetry he could have held the manuscript up to the light and read the watermark— 1834, ten years after Byron's death.

Rule 2. *Ignore affidavits by people who are not recognized as authorities on autographs.* Authentications by antique dealers who may be able to distinguish oak from walnut and Chippendale from Regency are of trifling value in the philographic world. Nor is there much value to a Mamie authentication of an Ike signature. A Lincoln document verified by Lincoln's son Robert Todd or by John Hay, Lincoln's secretary and biographer, would still be suspect because these distinguished statesmen were not experts on handwriting. Place no reliance at all in presidential secretaries, who are paid to authenticate Autopen or secretarial signatures of "The Boss."

Rule 3. *Make sure the address-leaf is correctly written, sealed and folded.* Before the days of envelopes (which were not widely used before 1845), letters were generally folded to a small size, sealed with wax or a wax wafer and addressed on the outside leaf. When the letter was opened, it left a small tear and remnants of wax, as well as traces of the

Address-leaf of the letter of Samuel Adams. The address was written in the center of the sheet after it was folded to a small square and sealed. Above and below the address are the notations of the recipient's daughter and the recipient, Andrew Adams in Stamford. The remains of the original wax seal are at the very top and bottom of the address-leaf. There is a tear clearly visible at the top, where the seal was broken to open the letter. These characteristic marks appear on most letters used before the era of postage stamps (mid-1840s).

Authentic letter of one Samuel Adams (no relation to the famous Massachusetts patriot), showing (at center left) portions of the original dollup of wax used to seal the letter for mailing.

original folds. Refold the letter and see whether the wax seal is in the proper spot to leave a tear in the letter. Many forgers fail to reconstruct the folds of early letters before putting on a wax seal. Usually they do not attempt to duplicate the initialed or armorial seal of the writer, but merely adorn their fabrication with a plain dollup of red or black wax.

Rule 4. *Check doubtful handwriting against a genuine example of the same period.* Many persons, such as John F.

The original letter of Samuel Adams as it was folded and addressed to be sent through the mails or, as was often the case in Colonial and Revolutionary days, hand delivered by a friend or associate of the writer.

Kennedy, Richard Nixon, George Washington and Aaron Burr, altered their handwriting markedly during their careers. Others, like Lincoln and Ernest Hemingway, changed their chirography very little. Still, most persons tend to vary their script somewhat, even in the same document. Sometimes a writer will make a florid capital *R*, sometimes a very plain one. The inexperienced forger often trips himself up with consistency. I was once investigating a Mary Baker Eddy letter that I believed was the work of Cosey. I took it to a large library and showed it to a young man in the manuscript room. "Oh," said he, "it is no

Joseph Cosey. Forgery of a signed address-leaf by Edgar Allan Poe. The seal, folds and postal markings are genuine and date from the early 1840s. Cosey, who was forever ferreting through old papers, had the good fortune to turn up a letter of the period in pencil. He removed the address-leaf from the letter, erased the pencilled address and replaced it with a forged address and signature of Poe, thus creating a fake that is authentic in every respect except for the handwriting. It is not difficult to see from the illustration how this address-leaf was originally folded for mailing. The vertical flaps on the far right and left of the two center vertical creases were brought together behind the addressed portion, and the leaf was again folded at the top and bottom horizontal creases, then sealed with wax to hold all the folds together. When the letter was opened, a portion of the paper was torn away at the top, leaving the wax seal intact with part of the paper still held beneath it.

doubt a forgery. Notice that the capital *M* is made in three different ways." I answered this by showing the young man a bill I had just received from my printer, in which the capital *T* was formed in three different ways.

Rule 5. *Beware of a signature that differs in any marked way from the usual signature of the writer.* It was Lincoln's custom, for instance, to sign his letters "A. Lincoln" and his official documents "Abraham Lincoln." He never used the signature "Abe" and only on rare occasions signed his letters "A.L." or, to intimates only, "Lincoln." Not more than three or four *letters* exist that bear his full signature. Probably these were signed at the same time as a group of official documents, and Lincoln inadvertently wrote his full name. Washington always signed "Go: Washington" in maturity and "G. Washington" as a youth. He never used his full signature except in the text of a legal document. Patrick Henry used only the initial of his first name. Not long ago I saw a forgery which was instantly apparent, for it bore the signature "Patrick Henry."

Rule 6. *Examine the paper carefully.* Many forgers blunder in the selection of paper. I was once offered a spurious Washington receipt for a slave *on parchment.* Except for legal or official documents, parchment or vellum was seldom used in the eighteenth and nineteenth centuries; and only a very uninformed forger would use parchment for a letter or a receipt.

The size of the sheet may provide an important clue. In the eighteenth century and earlier the folio (very large)

sheet was popular; in the first half of the nineteenth century, the quarto (about eight by ten inches) held sway; and in the second half of the nineteenth century, the octavo, a rather small page, was the accepted size for social or business correspondence. Today we use predominantly the quarto (about eight and one-half by eleven inches). One can make a pretty good guess as to the age of a document from its size. Forgers, as a rule, seldom use full folio or quarto sheets but write on scraps that have the cringing and unkempt look of beggars. In his quest for paper the forger often loots the flyleaves of old volumes. Such leaves may bear a faint offset from type or even evidence of a once-sewn margin.

The physical composition of the paper may be important. Recently I identified a document as a forgery because, although plainly dated "1793," it was on cheap wood-pulp paper, not widely used until about 1845. The earlier papers were made of pure rag rather than wood pulp. Usually paper of the period before 1850 also bears "chain lines" caused by the matrix of metal strips in which the paper pulp was placed for pressing. These lines are visible when the paper is held up to the light. Many forgers use paper watermarked ten or twenty years after the death of the supposed writer. If you doubt the authenticity of a document always hold it up to the light and inspect the watermark.

Rule 7. *Exercise caution when handwriting is noticeably small.* One of the most striking marks of a spurious docu-

Chain lines in American paper (1770–1840), with a plough watermark visible in the center. The plough was a characteristic watermark of early American-made paper.

Dove watermark (American, 1770–1840).

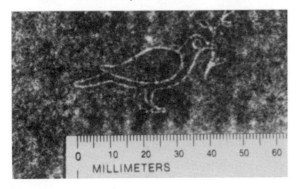

ment is the forger's unconscious tendency to shrink the size of his subject's handwriting—probably because of a psychological desire to conceal his fraud by making it less easy to read. Robert Spring used a diminutive handwriting in his Washington fakes. The average length of Washington's own signature was about three inches, but Spring's puny imitations run to around one and two-thirds inches, about half the size of Washington's. The forgeries I have seen of Richard Nixon's signature are almost always cramped and much smaller than his own sprawling signature, which often measures four inches in length.

Rule 8. *Do not be misled by dealer markings on a document, or by penciled notations or by repairs or by evidences of prior mounting or framing.* Skilled forgers often rig such details, thus beguiling their victims into the belief that the document has long been accepted as genuine and has already passed under critical eyes. Printed descriptions of the suspect document from old sales catalogues are of very little value, since many oldtime autograph dealers and auction houses sold autographs "as is," and the philographic market is peppered with fakes that have passed through the hands of various dealers during the last century.

Rule 9. *Compare the ink with that of a genuine document of the period.* You may imagine that the study of inks is very complicated and is the province of a few specialists. Yet it is not difficult to recognize ink that is "wrong." Earlier inks bite into the paper. An almost imperceptible brownness is sometimes visible at the edge of the pen strokes. Ink used before 1875 may show evidence of corrosion due to the iron content in the early ink. Many of the letters of Zachary Taylor and Andrew Jackson, for example, reveal ink corrosion which has cut tiny holes in the heavy quill strokes. Forgeries, on the other hand, have a washed-out brown or reddish brown or blackish purple cast quite unlike genuine old ink. Even the faint brown of pokeberry ink or the watery, speckled black of gunpowder

SOME FAMOUS EARLY WATERMARKS

Common British watermarks of the sixteenth and seventeenth century—and later—that are sometimes found on imported paper used in Colonial and Revolutionary America.

Bull's head
(sixteenth century).

Open hand and star
(sixteenth century).

Post horn
(seventeenth century).

Flagon
(seventeenth century).

Cardinal's hat
(seventeenth century).

Fool's cap
(seventeenth
century).
This common
watermark gave its
name to the large
sheets of paper
(13½" x 17") in
which it first
appeared.

ink, both widely used on the American frontier, do not look like the products of recent forgers. The Lincoln fakes of Cosey, often written in ink mixed from iron rust, an improvement on his earlier Waterman's brown ink, are unlike the rich deep brown or almost jet-black ink used by our Civil War president.

Rule 10. *Carefully investigate any autograph of exceptional rarity or with extraordinary contents.* Forgers often attempt to fabricate very rare and costly signatures, such as those of Button Gwinnett, Thomas Lynch, Jr., Abraham Lincoln or John F. Kennedy. The earlier fakes may often be detected because of the slight fuzziness, or featheriness, of the ink, which tends to blur when it goes on old paper. Signatures of the four men mentioned above must be examined with great caution when they are found in old books. A favorite trick of fakers is to add the signature of a famous person to an otherwise genuine document of little or no value. The forged signatures of Gwinnett and Lynch are often found on authentic old documents, usually as witnesses on a deed.

Rule 11. *Check the contents of the document or letter against known facts.* With remarkably well-executed forgeries, the primary suspicion may depend upon internal evidence, or what the document says. Little errors of place or date, tiny facts which fail to dovetail with our other knowledge, premature mention of books and ideas—these were the evidences on which Major Byron's adroit forgeries of Byron and Shelley were first condemned. Of equal significance are blunders in syntax and language of which the supposed writer would not be guilty. Most Lincoln forgers slip into a verbosity that does not tally with the terseness in Lincoln's authentic letters. If the letter of an eighteenth-century notable were to conclude with the words "Cordially yours" instead of something like "I am, Sir, Your humble Servant," or a similar extravagantly polite phrase, the deviation would justify a careful scrutiny of the letter.

Rule 12. *Be suspicious of shaky handwriting or any evidence of erasures or tracing.* Few forgers ever master the handwriting of their subject to the degree that they can write it with

"To Make Black Ink" (from an original recipe book, about 1770, in the possession of the author)

Take four Ounces Nutt Galls beaten & infused a Week in One Scots pint of Rain or River Water. Set in the Sun or near the fire, and Shaken or Flared frequently after which add half an Ounce Green Coperas and a fourth of an Ounce Roman Vitriol, one Ounce Gum Arabic and a few specks of Logwood. N.B. too much Coperas makes the Ink Black at first but it soon grows Brown Upon the paper but with the above preportion it always grows Blaker & never degenerates.

This two-century-old recipe is archaic and complicated enough to deter the most determined forger. And so long as forgers use modern brown ink or iron filings or tobacco juice their handicraft will be easy for an expert to spot.

great speed. Labored writing is often a giveaway. Retracing of words is a trumpet blast of the forger's work. Sometimes in a forgery the lines or even the individual words will weave up and down, showing that the writer was concentrating on the formation of individual letters of the alphabet rather than penning complete words or sentences. Some forgers trace or draw their fakes in pencil, then go over them in ink and afterward erase the pencil marks. A careful look under a magnifying glass may disclose such damning evidence.

Rule 13. *Keep an eye out for Autopen signatures.* Although signatures produced by Autopen or Signa-Signer, two modern devices which, by using a mechanical signature pattern, exactly counterfeit one's handwriting, are not technically looked upon as forgeries, they are not genuine signatures, and the message to which they are affixed may not be written by the signer. The difficulty in identifying them is that they are usually signed in ink with the owner's own pen, ballpoint or felt-tip, and exactly duplicate his signature. It is safe to say that most men and women who have very large correspondences use a robot to sign their names. Nearly all presidents since John F. Kennedy, all congressmen and senators, astronauts and cosmonauts, and a great many motion-picture stars employ the Autopen for signing their correspondence, souvenir items and photographs. If you encounter two signatures which appear identical—it is probable they were signed with a machine. If the signatures superimpose when one is placed over the other and they are held up to the light, then they are robot signatures.

Most forgeries—and we can be thankful for this—are not too difficult to spot. A wholesome skepticism, a sharp mind and some knowledge of the facts behind a document will enable you to detect almost any forgery.

The Autopen in action. Posed by Diane Hamilton; photographed by Roy Schatt.

Acknowledgments

For the immense assistance and enthusiastic cooperation of the philographers of America—collectors, librarians, archivists and historians—I wish to express my gratitude. Their willingness to help has made possible this book.

For permission to reproduce facsimiles or publish material I am indebted to Edward C. Hyers of Bradenton, Florida, who furnished information about Henry Woodhouse; George Rinsland, the noted mail auctioneer, Allentown, Pennsylvania; Howard Peckham of Hendersonville, North Carolina, who entertainingly recounted for this book the tale of a spoof forgery; Paul U. Congdon, academic dean, Springfield College, Springfield, Massachusetts, and Janice Gallinger, librarian of Plymouth State College, Plymouth, New Hampshire, for important information about Thomas McNamara's college and teaching careers; Jane A. Kenamore, archivist of the Rosenberg Library, Galveston, Texas; and Julia Sweet Newman, autograph dealer of Battle Creek, Michigan, who sent me biographical data about her father, Forest H. Sweet, and generously permitted me to publish some of his letters.

Others who helped were Paul T. Heffron, acting chief of the Library of Congress, Washington, D.C.; Philip Silver, Elberon, New Jersey, who sent his reminiscences of Henry Woodhouse; Princeton University Library, Princeton, New Jersey, which provided a photograph of a rare forgery of John Paul Jones by Robert Spring; Thomas A. Lingenfelter, Franklin Autograph Society, Hatfield, Pennsylvania, who generously submitted for my use a small but significant group of forgeries; James Camner, a good friend from Plainsboro, New Jersey, who supplied me with a much traveled and often misidentified forgery of Stephen Collins Foster; and Constance Camner, his attractive wife, who made a sketch of Charles Weisberg from a police mug shot for this book.

My gratitude is extended also to Bruce Gimelson, the noted autograph expert of Chalfont, Pennsylvania, who supplied me with a rare franking signature of Lincoln as congressman; Thomas

269

L. Gravell of Wilmington, Delaware, a distinguished authority on American watermarks; Barry Cassidy of Barry Cassidy Rare Books in Sacramento, who turned up a collection of Theodore Roosevelt forgeries; and David Lowenherz of Lion Heart Autographs and Fred Poggi, both of New York City, for their help in obtaining two scarce Cosey forgeries.

I am further indebted to *Manuscripts,* a publication of the Manuscript Society, which first printed an account by me of Thomas McNamara's forgeries; John Howells, Houston, Texas, for important data and opinions on John Laflin, alias John Laffite; the Scriptorium, Beverly Hills, California, for a Daniel Boone forgery; John Taylor, the distinguished author of books on autographs, for the use of material from his excellent book *From the White House Inkwell;* John Fleming, the celebrated New York book dealer, who cooperated with me most enthusiastically; Thomas A. Frayne of Cleveland Heights, Ohio, for the gift of a Poe forgery by Joseph Cosey and for various comments on Cosey's work; Dr. Daniel L. Thomas, Jr., Wooster, Ohio; Richard Burke, for the loan of a very early Franklin pay warrant forged by Joseph Cosey; Estelle Ward, director of the Plattsburgh Public Library, Plattsburgh, New York, for permission to use a few lines from a Charles Weisberg forgery of Washington; Ripley International Ltd., Toronto, Ontario, Canada, for authorization to reproduce a cartoon by Robert Ripley; Byron L. Troyer, Fort Myers, Florida, who provided several unusual forgeries by Eugene Field II; and Miriam E. Phelps, research librarian, *Publishers Weekly,* New York City.

Of great help to me was the assistance furnished by Mrs. Frances H. Stadler, archivist, Missouri Historical Society, who went out of her way to assist me by furnishing important data and documents about the career and work of John Laffite; W. H. Bond, librarian of the Houghton Library, Harvard University, Cambridge, Massachusetts, who furnished from that library a Keats forgery by Major Byron; Yale University Library, Yale University, New Haven, Connecticut; O. E. Elvgren, St. Paul, Minnesota, for permission to use several forgeries; John Scholz, Eugene Field House, St. Louis, Missouri, for his helpful cooperation; Robert Denniston, Lighthouse Point, Florida; Paul C. Richards, an old friend and the world's leading expert on Robert Frost, for the use of his splendid catalogues and many helpful suggestions; Larry D. Lewis, Springfield, Massachusetts, who munificently presented me with his own tiny but choice collection of forgeries; Thomas W. Pooler, Grass Valley, California, for the loan of Nazi forgeries from his great collection; and Robert W. Conrow, Santa Cruz, California, for important data on Eugene Field II.

I am also very grateful to Sotheby Parke Bernet, the famed auction gallery of New York City, and Swann Galleries, also of New York City, for permission to reproduce facsimiles from their catalogues; Robert Batchelder of Ambler, Pennsylvania, for his suggestions and cooperation; World Wide Photos, Inc.,

New York City, for permission to use photographs of Howard R. Hughes and Clifford Irving; Herman Herst, Jr., Boca Raton, Florida, who cooperated enthusiastically in this book and sent personal recollections of Joseph Cosey and Henry Woodhouse; William R. Cagle, Lilly librarian and Saundra Taylor, curator of manuscripts, both at Indiana University, Bloomington, Indiana, for their splendid and all-out assistance; Mary L. Robertson, curator of manuscripts, and Virginia Rust, associate curator of manuscripts, both at The Huntington Library, San Marino, California, for their enthusiastic help, and Donald H. Woodward, librarian, who waived the usual reproduction fee when informed of the scholarly nature of this book; Professor Howard J. Pollman, East Lansing, Michigan, an old friend from my boyhood, who volunteered many helpful ideas and suggestions; Robert Tollett, Altman's department store, New York City, an old friend who came to my assistance with several very significant items by Robert Spring; and Rosejeanne Slifer, distinguished autograph expert of New York City and a dear friend, who lent me a handful of interesting forgeries from her private collection.

Of enormous help to me were Kenneth and Diana Rendell, great autograph experts of Newton, Massachusetts, who placed at my disposal without reservations their personal archive of forgeries; Robert C. Vogel of the Department of Geography at the University of Minnesota, Minneapolis, Minnesota, the world's greatest expert on John Laflin, alias John Laffite, who offered unstintingly the use of his files on Laffite, photographs and other data which it required years of effort to gather; Louis Cohen, noted bookman and proprietor of the great Argosy Book Stores, New York City, who related many anecdotes about Charles Weisberg and Henry Woodhouse and placed several important documents at my disposal; Arthur Sutton, a former forger and now an honest and useful citizen, who cooperated generously in providing vital information for the chapter on his activities as a forger; Calvin N. Smith, the noted United States postal inspector whose sleuthing skills led to the arrests of Arthur Sutton and Thomas McNamara, and who cooperated in every way with the writing of this book and supplied many important illustrations; Raphael Gould of the American Library Service in New York City, who not only turned over to me his huge file of forgeries by Henry Woodhouse but spent three hours regaling me with tales and anecdotes about Woodhouse; James T. Hickey, curator of the famed Lincoln Collection, Illinois State Historical Library, Springfield, Illinois, for his superb cooperation in furnishing important details on the forgeries of Lincoln by Harry D. Sickles and Eugene Field II, together with photographs of their forgeries; David C. Sheldon, executive director of the Hildene Estate, Manchester, Vermont, whose great cooperation in sending me examples of the handwriting of Abraham Lincoln II, as well as biographical data about him, vastly improved this book; and Neale Lanigan, Jr., close friend and prominent autograph expert of Fairview Village,

Pennsylvania, who worked hard with me on the Sutton case and supplied many Sutton forgeries and other vital documents used to effect Sutton's arrest.

Of inestimable aid to me were the efforts of the librarians at the William L. Clements Library at the University of Michigan in Ann Arbor. Their friendly and enthusiastic cooperation contributed greatly to making this volume more complete and more useful, and I should specifically like to thank Arlene P. Shy, Barbara Mitchell, assistant manuscript curator, and Glen R. Wilson, assistant map curator. I am also grateful to the Museum of Anthropology at the University of Michigan for permission to reproduce a forged clay tablet. The efforts of the William L. Clements Library in the cause of scholarship were equaled if not surpassed by the New York Public Library, which owns one of the great forgery collections of the world. Its holdings have vastly enriched this book. My thanks go to the library's Forgeries Section, especially to Paul R. Rugen, who made a special effort to be helpful and who placed at my disposal all the fakes, filed and unfiled, identified and unidentified, classified and unclassified, in the Manuscripts and Archives Division, the New York Public Library, Astor, Lenox and Tilden Foundations. The librarians in the Rare Book Room also were most helpful and went out of their way to locate for me documents concerning the forgeries of Thomas Chancellor. I am further indebted to the great Berg Collection at the New York Public Library, with its superb Owen D. Young additions. Finally, I wish to thank Faye Simkin, Executive Officer of the Research Libraries, for arranging that I be given permission to reproduce material from the New York Public Library archives without a fee, since this volume is essentially a scholarly work and will, I hope, be useful to all who work in the field of manuscripts.

Finally, my indebtedness to those who worked closely with me is very great. Nicholas Hentoff of New York City was most helpful in doing preliminary library research. H. Keith Thompson, Jr., executive vice president of Hamilton Galleries, offered many useful suggestions as well as valuable reminiscences of Henry Woodhouse, George A. Van Nosdall and Samuel Loveman; Gretta Jacobson, my assistant, patiently endured my outbursts and epithets during an entire day at the library; Dianne Gomez, my secretary, aided greatly with her punctilious skills in taking dictation and adroit maintenance of the large file of correspondence necessitated in writing this book; Nancy Panarella, secretary to Herbert Michelman, gave me the friendly aid that only an editor's secretary can provide and finally my editors, Herbert Michelman and Peter Burford of Crown Publishers, Inc., provided the skilled professional assistance, with some deft excisions, that helped to make this volume more readable.

Lastly, and most important of all, I want to thank my wife, Diane, whose reading and rereading of the manuscript, always with the proffer of many worthwhile suggestions, has tremendously improved this book.

Index

Page numbers in boldface type refer to illustrations